WORLD–POWER AND EVOLUTION

WORLD-POWER AND EVOLUTION

BY

ELLSWORTH HUNTINGTON

RESEARCH ASSOCIATE IN GEOGRAPHY
IN YALE UNIVERSITY

LVX ET VERITAS

NEW HAVEN
YALE UNIVERSITY PRESS
LONDON · HUMPHREY MILFORD · OXFORD UNIVERSITY PRESS
MDCCCCXIX

TO

R. B. H.

WHOSE SUGGESTIONS DOT THE
PAGES OF THIS BOOK

PREFACE

EVERY important aspect of human knowledge must be considered in its relation to both space and time. In "Civilization and Climate" the problem of the effect of physical environment upon human progress was discussed in its relation to space. It was shown that the distribution of civilization upon the earth's surface is closely in harmony with the distribution of climatic energy, which appears to be the most important factor in physical environment. In the present volume the same problem is considered in its relation to time. Beginning with the present day we find that from year to year business activities vary in extraordinary harmony with health. Further study shows that variations in health from year to year depend upon the weather far more than upon any other single factor. Turning to the distant past we find that from the earliest geological times the evolution of man's ancestors, even before they had assumed the form of man, was largely guided by climatic environment. This was especially true of mental evolution. Periods of climatic stress not merely weeded out old types, but apparently caused new types or mutants to arise, so that new species and races came into existence. In historical times the same extraordinarily close relationship between the air that men breathe and the deeds that they do is apparent. Rome furnishes a striking example. Turkey is today one of the world's most puzzling problems partly because of the economic, physiological, and political conditions arising from the uninvigorating climate and the arid summers. Germany, in like manner, was able to defy the world largely because no other country has so many people who live under a highly energizing climate and are also under a single government.

Some readers may feel that the importance of environment is exaggerated in this book. That will be largely because they do not attach as much weight as does the author to the qualifying phrases which he has used. A few generations ago the emphasis was all upon the various agencies which combine to furnish *training*. In a broad sense these include the Church, the Home, the School, the State, and other institutions. Recently tremendous emphasis has justly been given to another factor, namely, *heredity*. We are told that heredity plays nine parts and training one in determining what a man's character shall be. According to such an extreme view *physical environment* is scarcely worthy of mention. Yet training, heredity, and physical environment are like food, drink, and air. One or another of these may be placed *first* according to the individual preferences, and one or another may demand more attention according to circumstances. It is idle, however, to say that one is any more important than the others. All are essential. Until the world learns this vital lesson, it will be necessary that some students should lay special stress upon heredity because its importance is not as yet so fully recognized as is that of training. Other students must lay still greater stress upon physical environment because its importance is still less appreciated. When the world realizes that the human race must be bred as carefully as race horses, and that even when people inherit perfect constitutions their health must receive as much care as does that of consumptives, it will be time for a book in which training, heredity, and environment receive exactly equal emphasis.

Part of the material here used has already been published in the *Journal of Race Development* and in the *Quarterly Journal of Economics*, but most is new. In writing this book, many sources have been drawn upon, some of which are acknowledged in the list of references in the Appendix. The author has also drawn

on many sources which cannot be thus acknowledged. He un-
blushingly confesses that when he hears or reads a good idea he
often assimilates it, and later gives it out as if it were his own,
not knowing where or when it came to him. So to the great host
of persons who have unconsciously given him help he offers his
thanks, with the hope that they may not object to his use of
their ideas.

Washington, D. C.
December, 1918.

TABLE OF CONTENTS

LIST OF ILLUSTRATIONS

CHAPTER I

THE CHART OF EVOLUTION

ON a fateful day in August, 1914, the ship of human progress crashed upon a rock. Though battered and broken by a terrific tempest, she still hangs together after four years of pounding on the reef of militarism. Clearly at this time of crisis it is well to reëxamine the route by which the world has come to this disaster. Has there been some wind, some current—some widespread tendency, or some unnoticed agency—that has carried us out of our true course? Many students are already engaged in the study of this great problem. In the future it will occupy the attention of thousands of the world's best minds. One inquirer studies the currents of philosophy. He judges that the teachings of Nietzsche, for example, were responsible for a swerve in German thought which changed the direction of progress and thus brought shipwreck. Another investigates the eddies of religion. He finds that lack of altruism in the great commercial centers and the setting up of a home-made God in Germany were potent causes of the wrong course which the whole world now deplores. Again, an historian concludes that the wind of junkerism and the militaristic spirit had been blowing more strongly than people realized. Thus before mankind knew what was happening the ship had run aground. Still another inquirer, impressed by the importance of trade and commerce, finds in them the deflecting force. The jealousy of England and Germany formed a perfect network of conflicting currents which drifted the ship first this way and then that. Where one student feels that the Bagdad railway was a dominating influence, another is sure that the Serbian question was the unexpected event which finally brought disaster. A third believes that a more important influence was the wind of Pan-Slavism which blew gently for many decades, and then came up as a sudden gust when Russia supported Serbia.

Each of these students is right. If any one of a thousand conditions had been different, the war would never have happened in the way that the world now rues so keenly. Yet probably it would have happened in some other way. The course of evolution has brought the human race to a certain stage of development. In that stage selfishness, short-sightedness, lust, and jealousy still dominate a large part of mankind. Vast numbers of people are intellectually so weak or sluggish that they can easily be dominated by stronger wills, no matter whether those wills are right or wrong. Therefore strong nations are able to exploit their weaker neighbors; a ruling class is able to persuade their fellow countrymen that world-power is the only alternative to downfall; and a group of selfish politicians is able to hoodwink this so-called land of freedom and wallow in graft to the neck. When the world is in such a stage, war, graft, labor troubles, and a host of other ills are inevitable. We think that we have found palliatives and even cures, but the old ills keep breaking out in new places. Something is radically wrong with the human race, and we must find out how to right it.

The teachers of religion were the first to announce a cure for the fundamental ill from which all other troubles take their rise. "Ye must be born anew." That was the message of religion. But three thousand years of Judaism, Buddhism, Mohammedanism, and Christianity have not brought that new birth except to scattered individuals here and there. Why? Because the message was wrong? No, but because the teachers of religion have insisted that a spiritual birth was sufficient. Seeing this error the educators took up the cry. "Ye must be born anew," they shouted, "but your minds as well as your souls must be reborn." So education became the panacea—education of rich and poor, brilliant and stupid, savage and superman—but still the old evils persisted. Next religion and education called in their little sister, philanthropy. She, too, insisted on the necessity of a new birth, but her method was different. She devoted herself to the poor and wretched quite as much as did her elder sisters, but she began with the body, worked next on the mind, and believed that when body and mind were right, the spirit would also be regenerated. Yet the old misery persists, and is perhaps today as great as ever. Good government is another little sister who has vainly made the same attempt. She, too, has failed to prevent the world's worst war, the world's worst massacres, and the world's most awful collapse of civilization.

Have religion, education, philanthropy, and government failed? Shall we despair because the Church, the School, the Charity Organization, and the State have not yet destroyed war, pestilence, lust, greed, cruelty, and selfishness? Far from it. These agencies cannot possibly play their proper parts unless science comes to their aid. Not mechanical science, although that has its useful part to play, but biological science. The sum and substance of biology is evolution, the Darwinian idea that no type of living creature is permanent. With his splendid sweep of vision Darwin saw that neither man nor any other creature is a finished product. Variations occur, and natural selection by means of the environment ruthlessly exterminates some of them and preserves others to form new species. The variations are possibly sudden and marked rather than gradual and slight as Darwin supposed, but that does not alter the main idea. Darwinism, as we here use the term, means biological evolution, and evolution means constant change in species and in races. The idea is still so new that we have not yet learned to apply it on any wide scale. We are indeed applying it to plants and animals, and hence are improving them immensely. We are also beginning to apply it to the study of disease, and are thereby working wonders. Yet thus far we have scarcely begun to apply the principles of

Darwinism to the great problems involved in the evolution of races, nations, and ideals.

It has taken millions of years to evolve the human race. The impress of those millions of years is engraved upon everything that we do. Perhaps the greatest mistake of the thinkers of the past has been the idea that religion, education, philanthropy, good government, or any other products of the last few thousand years can eradicate or even neutralize tendencies which are the product of a hundred million years of evolution. The only way to eradicate them is to change the course of evolution. Such a procedure takes time, but it can be done. Nature has done it again and again in the past. We have been doing it unconsciously for several thousand years. The case of mankind is like that of a ship that has been drifting with the current, but which now finds at its helm an ignorant child who twists the rudder according to his whims. He steers the ship into slavery, monasticism, commerce, manufacturing, warfare, nationalism, a sedentary life, the use of machines, and a host of other habits totally different from the conditions under which most of man's evolution took place. The human animal now rides instead of walks; lives in stuffy houses instead of out of doors or in caves; wears clothes instead of exposing his body to the weather; and eats soft, cooked, concentrated food instead of that which is raw, tough, and bulky. He preserves the sick and weakly instead of letting them die; he permits an economic and social system which causes the people with greatest mental power to have the fewest children, while the stupid breed like rabbits; and he moves recklessly from one kind of environment to another without regard to the possible effects. In addition to all this, modern civilization imposes upon mankind a tremendous burden of mental and moral responsibility. We expect the ordinary farmer or laborer to restrain his passions; to abide by a multitude of laws and customs which he had no voice in framing; to feel a sense of responsibility for affairs of state which neither he nor the profoundest scholars can really understand. More than this, we demand that such a man, framed of ordinary clay, shall right the wrongs of nations thousands of miles away; shall give of his substance for starving millions in Turkey or China; and in a hundred ways shall act as if he were more than human.

Thus we have built up a wonderful fabric of civilization, and at the same time have actually weakened the human race by diminishing its vitality and hence its will power. We have also lessened its adaptation to its environment. Our foolish hands have turned the rudder in such a way as to check the reproduction of the bravest warriors, the people of deepest religious zeal, the men and women of highest self-control, and those with the greatest power to think and act. Today, as Conklin well puts it, "social heredity has outrun germinal heredity." In other words we have woven a complex fabric which makes the most strenuous demands upon human character, but we have weakened the fiber by interfering with the course of evolution and by subjecting the human race to new and unfavorable conditions. Thus, when some great crisis comes, the social fabric is suddenly rent, as it was in the Great War, and we see man in all his nakedness. We realize that in many ways he is still a weak-willed brute.

When it comes to the problem of strengthening the social fabric all the many methods may be grouped under three great heads. First, we may improve our systems of religion, education, philanthropy, and government. Work along such lines may all be summed up under the general heading of *training*. No one will question that our efforts to train the next generation in the right way must be redoubled. Second, we must give tenfold or a hundred-fold greater weight to the great problem of eugenics. Our country's children must have a good *inheritance*. The best inheritance and the finest training, however, are not enough. Between the two stands *health*. How many human ills arise because well-trained people with a good inheritance fail to do their part through ill health or nervousness? Think of the business failures, the labor troubles, the bitter heart-burnings, and the lapses into sin which occur because people's nerves are unstrung. Surprising as it may seem, we shall find that financial depression in the United States is apparently a regular consequence of widespread ill health. The lamentable and most ominous failure of the more competent parts of the community to reproduce themselves and maintain their proportion among the general population is due in part at least to the weakened physique which results from a life of ease and luxury, especially among women. In a thousand other ways health is equally vital to the general welfare. Watch the laborers loafing on their job in the street. If those men had been born with the minds and bodies that they ought to have, and if they were blessed with the perfect health that they ought to enjoy, would they be content with such dilatory work even though they are employed by the city? Would you, with your quick mind—if you were in perfect health—be willing to work so slowly?

Consider for a moment the actual figures as to health in the United States. In his book on "The Hygiene of the School Child" Terman says that of the 20,000,000 children enrolled in the schools of the United States about 14,000,000 are handicapped by some kind of physical defect. "Not far from 2,000,000 are suffering from a grave form of malnutrition; 10,000,000 have enough defective teeth to interfere seriously with health; at least 2,000,000 suffer from obstructed breathing due to adenoids or enlarged tonsils; probably 2,000,000 have enlarged cervical glands which need attention, many of these being tuberculous; at least 10,000,000 are, or have been, infected with tuberculosis, of whom about 2,000,000 will later succumb to the disease; 4,000,000 have defective vision; over 1,000,000 have defective hearing; about 1,000,000 have spinal curvature or some other deformity likely to interfere with health; not far from 500,000 have organic heart trouble; and at least 1,000,000 are predisposed to some form of serious nervous disorder."

We are apt to say that the figures just given are not so bad as they seem, for they include many minor ailments. True, but great oaks from little acorns grow. What did our draft show during the Great War? Only preliminary figures are yet available. Judging by 9,256 men who were examined at eight camps, however, men were rejected for defects and diseases in the following ratios per thousand men:

(A) Defects of eyes	80	
Defects of teeth	31	
Defects of ears	22	
	—	133
(B) Physical undevelopment . . .	15	
Flat foot	14	
Underweight	6	
	—	35
(C) Venereal diseases	16	
Alcoholism and drugs	3	
	—	19
(D) Mentally deficient	17	
Nervous disorders	14	
	—	31
(E) Diseases of the joints	12	
Diseases of the bones	11	
Diseases of the skin	4	
Diseases of the muscles . . .	2	
	—	29
(F) Diseases of the heart	22	
Diseases of the blood vessels . .	7	
	—	29
(G) Hernia	28	
Diseases of the genito-urinary organs (non-venereal)	5	
Diseases of the digestive system . .	3	
	—	36

(H) Tuberculosis   20
     Respiratory diseases   6
                                     —
                                       26

       Grand total   338

Even if we admit that most of those in groups A and B are not seriously incapacitated for the work of life, there remain 165 out of every thousand who have some grave physical or mental defect. This means that in the very prime of life one in every six of the young men in the United States is terribly handicapped, and is thus handicapping his home and his country.

Other countries are almost equally afflicted. In Germany, before the Great War, over 20 per cent of the school children were anæmic, in part from malnutrition, and in part from other disorders. In England conditions are not much better. In Italy they are worse. It is impossible to obtain exact figures, but ordinary observation is enough to indicate that in countries like Turkey, Persia, and China, a large part of the children are anæmic. Even in our own country the proportion rises as high as 50 or 60 per cent in parts of the southern states. Taken as a whole the situation is exceedingly grave. Its seriousness gives good ground for the suspicion that a large share of the moral, social, and political evil in the world has its root in unfavorable conditions of health. On the side of religion, education, philanthropy, and government, that is, in those conditions which depend primarily upon training, the advanced nations of the world have not failed so badly as many people suppose. There have indeed been sad failures, but have not these generally been due to the poor quality of the material that has been trained? That is what we most need at present—better human material. In the course of many generations the eugenists will greatly improve the hereditary quality of the material, but meanwhile proper attention to health will do wonders.

In this book we do not propose to study health from the standpoint of the physician. Instead we shall view it from the standpoint of the geographer and evolutionist. First we shall examine the astonishing relationship between health and business in the United States. We shall see that conditions of health not only cause great differences in man's activity from region to region but from decade to decade. Incredible as it may seem, health seems to play a predominating part in the ebb and flow of the stock market, in the rise and fall of prices, and in the fluctuations of prosperity and of immigration. A realization of this will lead us to inquire minutely into the causes of fluctuations in health from year to year and from day to day. We shall discover that far and away the most important cause of fluctuation is variations in temperature and in other climatic elements. Then we shall take a backward look into geological times to see how man acquired his wonderfully delicate adjustment to climate. That will lead us to the most far-reaching of all our conclusions, namely, that brief extremes of weather are among the most potent causes of biological mutations and thus may lead to the origin of new species. Coming down to historic times we shall study Rome as an example of the effect of health upon the greatest of ancient empires. Next Turkey will occupy our attention as a modern example of the way in which unfavorable conditions of health retard a nation and cause untold trouble to the rest of the world. Finally the dilemma of Germany will make clear the way in which mere strength of body and mind without the safeguards that come from the right kind of training may turn the world upside down.

Germany furnishes an example of nervous energy like that which is both the pride and the danger of the United States. It also furnishes an example of the aggressiveness which caused Rome to wield so wide an empire. Both the nervousness and the aggressiveness appear to be largely matters of climate, not only in Germany, but in the United States and Rome. A nation with the German inheritance, the German climate, and the German geographical position is bound to expand. We shall find that the part played by that country and also by all the other belligerents in the Great War corresponds closely with what we should expect from the health and climate on the basis of our previous studies. We shall also find that the expansion of the great nations of the world is to a large extent determined by climatic conditions. We talk, indeed, about trade, but back of trade, as we shall see in our study of the United States, lies the question of health. Health, however, depends chiefly upon air, food, and water; and all three of these depend upon climate. Every nation that has been stimulated by an energizing climate has apparently spread its power over neighboring regions either by land or by sea. Germany cannot be an exception. Unless we destroy her, she is bound to act in accordance with the biological principles which have guided the action of every race upon the face of the earth. We do not propose to destroy her, even if we were able. What we do propose is somehow to defeat her and shame her until she recognizes that the only salvation both for herself and the world lies in allowing her biological propensities to be directed by higher motives. That is today the world's greatest problem.

It is our problem quite as much as Germany's. Our strength is due largely to the fact that both we and our remote ancestors have dwelt in an environment favorable to mental activity. In the future the struggle between nations will inevitably continue, but will change its form. As war becomes rarer, as commerce becomes more thoroughly international, the great contest of the nations will be to see which can produce the type of people that is strongest not only physically, or even mentally, but also morally. The science of health must see that the bodily strength and mental activity that belong to a good inheritance do not degenerate because of unfavorable surroundings. Darwin declared that the trouble with mankind is not so much lack of inherent ability as lack of the zeal and energy to make the best use of the powers that we actually possess. We have the talents, but they are buried in a napkin. The way to bring them out into the light

where they can be used is to give to each individual, however
humble, the most stimulating environment and the most perfect
health.   Then all our activities will assume far higher forms than
is now possible, for they will have far better material upon which
to work.   In a single book it is impossible to discuss all the winds
and currents which bear the ship of human progress to this great
goal.   Therefore, while remembering that many other factors are
at work, we shall confine ourselves to the relation between business
and health, and between health and climate as illustrated both at
present and in the course of evolution and history.

CHAPTER II

HEALTH AND BUSINESS

EVERYONE knows that business is subject to a constant ebb and flow. This year there is a boom. Everyone expects to make money; credits expand; factories work full time; wages rise; new railroads are built; ocean freight rates increase; prices show an upward tendency; and all but the more thoughtful—and the dyspeptic—are full of overflowing optimism. A few years later despondency is the rule. Credit is so shortened that even well-established firms are hard pinched; factories work on part time; men walk the streets in search of employment; and their families starve even though prices have dropped. Such economic cycles occur in all countries, but most of all in America. Why should there be such a constant ebb and flow? A recent writer estimates that there have been two hundred and thirty distinct answers to this question. Some are fantastic, but the great majority contain some truth. All can be grouped under three heads—economic, political, and psychological. Which group is more important? Let us look briefly at each, and then turn to health, which we may call No. 231. We shall find that it occupies a surprisingly high place.

The economic causes of business cycles include crops, which are the most important and most variable of all man's material resources. How often the financial page of the newspaper contains articles on the crops. No wide-awake business man feels that he can safely estimate next winter's business unless he takes some account of the probable buying power of the farmers. When crops are good the farmers may have a billion dollars more to spend than in years of scarcity. Perhaps they will use those dollars for automobiles, new carpets, new pianos, or to send the boys and girls to college. Or possibly they will pay old debts, clear off mortgages, and fix up the old barns. In any case more than the usual amount of money is thrown into circulation; the railroads have more than the usual freight and passenger traffic; the factories get unusually large orders; and business in general is stimulated. At the same time other material resources, such as coal, iron, machinery, lumber, and manufactured goods, are likely to be produced in unusually large quantities. A few years later there may be too much of these articles on the market, while the farmers may have such poor crops that many are obliged to borrow instead of having money to spend. No wonder business is dull. When material resources can so alter the course of business, it is not strange that many economists think that variations in the quantity of such resources are the main cause of business fluctuations.

In spite of the importance of economic resources many people believe that business fluctuations would be of slight importance, and that hard times and panics would largely disappear, if only our laws were better. Consider the effect of excessive taxation, onerous banking restrictions, a currency that does not expand easily, or that is subject to inflation. Think of the laws that restrict the legitimate expansion of business. Surely it needs no demonstration to show that many a factory has shut down because a change in the tariff made it impossible to do business. So, too, it has happened more than once that a railroad has gone into the hands of a receiver because it could not comply with new laws and restrictions. Bad financial legislation unquestionably precipitated the panic of 1837 when the government of the United States insisted on payment for public lands in gold or silver coin, and thus destroyed the value of bank notes. Here, then, there seems good ground for the idea that business cycles are largely the result of bad laws.

It might seem as if economic and political causes were enough to explain the ebb and flow of business, but business men themselves are apt to favor a psychological explanation. The greatest study of mankind is man, they say, and business cycles are a reflection of man's mind. Of course bad crops do not improve business, but after all, in these days of easy transportation, poor crops would not do much harm if only people would not become panicky. So, too, overproduction would not occur if people did not have the curious habit of becoming overconfident. If one man did this at one time and another at another, no great harm would result. For some reason, however, when overconfidence appears in one place, it appears also in others. It is almost like a contagious disease. If it seizes men of influence it spreads through the whole world of business. The same with depression. So subtle is man's mind that the whole community is swept by waves of fear which make large numbers of people restrict their output, try to sell off their surplus stock, reduce their orders, and keep their money in safe places instead of putting it into legitimate business. Such causes, say the thinkers of the psychological group, are much more important than either economic or political factors in causing fluctuations in business.

Until recently I was inclined to sympathize with the economic group. While recognizing the importance of laws and of psychology, I felt that economic conditions and especially the volume of the crops are the most important cause of cycles of prosperity and depression. Being anxious to discover the main factors which influence the health of the community from year to year, I reasoned that variations in rainfall and in other climatic conditions are the cause of variations in the crops. Therefore they must also be the cause of variations in the deathrate. Bad crops are followed in a few years by hard times, so the reasoning ran. During hard times many people are out of work; the children of the laboring classes are often ill nourished, there is no money for medicines, delicacies, and doctor's bill; even the more prosperous parts of the community are under a nervous strain. Hence at such times there must be more deaths than during the prosperous times which are supposed to follow good crops. Hence I looked for a rise in the deathrate during hard times and a fall in good.

This line of thought may sound reasonable, but it is fallacious. The statistics from 1870 to the Great War show that a high deathrate regularly *precedes* hard times, while a low deathrate precedes prosperity. By no possibility can the reverse be made to appear the case. Health is a *cause* far more than an effect. Apparently fluctuations in health are a cause of changes in mental efficiency, in drunkenness, in bank deposits, in prices, and in immigration. I know that this seems incredible. When I first compared the curve of health with that of business in one form and another, such a close connection seemed impossible. Now, however, I see no escape from it. The psychologists are apparently right. Business cycles appear to depend largely on the mental attitude of the community, and the mental attitude depends on health.

So sweeping a conclusion can be accepted only on the basis of most thoroughgoing proof. Let us begin with the variations in health. The most delicate index of the health of a community is the deathrate. Figure 1 illustrates the changes in the deathrate year by year from 1870 to 1910 in Massachusetts, Connecticut, New York City, and Chicago. Strange as it may seem, these places are the only parts of the United States where an approximately reliable record of deaths is available as far back as 1870. In Figure 1 and subsequent diagrams, as is shown in Appendix A, the gradual change from decade to decade, the so-called "secular trend," due in this case to improvements in medical practice, has been eliminated. Hence in Figure 1 the numbers on the left show the percentage by which the deaths in the various years exceeded or fell short of what would have occurred if the improvements wrought by medical science had been the only reason for changes

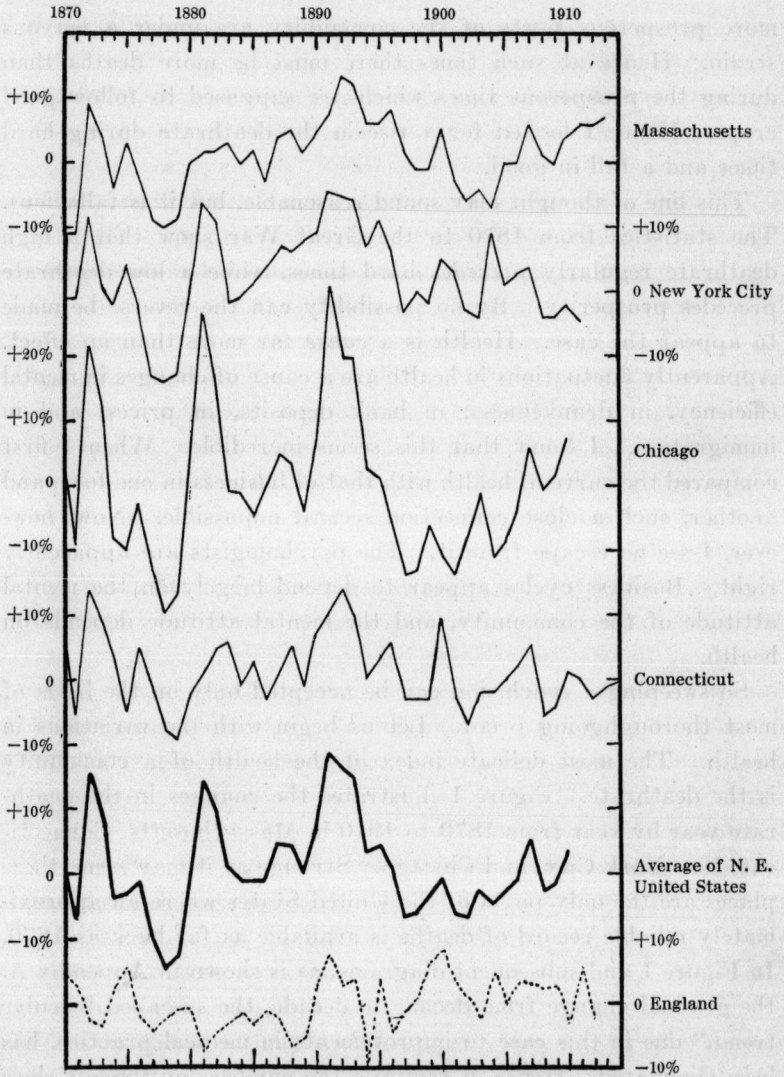

FIGURE 1.   Variations in the Deathrate from 1870 to 1910

in the deathrate. These *departures* from the normal are the subject of our study.

Notice how closely the four curves of Figure 1 agree. All are high in 1872; they sink to a low level about 1878; rise again at the beginning of the eighties; fall about 1885; rise markedly in 1891 or 1892; fall once more in 1897; rise a little about 1900; fall in 1902 or 1903; and finally rise again about 1907. The only marked discrepancies are 1903 in Chicago and 1904 in New York. The average for all four regions is given at the bottom. Double weight has been given to Chicago because it is the only representative of the great interior. It is true that the early Chicago statistics are not particularly complete, but this applies only to a short time. Moreover it makes no essential difference, for the main features of all the curves are substantially the same. Even if Chicago were omitted, the average curve would look almost as now except that the fluctuations would be somewhat less extreme. Yet they would be large. Is it not surprising that the difference between the highest and lowest points of the Connecticut curve in Figure 1 is 23 per cent, Massachusetts 24 per cent, New York 29 per cent, and Chicago 51 per cent, while in the average curve it amounts to 32 per cent? Clearly some powerful agency causes similar variations in health all over the eastern quarter of the United States. That agency, as we shall see later, appears to be the weather.

For the present let us pass by the cause of such widespread variations in health and study their effect. Our statistics of deaths represent the northeastern quarter of the United States. This region from New England and New York westward to the Mississippi River includes more than half the people of the United States and a much larger proportion of those who are active in business. Hence when the curve of deaths is inverted it represents the health of the business section of the United States. This health curve appears at the top of Figure 2. Below it comes a curve showing the percentage of persons who passed

the Civil Service Examinations. The number of persons taking
the examinations increased from about 14,000 in 1883 to well
over 200,000 in 1910. The applicants for Civil Service positions
represent all classes of society. They come from all over the
country, although the great majority live in the northeastern
quarter represented by the health curve. The examination papers
are graded by a large number of persons representing a variety
of bureaus. There is no reason to think that there have been any
marked changes in the severity with which the papers are graded.

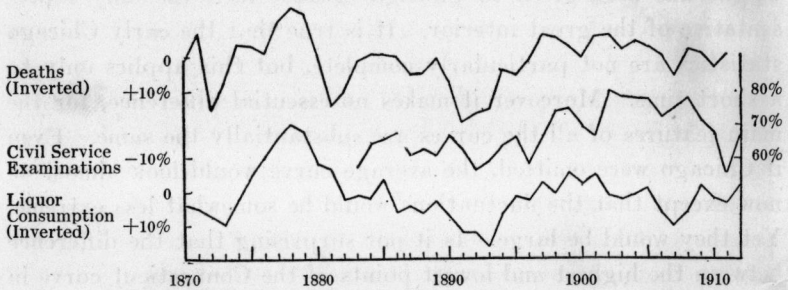

FIGURE 2.   Health, Examinations, and Temperance

Psychologists have concluded that such examinations furnish an
admirable test of mental capacity, and that they can be graded
with much accuracy. Hence this set of statistics probably gives
a good idea of the general mental alertness of the American people
as a whole. The curves of health and of examinations in Figure 2
show a marked agreement. Good health from 1884 to 1886 is
followed by a high percentage of success in the examinations of
1886. A slight drop in both lines is followed by good health in
1889 and good examinations in 1890. Then comes 1891, a year
of many deaths and poor health. See how the examinations fall
off the next year. It is not necessary to trace the curves further.
They rise and fall almost in harmony except that good or bad
health systematically precedes success or failure in the examinations by about one year.

The lower curve in Figure 2 represents temperance. In other words, it is the inverted curve of the consumption of alcoholic liquor per capita. The general increase in consumption has been eliminated as explained in the Appendix, and the curve shows the percentages by which the actual consumption departed from what would be expected if the increase from year to year were steady. The curve has been inverted so that good conditions are represented by high parts and bad by low. The resemblance between the curves of health and temperance is obvious. Notice how they both rise to a high level in 1878, 1885, and in the period from 1897 to 1901. The temperance reformer may say, "Ah, here we have the widespread cause of variations in the deathrate. It is drink which does the business." Further study, however, shows that this is not the case. Doubtless the use of alcoholic liquors increases the deathrate, but something else is the main controlling factor both in health and in business. The proof of this lies in an examination of the lowest points of the two curves. Almost always health reaches its lowest ebb before the consumption of liquor becomes greatest. Poor health in 1872 is followed by much drinking in 1873, the same relation holds between 1881 and 1882, between 1887 and 1888, between 1891 and 1893, between 1895 and 1896, and between 1910 and 1911. In other cases, such as 1900, 1903, and 1907, the two curves drop together, but as a rule the temperance curve lags behind the other.

How shall we interpret this relationship between health and temperance? In the United States the drinking of alcoholic liquors is to a large degree a question of moral strength. The case with us is not the same as in Europe. There, before the Great War, beer, ale, and similar drinks were a regular part of the food supply. No moral question was generally involved in their use. Hence their consumption varied almost directly in proportion to the buying power of the community. In the United States, however, the proportion of people who drink in this way is comparatively small. The vast majority think that drinking is not a good plan. Therefore they drink only because they feel the need of something to brace them up, or because they have not the strength of mind to refuse invitations or to resist their own desires. The steady drinker perhaps drinks most when out of work. The far larger army of moderate drinkers use most alcohol when they are physically or morally weak. This, then, is the meaning of the agreement between the curves of health and of temperance. When people's health is good they do not crave liquor so much as when they are weak. They are weak at times of many deaths; each death means that perhaps ten times as

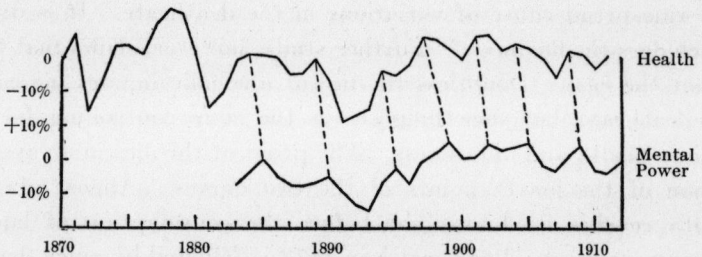

FIGURE 3.   Health and Mental Power

many people are seriously sick and a hundred times as many have some slight ailment.   Is it not notorious that anæmic women resort to so-called "vegetable" tonics which are really nothing but disguised alcoholic liquors?   Thus when poor health is widely prevalent many people get the habit of drinking. When better health and stronger wills prevail, people do not give up the habit at once, for it takes longer to get rid of a bad habit than to form it. Thus at the lowest ebb the curve of temperance generally lags behind that of health. On the other hand, when people's health is good they have the moral strength to say "No." Hence the highest points of the two curves generally coincide.

In the lower line of Figure 3, I have combined the curves of Civil Service Examinations and of temperance, giving equal weight to each. The one may be regarded as representing mental alertness; the other as representing strength of will. Combined they represent mental power. Such power, especially when united with physical vigor, gives a nation the ability to do the things that cause progress and promote civilization. Of course such ability may be exerted in the wrong direction, but our present concern is merely to find out what causes it and how it is modified. Above the curve of mental power in Figure 3, I have again placed the curve of health. The two curves agree even more closely than do the curves of Figure 2. Without exception each upward or downward movement of one is reflected in the other. The dotted lines connecting the maxima bring this out clearly. With one exception the maxima of mental power lag a year behind the maxima of health. In the exceptional case the lag is two years. From the early nineties to the first few years of the twentieth century the general health of the United States improved about 20 per cent more than would be expected on the basis of the improvement in medical practice and hygiene. During the same period mental power apparently increased in almost equal ratio. I know that it sounds unreasonable to place these two things in such close connection, but the facts are stubborn. What can they mean except that man's power of achievement is closely dependent upon his health?

Here is the apparent sequence of events. This year the death-rate is low; people have relatively few serious illnesses; they are comparatively free from anæmia, colds, and other minor ills that constantly prevent us from doing our best. As a result the young people who are going to take the Civil Service Examinations study unusually well; the young men who have begun to drink a little swear off; those who have not yet begun to drink do not yield to temptation so easily as they would if they did not feel so strong and vigorous. Hence the community is in a fit condition to make progress, and a year later the effect is evident in the Civil Service Examinations and in the drink bill.

If health is so potent in controlling man's mental power, has it any effect upon his other activities? The answer is found in Figure 4. There the upper line is the curve of health—the foundation, so to speak, of our present discussion. Below it comes the curve of mental power in the United States. These two curves are identical with those of Figure 3 except that the line representing mental power has been pushed one year to the left. If the dotted lines of Figure 3 were inserted in Figure 4 they would

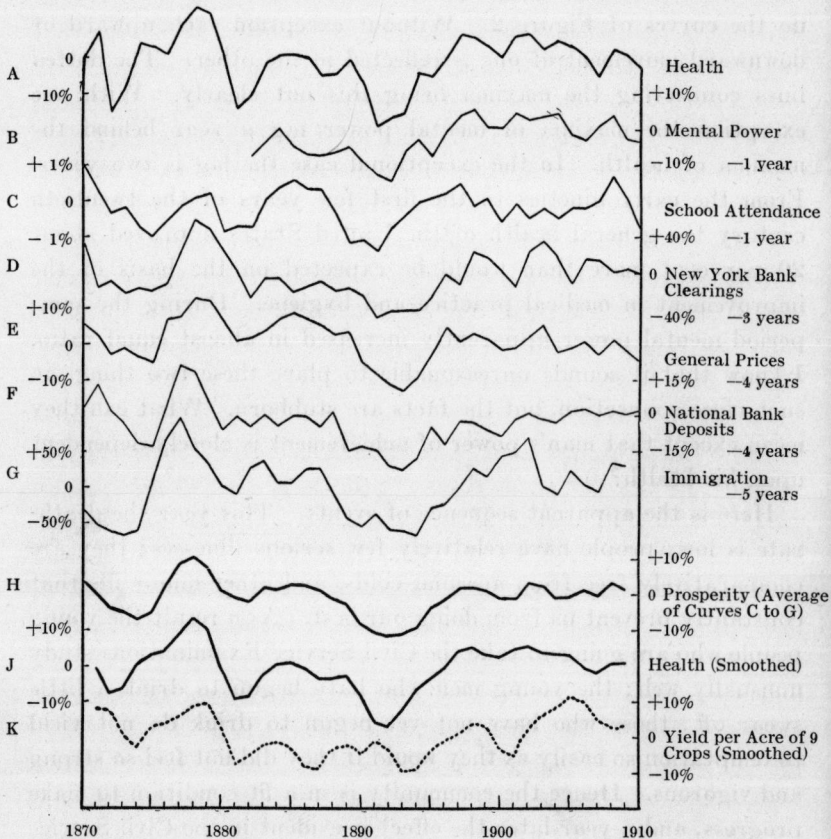

FIGURE 4.   Health and Business in the United States

become vertical. Thus the lag of a year between the conditions of health and the succeeding conditions of mental achievement is eliminated. The next curve, C, illustrates the attendance of children at school. Where it is high the attendance is good and vice versa. If absences depended only upon health, the school curve would be expected to follow the health curve directly. As a matter of fact, absences depend upon many other factors. One of these is the amount of employment. In good times there is a tendency to take children out of school and send them to work; whereas, in bad times there is nothing for children to do, and they are better off in school than anywhere else. Another factor is the mental attitude of both parents and children. When health and energy are at their best the parents are more likely to keep their children up to the mark than when the community as a whole is anæmic. Thus curve C shows not only the direct influence of health but also the influence of employment and of mental energy. It has been shoved back, that is, to the left, one year because here as in many other cases the effect of habit lasts after the original cause ceases to act. In this position it shows an unmistakable resemblance to the curve of health.

Curves D to E in Figure 4 represent business conditions. In D we see what happens in New York. The curve represents the amount by which the transactions of the New York clearing house depart from the normal that would be expected if business increased steadily without the pulsations which are so notable a feature. This curve has been shoved to the left three years, so that the year 1873 lies in line with 1870 of the health curve. The agreement of the two curves is so close that one can scarcely doubt that there is some connection. Notice the decline in business corresponding to the poor health of the early seventies. Then see how good health in 1878 is followed by great activity in New York's finances three years later. Thus, as our curves are arranged, the two high points come together. A little later there comes a decline in health and business, followed by rather poor conditions throughout the rest of the eighties. Next, bad health in 1891 is the sign for the relatively poorest business ever done upon the New York clearing house from 1870 to the Great War. Of course the low state of business in 1894 and for the next few years was due to the panic of 1893. But why did the panic occur just after a period of peculiarly bad health—the worst during the period under observation? Why, too, did the panic of 1873 come just after a period of bad health, the severity of which was next to that of 1893?

A similar line of reasoning applies to E, which shows the variations in the prices of all commodities. It is based on Falkner's figures from 1870 to 1889, and those of the Bureau of Labor from that time onward. Like all the curves in this chapter it does not indicate the absolute changes. Instead of this it shows the fluctuations from the level that would exist if certain permanent tendencies, such as the improvements in manufacturing and transportation, or the decline in the value of gold, worked steadily without interference from other factors, such as the weather. The resemblance of the curve of prices to that of health is remarkable. The chief difference is that when the prices once fall they do not recover again so quickly as does health. Notice how the low prices corresponding to the poor health of 1872 continue for four years. Similarly those corresponding to the sickness of 1881 last two or three years, while those attending the bad period of 1891 continue still longer. Another point should be noted. The price curve has been shoved back four years instead of three as in the case of the New York clearing house. In other words, general prices do not change quite so quickly as does the amount of bank clearings in New York.

If anyone objects to using general prices as a measure of the conditions of business in general, the national banks can be used as a yardstick. The fluctuations in the deposits in such banks are shown in curve F of Figure 4. Here we have essentially the same fluctuations as in the curve for prices. The two most prominent features in this curve, as in all the others, are the maximum following the good health of 1878 and the minimum following the poor health of 1891. The bank deposits, like the prices, lag about four years behind the conditions of health. This is because when bank clearings become active there is a certain amount of lag before the money actually on deposit reaches a maximum.

A still greater lag, about five years, occurs in the case of immigration, curve G in Figure 4. The greatest forces in bringing immigrants to this country are the reports of their friends as to high wages and the money that those already here send over to pay the passage of their relatives. Activity in the New York market, high prices of commodities in general, and abundant deposits in the national banks are all signs of business activity, plentiful work, and good wages. Thus it is not surprising that the high tide of immigration follows a year or two after high-water mark in these other lines. The surprising thing is to find that the curve of immigration at an interval of five years almost reproduces the curve of health. Compare the two once more. Remember that during five years many other conditions aside from health have an opportunity to act. Remember also that, although the prosperity of the United States is a deciding factor in the volume of immigration, hard times, political disturbances, and racial jealousies across the water are highly important. Yet, in spite of all these other factors, the curve of immigration faithfully reflects the main fluctuations of the curve of health.

Finally, for the benefit of the reader who does not believe that any one condition gives a true picture of the prosperity of the country, I have prepared curve H. It is the average of C to G. Each of these five is reckoned as of equal importance, and each is given a lag corresponding to that shown in Figure 4. This is legitimate, for it takes time for health to be converted into good habits, for mental activity to be converted into bank clearings, for a business decision to be converted into a factory, and for high wages to be converted into immigrants. Thus we may say that curve H represents the total effect that good health may be expected to have upon the country, although some effects come sooner and others later. The faithfulness with which children attend school; the volume of bank clearings in New York City; the general level of prices of all commodities; the size of the deposits in national banks; and the number of immigrants reaching our shores;—these are the elements which have been combined to represent the general prosperity of the United States.

Below the curve of prosperity the curve of health has been repeated and labelled J. This time, however, it is smoothed by the formula $\dfrac{a+2b+c}{4}=b$. This merely means that the health of a single year cannot be expected to produce all the observed effects. Other years play their part. Therefore in any given year, such as b in the equation, instead of reckoning the health of that year alone, I have averaged its health with that of the preceding year (a) and the succeeding year (c). Double weight, however, has been given to the year in question. Thus curve J represents the effect that the weather, acting through health, might be expected to have upon the general prosperity of the next four or five years. The actual effect is shown in curve H.

The resemblance of curves H and J is so pronounced that it scarcely needs emphasis. Remember that both are based upon the fullest modern statistics. In no case has any change been made in the statistics except to eliminate the features due simply to normal growth. By thus eliminating the tendency for bank deposits, for example, to increase from decade to decade, however, we cannot possibly *add* anything to a curve. We simply prevent the minor fluctuations from being concealed by the fact that the total volume of deposits is now much greater than in 1870 because the country has grown. I emphasize this point because one reason why people have not seen the relationships here pointed out is that they have looked at the growth of business, the growth in immigration and so forth, and have not realized that in 1870 a change of a million dollars in bank deposits or of a hundred thousand in immigration was as important as a change of ten million or four hundred thousand now. We have shoved our curves backward only in accordance with the known facts as to the delay that inevitably occurs between the making of a decision or the birth of an idea and the fruition of the decision and the idea. First, the idea must be carefully examined; then other men must be interested in it; next, ways of financing it must be found; then orders have to be placed; next, machines must be made, factories must be enlarged; and finally, after new goods are being made, there is a certain lapse of time before they have much effect upon prices, bank deposits, and immigration. How important such delays are was brought home to the United States in the Great War. We made a great decision in April, 1917. A year later the aeroplanes, ships, and other indispensable articles which that decision involved were only beginning to be ready. Yet that was a case in which urgent haste was demanded and in which, in spite of mistakes, the most strenuous efforts were made to produce such haste. Notwithstanding the complaints of the critics, private enterprise could not possibly have accomplished so much in so short a time and under so many difficulties. No private concern, for example, can hasten production by demanding the right of way on railroads. Thus the shoving back of our curves is the only reasonable thing to do. If they were moved in the other direction or by any amount not in accordance with reason, they would not fit the curve of health. The business conditions of the country thus act exactly as if they were the result of the preceding conditions of health.

The truth of this last statement is emphasized by comparing the curve of prosperity with the curve of crops. If any economic factor has a dominating effect upon American prosperity, it is surely the crops. Yet look at curve K in Figure 4. It represents the average yield per acre of the nine chief crops which make up more than 95 per cent of the products of our soil. The figures are taken from Moore's interesting little book on "Economic Cycles." This curve has been smoothed in the way employed for curve J above it. The unsmoothed curve is compared with the health curve in Figure 5. When the smoothed crop curve is com-

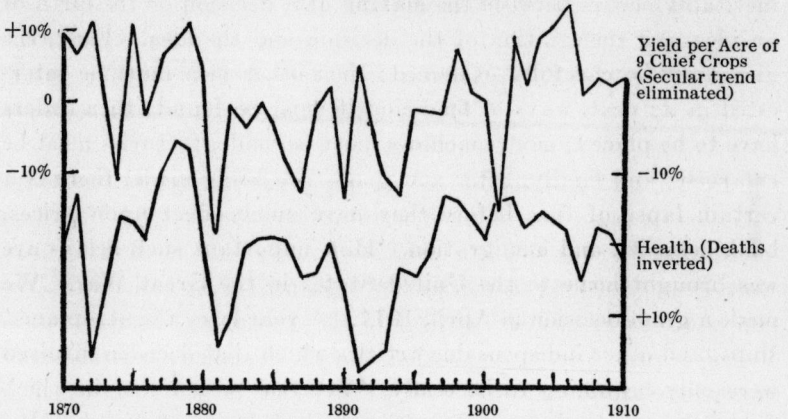

FIGURE 5.   Crops and Health in the United States

pared with the curve of prosperity, H, a certain resemblance is indeed apparent. But look at the crop minimum in 1887, the maximum in 1891, the minimum in 1901, and the maximum in 1905. These features by no means accord with the conditions of prosperity. Certainly the crops must have an important effect upon prosperity. When crops and health are both favorable, as they were to a notable degree about 1878 and 1898, and to a less degree in 1884, prosperity is doubtless much enhanced. When crops and health act in opposite directions, however, there can be no question as to which has the greater effect upon business. The prosperity curve follows the health curve with no apparent regard for the crops. Contrary as it seems to our established convictions, there appears to be no way of avoiding the conclusion that economic cycles of adversity and prosperity in the United States depend upon health far more than upon any other factor. And health depends largely upon the weather.

CHAPTER III

BUSINESS CYCLES IN FOREIGN COUNTRIES

IF the business conditions of the United States depend so closely, upon health, how about other countries? The data for answering this question are scanty. It is easy to show that in agricultural countries like Russia, India, and Spain, the ebb and flow of business appear to be almost entirely determined by the crops. It is quite possible that in those countries the same conditions which cause poor crops are also the direct cause of ill health, but as to that we cannot yet speak with certainty. What we want to know, however, is how far conditions of health determine the course of business in countries where manufacturing and commerce are highly developed. It will scarcely pay to consider small countries like Belgium and Switzerland, for their prosperity and adversity are largely dependent on those of their large neighbors. Austria and Italy, like Russia, are too purely agricultural to answer our purpose. Moreover, for all three of these countries it is difficult to obtain homogeneous statistics covering a sufficiently long period.

This limits our investigation to France, England, and Germany. In France, however, the conditions of business are radically different from those of the United States. In the first place, in spite of her manufactures most parts of France are self-supporting. There is no large section like the North Atlantic States where manufacturing industries completely overshadow agriculture. Hence the foundations of prosperity are more stable in France than in this country. In the next place, the manu-

facturing industries of France cannot be expanded anything like
so easily as those of the United States. This is partly because
the French population is stable and there is relatively little opportunity to draw labor from abroad. We talk about the value of
free immigration in stimulating industry, but we might more
wisely talk about the harm done by free immigration in stimulating hard times. As H. P. Fairchild points out, immigration
helps to rob us of that stability which is so valuable in France.
When good times are upon us immigrants flock to our shores.
They are so eager to work that they keep wages low. Thus at
times when undue expansion is under way the condition of the
labor market does not act as a check as it ought. During the
Great War we saw that scarcity of labor checks many enter-
prises. At that time the scarcity was harmful, but at times of
ordinary industrial expansion our most urgent need is some
agency that will prevent overproduction. In France the fixity of
the labor supply provides such an agent. If factories and other
productive works begin to expand, wages go up because there are
not enough workmen and there is no great foreign supply waiting
eagerly for a chance to fill the gap. Hence the tendency to overproduction is checked instead of being stimulated as it is by our
unreasonable system.

France possesses still another stabilizing influence in its pro-
verbial thrift. Almost every French family considers that savings
are as necessary as earnings. Hence there is always a large body
of capital ready to be drawn upon in every community. This
obviates the danger of contraction of credit which does so much
to accentuate hard times in America. Another effect of the
thrifty habits of the French is, that when there is a slight tendency toward depression, the expenditures of the general public
do not fall off so rapidly as with us. If people's incomes decline
a little they either save less for a while or draw on what they have
already stored up. Many Americans, on the contrary, especially
the recent immigrants, have nothing stored up and have not

learned to save. So long as wages are good they spend all they earn, and thus intensify the overproduction which is the cause of their prosperity. Then, when hours are curtailed, or when they lose their jobs, they have nothing to live on. Not only do they fail to perform any appreciable part as consumers, but they act as a drag on the rest of the community. Their very presence loafing on the streets or hanging about the factory doors in hope of work increases the feeling of insecurity which is one of the prime factors in causing depression. France, being relatively free from this evil, as well as from others that beset America, is also relatively free from financial crises.

England is less thrifty than France, and hence might be expected to show the psychological effect of health much as does the United States. She also depends upon manufacturing and buys food from other regions much as do the North Atlantic States. Moreover, her statistics are very full and reliable, so that she might seem to be ideal as a test of the relation of health to business. Nevertheless a comparison between the deathrate and business activities fails to disclose any such relationship as we have found in the United States. At first sight this may seem to prove that health is not so important as we have supposed. Such a conclusion, however, is scarcely warranted. In the first place, the prosperity of England does not depend upon her own resources to anything like the extent that ours does. One of her greatest lines of business is the carrying trade. That depends on the prosperity of many other countries scattered all over the world. In the same way her food supply does not depend upon her own climatic conditions, but upon those of the United States, Australia, Argentina, India, and Russia. Thus unfavorable conditions of health and of crops at home are apt to be neutralized by favorable conditions abroad, an advantage which we do not possess. Moreover, the British labor supply is less mobile than ours. In this respect conditions are more like those of France. Of course all the European countries draw some labor from their neighbors, but on nothing like the American scale. Moreover, prosperity in all the countries of western Europe is likely to occur at the same time. This of course diminishes the ease with which labor can be diverted from one country to another, and thus lessens the dangers of overproduction. America, on the contrary, possesses a potent attractive force not only in her immediate labor conditions, but in her magic charm as a supposed land of freedom.

There is another and stronger reason why England's deathrate shows so little relation to her economic life. In order to understand this we must anticipate a conclusion which will be fully discussed in the next chapter. The conclusion is that variations in health from year to year are due largely to climatic conditions. This carries with it the corollary that under certain climatic conditions people are mentally stimulated, while under other conditions they are depressed. In England such variations both in health and in feelings are not nearly so marked as in the United States. The extreme fluctuations in the deathrate there are only about half as great as here. More than this, the fluctuations do not appear to be of great importance in their nervous effects. England is located in a fortunate climate where extremes are rare. That is probably one reason why Englishmen seem to Americans phlegmatic. They are not inactive in the sense that tropical people are inactive, but they are not nervous in the way that Americans, Canadians, and Australians are nervous. Nor do they go to those extremes of elation and of despondency which are characteristic of the Russians, and which seem, in part at least, to be the result of extreme fluctuations in climate. Hence the variations in the health of the English do not have nearly so much effect upon their mental activity as do the similar variations in this country. Thus even though England does not show the effect of health upon economic cycles, it amply supports the main thesis of this book. That thesis is, that climatic conditions, through their effect upon health, are largely responsible for differences of mental attitude both from place to place and from time to time. England's climate is bracing, even though it is not subject to extremes. In fact, for real excellence it is perhaps the best in the world. One of its great advantages seems to be that from year to year it does not vary enough to have much effect on the nerves, and thus helps to keep England's business life more steady than that of the United States.

This leaves Germany as the only European country where conditions are enough like those of the United States to furnish a conclusive test. In many ways the resemblance between Germany and the northeastern United States is surprising. In both there is the same great development of manufacturing, and the consequent importation of food. In Germany, far more than in the other countries of Europe, the labor supply is mobile. Although German immigration cannot compare with that which enters the United States, every period of industrial expansion brings a great wave of Poles from the east. Indeed, one of Germany's grievances against the rest of the world has been that while hard times see her own children migrating westward across the sea, good times see their places filled by aliens from the east. In addition to this, the effect of the German climate upon the nerves is somewhat like that of our own. It is not so extreme, to be sure, but it has much more effect than that of England.

Surprising as it may seem in view of Germany's statistical reputation, I have found it hard to obtain any statistics comparable with those available for the United States and England. I have gone through the *Statistische Jahrbuch* again and again, but imports and exports are the only available subjects as to which uniform figures are available for a sufficiently long period. Because of the recency with which Germany became a unified empire, good statistics for the country as a whole are not available earlier than about 1875 and in most cases 1880. Even where statistics are available, they are often divided into those for Prussia, Bavaria, etc., for part of the years, and are given for the whole country in later years only. For our present purpose, however, the figures for imports and exports are sufficient. They give a good idea of the economic condition of the country and that is what we want.

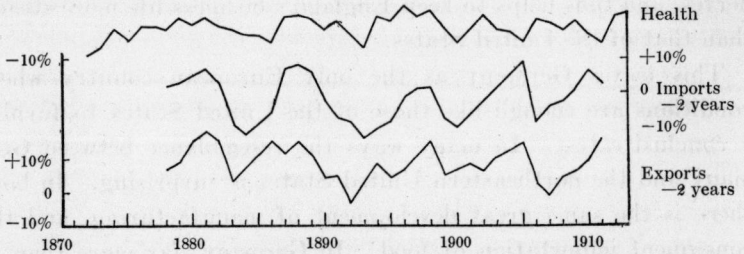

FIGURE 6. Health and Business in Germany

Figure 6 shows the German variations of health, imports and exports so far as the data are available. The curves for imports and exports have been shoved to the left two years, since this appears to be the amount of delay between conditions of health and those of commerce. Notice in the first place that the German curve for deaths does not move up and down anything like so violently as that of the United States. This is partly because it is based on the entire country instead of on only about a seventh of the total population, as in the United States. It is also because the variations from year to year are actually less than in this country. They are less because the Germans are undeniably ahead of us in the public care of health. They are also less because the climate of Germany is less strenuous than that of the United States. Examining the curves in detail it appears that in Germany both imports and exports vary in fairly close harmony with health. The health maximum of 1881 was followed in two years by a maximum of both imports and exports. In the case of the succeeding minimum, however, there was no delay in the case of imports, while the minimum of exports actually occurred a year before the absolute minimum of health. Hence, since the curves are drawn with the imports and exports shoved two years to the left, there does not appear to be much agreement. The health maximum of 1887-1888, however, is faithfully reflected in both of the business curves. So, too, is the minimum of 1893, which is delayed two years in imports and one year in exports. In all three curves the minor maximum of 1891 is apparent, although it is insignificant in the line for imports. Next comes the little maximum of 1894, which is evident in the exports but not in the imports. The general high level of health from 1894 to 1898 has its counterpart in an increase of both imports and exports reaching a maximum in 1900, which appears in Figure 6 as 1898. Then comes a rapid drop in all the curves. Taking the curves as a whole we may say that up to 1900 (or 1902 in the business curves) the course of health is closely followed by that of business, especially in the imports, which seem to be an excellent measure of general prosperity. After 1900, however, the other curves appear to have nothing to do with that of health. That was the time when the German imperial policy began to be effective. German business was not allowed to pursue its natural course as hitherto. It was officially boosted, guided, and, if need be, chastised. Notice the unnatural steadiness with which the imports increased from 1902 to 1907 (1900 to 1905 according to the health dates). The sudden collapse in 1907 may perhaps have had something to do with the American panic. Then once more the government's steady boosting began to have effect.

From this brief survey of European countries we conclude that in Europe as well as in America health has much to do with economic cycles. In countries like England and France the mildness of both the summers and winters causes the variations in nervous activity to be so slight that their effect is concealed by other influences such as the commerce and foreign relations of England and the thrift of France together with her lack of an expansive labor supply. Yet when further analysis is possible, even these countries will probably show a relationship of some kind between health and business. In Germany such a relationship seems clear. Business activities follow the lead of health so long as the government does not interfere. The waves of business are not delayed so long after the waves of health as in the United States, presumably because they are not so large. Otherwise the relationship is similar. Thus far it has been possible only to scratch the ground in this important field. When deeper ploughing is possible rich harvests will probably be reaped.

CHAPTER IV

HOW HEALTH DOES ITS WORK

IN the preceding chapters we have assumed that the relation of health to business is chiefly psychological. Unquestionably, however, the deathrate has an economic effect. In fact there is good reason to think that the economic effect is comparable to that of the crops. Let us examine this matter in the United States. From 1870 to 1910 the annual deathrate in the northeastern quarter of the United States averaged not far from eighteen per thousand. Reckoning in terms of the high prices with which the world is now familiar, it seems safe to say that economists are not extravagant when they estimate the value of the average human life at about $5,000. Of course this varies according to age, health, and ability. Nevertheless if we reckon the expense of bringing up children, the amount that people could earn if they lived to a normal old age, the harm done to business by the taking away of individuals of especial ability, the distress, sorrow, and actual incompetence which death causes among survivors, and the expense of hospitals, undertakers, doctors, nurses, insurance companies and the like, it seems probable that $5,000 is conservative. For our present argument, however, it makes no difference whether we say half as much or twice as much. Each death, as we have already said, means on an average perhaps ten cases of severe sickness and a hundred minor ailments such as colds, sick headaches, backaches, stomach aches, and so on. Probably the minor ailments number far more than a hundred, for practically no one is free from them. Most people, indeed, have at least ten or twenty days per year with some slight ailment,

while none of us dies but once. Since the average life in the
United States is now nearly thirty-five years, that would mean
at least three hundred and fifty minor ailments for each death.
Whatever the exact figures may be, such ailments are very
numerous and almost universal. It is a well-established medical
principle that when the deathrate increases, the amount of sickness
and the number of minor ailments also increase in essentially the
same proportion.

Each sickness, as well as each death, obviously involves a
financial loss to the general public. Not only does the sick person
lose time and wages, provided he is at work, but he is an expense
to the community for food, care, heat, and many other things.
He takes the time of people who ought to be otherwise occupied.
His absence does harm in office, factory, school, or home. Some-
one else has to do his work, and generally does it less efficiently.
The minor ailments are also an expense. The man with a cold or
a headache may go to the office, but he does less work than usual,
although he often will not admit it. Moreover, his work is not
so good, for he makes mistakes and loses his temper. Moreover,
most people lose at least one day each year because of some minor
ailment which does not send them to bed, or cause the doctor to
be summoned. Taking all these things into consideration it
scarcely seems an exaggeration to conclude that the ten major
sicknesses and three hundred minor ailments which accompany
each death cause at least $500 worth of damage. On this basis
each death means an expense of about $5,500, or approximately
$100,000 for the 18 deaths in each 1,000 of the population. In
other words, from 1870 to 1910 the deaths in the United States
cost at the rate of approximately $100 per year for every man,
woman, and child. Even half this figure would be a terrible tax.

This heavy death-tax is not the same from year to year. We
have seen that regardless of the improvement in medical practice
the deathrate may within a few years vary over 20 per cent in
New England and 50 per cent in Chicago. In the northeastern

quarter of the United States as a whole the maximum variation appears to have been about 30 per cent.   According to the present scale of population this would mean a difference of three billion dollars between the best year and the worst.   The labor supply of the country increases or diminishes because of this variation.   Remember that we are dealing not only with the actual losses through death, but with the days when men stay at home because their wives are sick, their babies are dying, or they are called to the bedside of their feeble parents.   Remember that the loss in efficiency includes also the anæmic work done by men and women with bad colds, with indigestion, and with sick headaches, and also the mistakes made by people with shaky nerves.   Think of the stock spoiled, the letters missent, the men wrongly discharged, the bad bargains, and the friction and misunderstanding due to these many causes.   The sum total is enormous.   Remember, too, that all these losses increase in the same ratio as the deathrate.   Can there be any question that when the general health is bad, the country pays a huge tax which would be unnecessary if people's health were good?

We rightly make much of variations in the crops from year to year, but why make so much more of the vegetable crop than of the human crop?   Expressed in dollars and cents the human losses of a year of bad health are of the same order as the material losses due to bad crops.   There is no sense in carefully watching one and neglecting the other.   On a purely economic basis the business men of the country ought to pay as much attention to the deathrate as to the crop reports.   Yet how much space do the two receive relatively in our papers?   How much do our cities spend for the conservation of health?   Is it not ridiculous that in the year 1916 the 213 cities in the United States having a population of over 30,000 spent only $14,000,000 on the conservation of health, while they spent $67,000,000 on the police department and $53,000,000 on the fire department?   Those same cities spent as much on hospitals as on the conservation of health. As much to cure people as to prevent them from being ill! It is as if the Department of Agriculture at Washington spent its money in picking the scale from the leaves of orange trees rather than in discovering how to eradicate this obnoxious blight.

Although I have thus emphasized the economic aspects of health, I believe that the psychological aspects are still more important. We might dwell upon the effect of poor health in promoting crime, vice, stupidity, and misery. Let us confine ourselves, however, to business, and let us see why there is reason to believe that the psychological effect of ill health is even greater than the economic effect. One of the chief reasons for this conclusion is that an obvious economic factor, such as the crops which are the greatest single material resource of the United States, by no means shows so close a connection with business fluctuations as does the deathrate. Important as is the economic effect of ill health, it can scarcely have so great an effect as the crops. The crops have not only their purely material effect but also the great psychological effect which comes from their constant discussion in the papers. The economic effect of ill health has no such reënforcement through publicity. In the second place, if the economic factor in ill health were dominant, it seems as if it would make itself apparent in England. The absence of any apparent effect there, as we have seen, is in accordance with the psychological explanation but not with the economic. The economic effects in England must be similar to those in America, but the psychological effect is apparently far less because of the less severe climate. Again, if it should be found that some of the minor movements of prices on the stock market are associated with fluctuations in the deathrate, it would be strong evidence of the psychological effect of health. Finally, the fact that business men themselves are so strongly convinced of the importance of psychology in business fluctuations seems to be a weighty argument. Their view, with slight modifications, coincides exactly with that to which we are led by a study of health.

In concluding this chapter we may well restate this view of the business man with the modifications suggested by our study of health. At certain times, says the business man, a wave of optimism goes over the community. Many men feel that now is the time for an advance. It is time for the railroad in which they are interested to double-track a new section, run a spur to a new manufacturing town, and improve the stations. Others say it is time to build a factory, boom a neglected mining property, open a new chain of drug stores, or make a market for a new brand of baking powder. One man's optimism, so it is said, communicates itself to another, and thus the idea of expansion is "in the air." Our study of health makes us believe that this phrase "in the air" is literally true. Because the air has certain qualities which we shall examine in the next chapter, good health prevails. Not only does the deathrate drop to a low level, but sicknesses are rare, people do not suffer so much as usual from colds and headaches, and those who are well have a feeling of strength and buoyancy. We all know that feeling, and we know that it makes us hospitable to new ideas. The ideas that have been floating in men's minds seem more feasible than formerly, the difficulties do not seem so formidable. Hence one man here and another there makes a final decision which may have been hanging fire for a long time. Thus a long train of circumstances is set in motion.

Consider your own case. Your financial, social, and moral condition may be exactly the same at two different times. Yet at one time you lie awake at night and wonder whether you can ever pull through. Something that cannot happen for a year—and that may not happen then—seems like a mountain of difficulty. You get up in the morning, determined to play your part perhaps, but dull and hopeless. No, you are not sick. You believe that your judgment is as good as ever, but something is wrong—with the world. A few months later everything is different. You drop asleep as soon as you go to bed; your worries seem to be gone; you can meet that debt, you can build that new wing of the factory, you can increase your sales. The man who seemed three months ago to be your greatest enemy is relatively harmless. Of course he did not do the fair thing, but after all he can't hurt you, and anyhow the poor chap deserves pity with a sick, nervous wife like that. So you go about your business hopefully, although the actual facts are no better and no worse than they were when you were so depressed.

I know that there are many men who say that they decide on their business policy from motives of judgment and not because of their feelings. But do they? One of the directors of a large corporation broaches a new scheme. Does not its reception by the others depend largely upon whether the president or some other particularly influential director happens to favor or oppose it? And does not that man's judgment vary according to whether he has been overworking or is thoroughly rested by a week-end yachting trip? He may not see that his judgment depends on his physical condition, but other people can see it plainly enough.

In claiming that health is of such importance I would not be misunderstood as minimizing the well-established conclusions of business men and economists. Human activities are like the various parts of an engine. Because we happen to be talking about safety valves, we do not thereby minimize the importance of levers and boilers. Each is essential. The piston rod cannot say to the wheels, "I have no need of you." Nor can the bell make the axles unnecessary. All human activities are run by human energy. The cause of that energy is as unknown as is the cause of life. Health is merely an expression of it. Or rather, health, as it were, turns on the steam. Then each part functions according to laws that are well understood. If the steam is turned on too fully, as it is when people feel that sense of elation and recklessness which we all know, the train dashes forward too fast and may jump the track if the curves are too sharp.   If there is not enough steam in the cylinders, as happens when people feel depressed, the engine cannot start on a grade, and the economic force of poor crops or of a scanty supply of ocean tonnage causes the train to slip back a bit on the rails.   What we need is steady good health, such as prevails more commonly in England than here.   If health varies greatly, and if elation and depression are consequently the rule, we may look for financial inflation and depression such as we have in this country, or for alternate waves of revolutionary zeal and dull reaction such as occur in Russia. A steady hand is needed on the valve of health which turns on the steam of human energy.

CHAPTER V

CLIMATE AND HEALTH

WE have already seen that health depends largely upon climate, and hence that fluctuations in the weather have much to do with the course of business. But can such a view be sustained? Granting that health may be the most potent cause of the psychological conditions which cause financial and economic expansion and contraction, what ground is there for believing that health depends primarily on the weather? Aside from a good inheritance, which is of course the first essential, good health depends upon three material factors—proper food, proper drink, and proper air. Exercise is merely a means of insuring that our food, drink, and air have the opportunity to reach all parts of the body, and to be readily eliminated after they have done their work. So, too, with sleep. We need it in order that food, drink, and air may repair the ravages of work.

Among these three factors air is by far the most variable. In civilized countries the water supply is generally fairly good, and its quality rarely varies much from year to year or season to season. Of course diseases like typhoid and dysentery are caused by polluted water, but in 1915, the last year for which figures are available at the time of writing, neither of these caused 1 per cent of the deaths in the registration area of the United States. Moreover, only a small part of this 1 per cent arose from variations in the condition of the water. In the same way, while millions of people may die from lack of food in countries like China and India, less than forty per year have been reported as dying from this cause in the United States since 1900. A

certain number die from malnutrition, and some from over-
eating or from eating unwholesome food, but the total from all
such causes is slight. Moreover, the excess of deaths in one
year over another because of variations in food is almost negligible. Thus while food and drink are highly important, they are
not really variables and cannot be appealed to as causes of the
great variability in the deathrate from day to day, week to week,
month to month, and year to year.

With air the case is different. "Air is the first necessity of
life. We may live without food for days and without water for
hours; but we cannot live without air more than a few minutes.
Our air supply is therefore of more importance than our food or
water supply, and good ventilation becomes the first rule of
hygiene." These words are taken from the beginning of the first
chapter of a book called "How to Live." It is extremely significant that they were written by Professor Fisher who has an
international reputation as an expert on food, and by Dr. Fisk
whose reputation is largely based upon his work in respect to
drink. These experts upon food and drink look upon air as the
most important factor in health because air is the great variable.
The air varies constantly in temperature, humidity, movement,
electrification, percentage of carbon dioxide, dustiness, and many
other characteristics. A room cannot be closed an hour without
causing a distinct change in the quality of the air. Coupled with
all this is the fact that the human body is far more sensitive to
the air than to any other feature of environment. A person who
without a tremor can eat raw oysters, hot soup, cold lobster
salad, frozen ice cream, and hot coffee, will become uncomfortable
in a minute if air at a temperature of 65° instead of 70° blows on
her neck.

As an example of the importance of the air, that is, of climate,
take New York City from 1900 to 1915. The following table
shows the average temperature of the months of March and July

and the percentages by which the deaths departed from the normal for the year in question.

DEATHS IN NEW YORK CITY DURING JULY AND MARCH, 1900-1915

July			March		
Mean Temperature	No. of Months	Departure of Deaths from Normal	Mean Temperature	No. of Months	Departure of Deaths from Normal
78°F	2	+19.4%	35°-36°	5	+21.4%
76°-77°	3	+9.6%	37°-38°	3	+11.7%
75°	4	+6.4%	39°-41°	4	+8.7%
74°	4	+4.3%	44°-48°	4	+7.5%
73°	2	−5.2%			
71°	1	−9.5%			

In July the higher the temperature the higher the deathrate. The difference between the hottest and the coolest years amounts to 28.9 per cent. In March the opposite is the case, for the warmest months had 13.9 per cent less deaths than the coldest. In both cases notice how regularly the deathrate declines as the temperature becomes more favorable. Under ordinary conditions no differences in food or drink ever cause one tenth as much variation. Neither do epidemics cause any such variations in the deathrate. Among the epidemic diseases of the United States pneumonia, diphtheria, and influenza cause much the largest number of deaths, provided we omit tuberculosis. Tuberculosis, however, acts very slowly so that the deathrate from this cause, which was 9.5 per cent of the total in 1915, shows only very slight variations from year to year. Pneumonia, although infectious, depends almost wholly upon the weather conditions. It caused 6.1 per cent of all the deaths in 1915. Influenza and diphtheria each accounted for only 1.2 per cent of the total deaths in 1915. Yet that was an uncommonly bad year for influenza. Even when these epidemic diseases are at their worst none of them causes a variation of more than 2 or 3 per cent of the deaths in the country as a whole.

Let us turn back now to Figure 1. We there saw that with slight exceptions the deathrate in various parts of the United States varies in harmony. We have already seen that variations in the food supply and water supply cannot be the cause of this. Hard times, as we have also seen, are preceded, not followed or accompanied, by a low deathrate. Therefore they cannot be responsible for the uniform fluctuations in health all over the country. Epidemics, as we have just seen, are not competent to cause such great fluctuations. Moreover, as will appear later, they are subject to the same sort of fluctuations as are other diseases, and the cause is apparently the same. This leaves the weather as the only factor capable of producing such marked variations in health over such wide areas. We have just seen that in New York a difference of 7°F in the average temperature of the month of July is accompanied by a difference of nearly 30 per cent in the number of deaths. Anyone who reads the daily weather reports knows that extreme weather in Chicago, for example, is almost sure to be followed by similar weather farther east. Thus in the weather we clearly have a factor which not only has an enormous influence upon health and thus upon business, but which also varies in the same way over vast areas.

Let us inquire further into the relation of health to the weather. Figure 7 shows how the average daily deathrate of several countries varies from month to month when hundreds of thousands or millions of deaths are considered. Finland, for example, is a country where the summer is never too hot, but where the winters are cold and trying. Notice how the deathrate reaches a maximum in winter and declines steadily to a minimum in summer. Next come curves for the eastern United States from Massachusetts to Washington. This is a region where the winters are cold enough to be harmful, while the summers are hot for at least a short time. In every case the deaths are most numerous in February or March, that is, at the end of the winter. They decline until June, or in the case of Washington until May. Then they increase during the hot weather, decline to an autumn minimum which generally comes in October, and rise again as cold weather comes on. In Massachusetts, where the summers are usually not oppressive for more than a few days at a time,

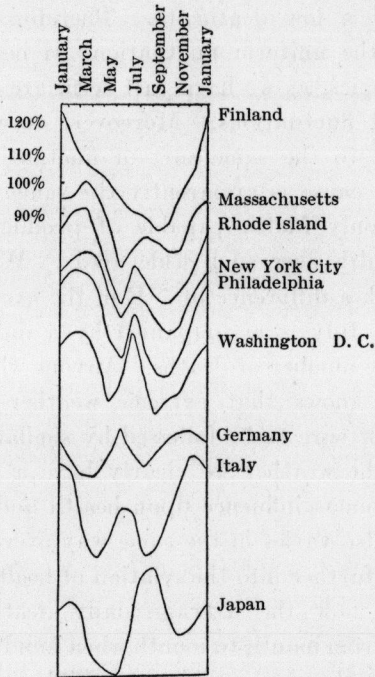

FIGURE 7.   Seasonal Distribution of
Deaths in the United States

The scale for Finland is indicated in
percentages of the yearly normal. For all
the other curves the scale is the same
except that the zero is at a different level.

the increase in the deathrate in summer is not nearly so great as in winter. As one goes southward, however, the relative harmfulness of the summer increases until at Washington the warm months are worse than the winter.

In foreign countries the same principles apply. In Germany, for instance, there is a bad time in August, but it does not last so long as the similar period during the winter. In Italy the summer is worse than in Germany, for the longer duration of the hot weather lengthens the period of increased deaths. The Italian winter is also much worse than the German winter, which seems surprising at first. This is partly because the Italians, like other people who live in relatively uniform climates with little variation from day to day, lack endurance. Moreover, the care of health receives much more attention in Germany than in Italy. The Japanese curve in Figure 7 also shows the dominating effect of climate. In Japan the late summer and early fall are very damp as well as hot. Hence this season is much worse than the winters or than any of the summers thus far discussed.

We might go on with a large number of other curves of this kind, for nearly sixty million deaths have actually been plotted in this way. They all demonstrate the dependence of health upon climate. It will be better, however, to inquire now into the precise conditions of climate which promote health and which thus influence the business and civilization of the world. For this purpose let us examine about 9,000,000 deaths in the United States, France, and Italy, and see under what conditions of temperature, humidity, and variability the deathrate is highest or lowest. To begin with temperature and humidity, Figures 8 B to 11 are what are known as "climographs" for the northern and southern halves of France and Italy respectively. A climograph is simply a diagram representing the effect of climate upon living beings. The method by which these have been prepared is explained in the Appendix. In the present diagrams the figures on the left indicate the average temperature taking day and night together. Those at the top indicate the average humidity in the same way. Dark shading means good health and light shading poor health. The unshaded areas mean that no months have the particular combi-

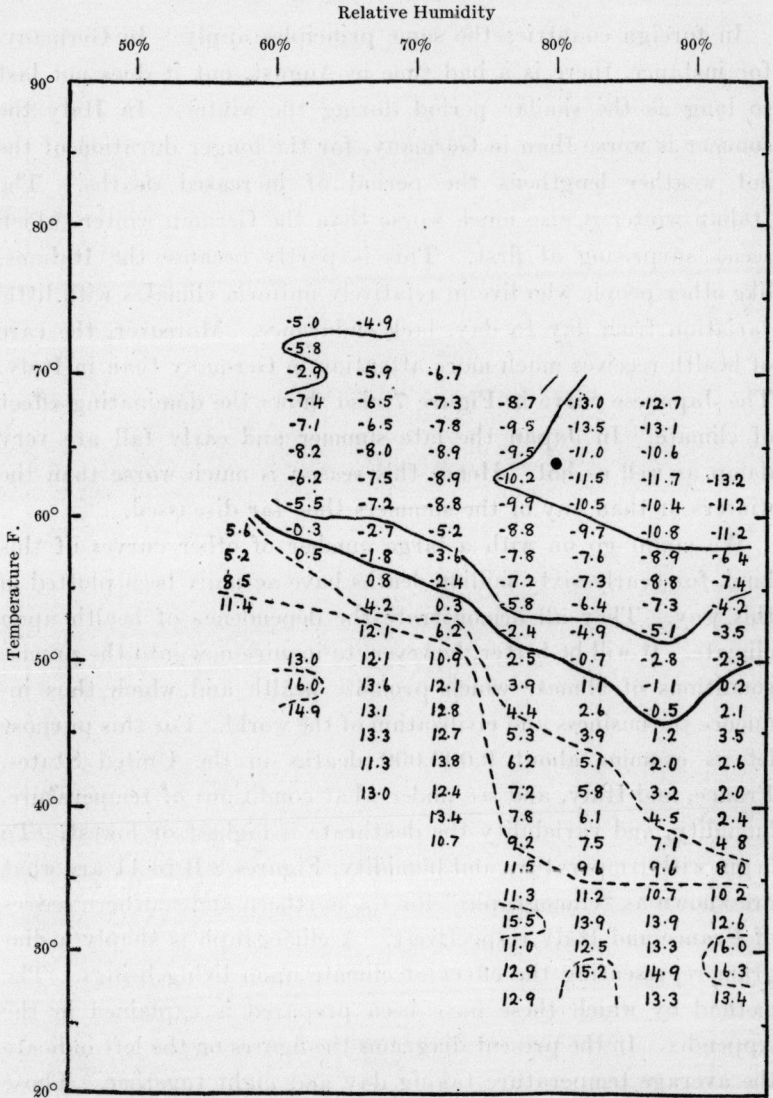

FIGURE 8 A.   Unsmoothed Climograph of Northern France, 1901-1910
Based on 1,315,000 Deaths

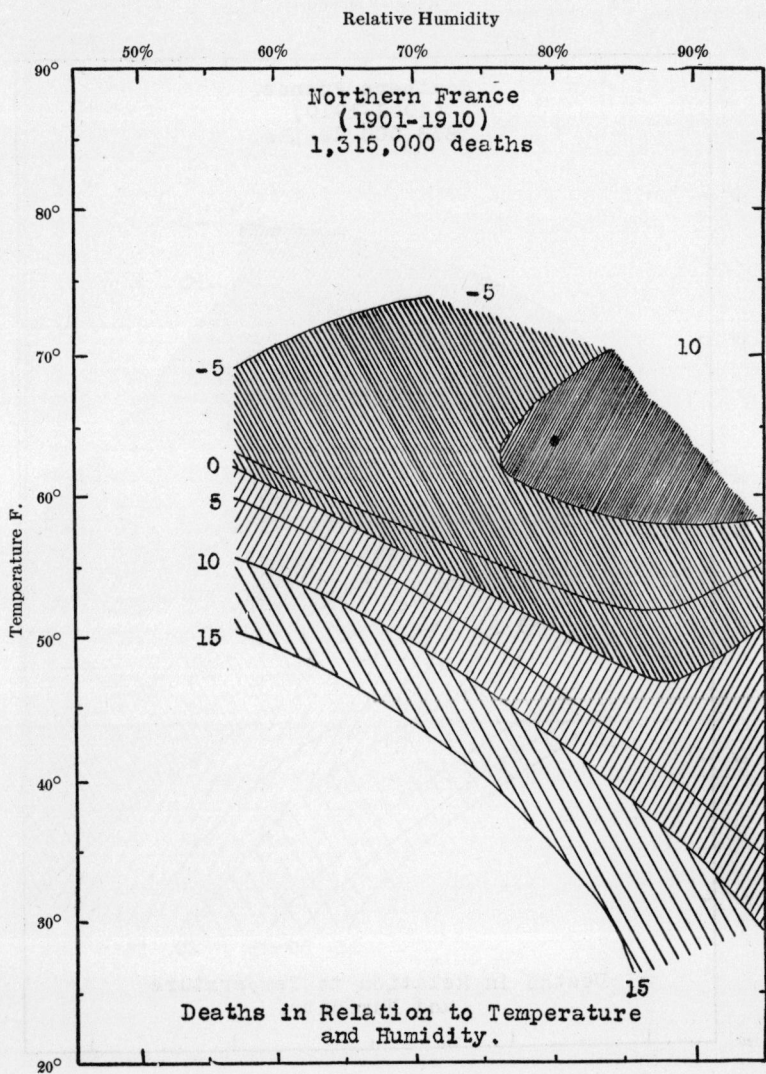

FIGURE 8 B.   Smoothed Climograph of Northern France

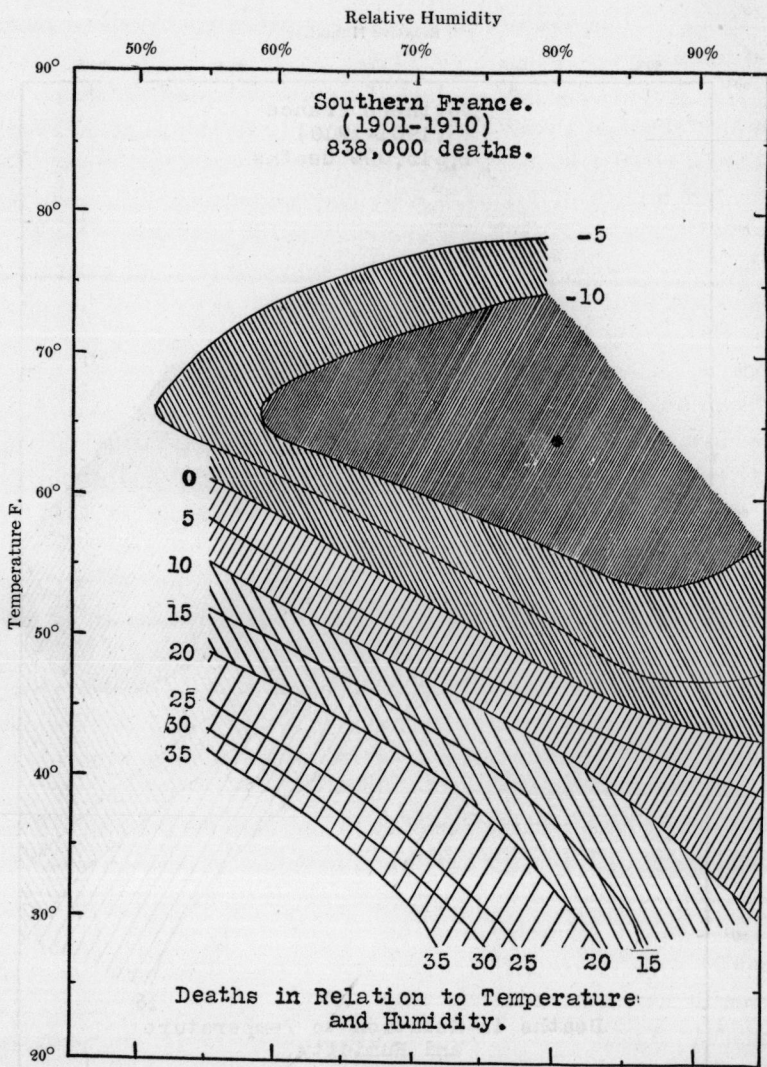

FIGURE 9.   Climograph of Southern France

nations of temperature and humidity indicated by those parts of the diagrams.

To take a concrete example, suppose we want to know the healthfulness of a month having a mean temperature of 60°F and a mean relative humidity of 80 per cent in northern France. On the left margin of Figure 8 B we find the number 60° beside the word "temperature." Then we ascertain the point where the level thus indicated lies directly below the figure 80 per cent among the humidity figures at the top. The point thus determined lies close to the curved line marked —10, and on the edge of the most heavily shaded part of the diagram. The curved lines are called "isopracts," or lines of equal efficiency. The numbers, such as —10, 0, +10, etc., mean that on an average all the months having the combinations of temperature and humidity included within the —10 line, for example, have an average deathrate at least 10 per cent less than that of the year as a whole. A month having an average temperature of 70° and a humidity of 80 per cent would also fall close to the —10 isopract, but on the upper side of the heavily shaded area. Similarly a month having a temperature of 65° and a humidity of 85 per cent would fall well within this isopract, which means that in such months the deaths usually fall below the yearly average by even more than 10 per cent.

On the other hand, suppose the temperature averages 60°, as in the first case, but the humidity is low, only 60 per cent. This combination of weather conditions occupies a position close to the isopract marked 0. That is, in northern France a very dry month with a temperature of 60° is not nearly so healthful as a wetter month having the same temperature. The health in such months averages no better than the normal for the year as a whole. Again, if the temperature averages only 50° and the humidity is very low—less than 60 per cent—the deathrate rises notably, for Figure 8 shows that in such cases it averages 15 per cent above the yearly average. In wet months, however, an equally high deathrate, as may be judged from the curve of the

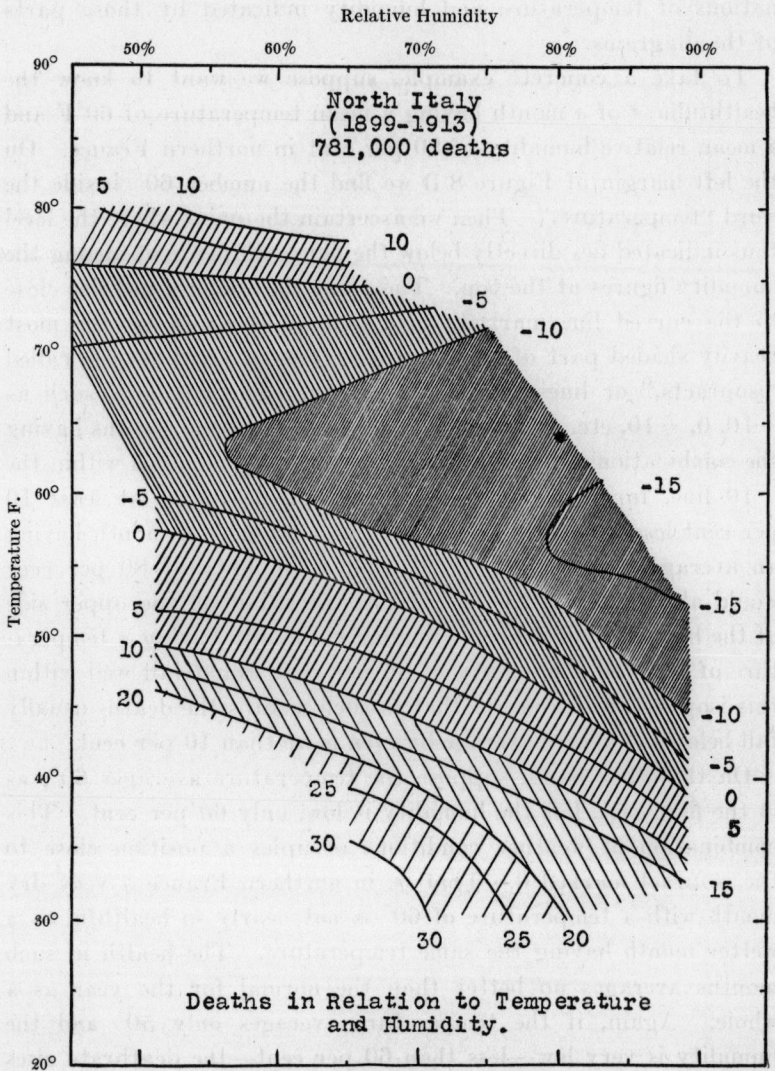

FIGURE 10.   Climograph of Northern Italy

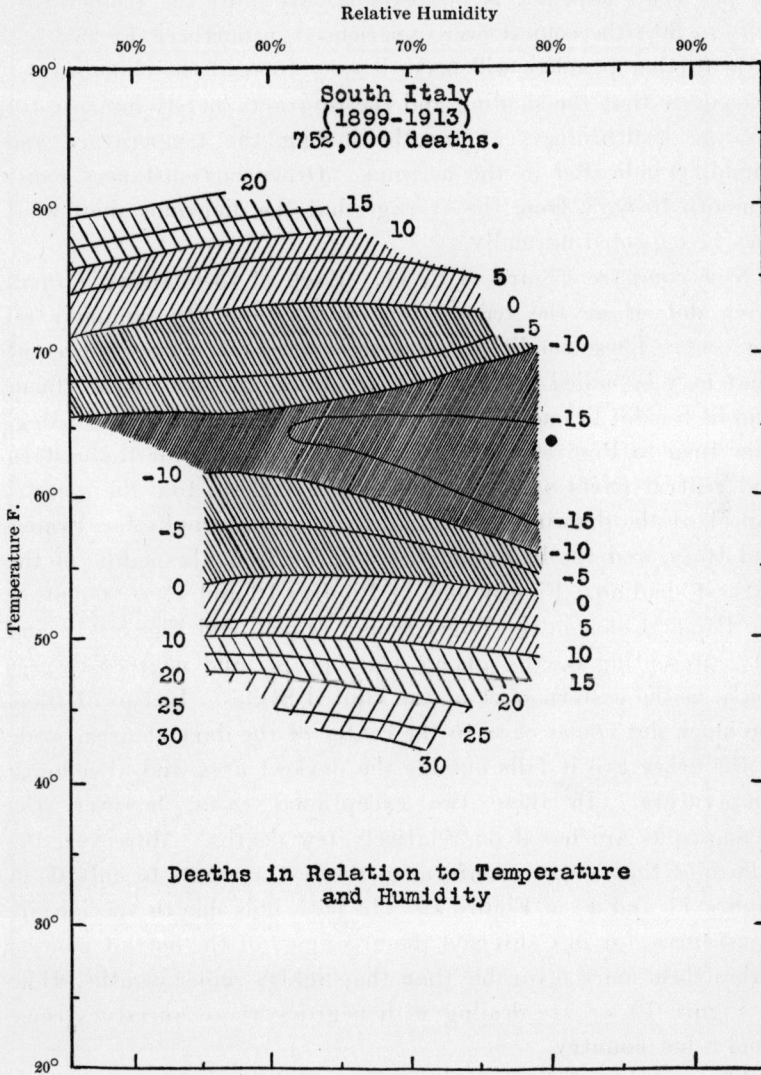

FIGURE 11. Climograph of Southern Italy

15 per cent isopract, is not experienced until the temperature falls to 30°, the coldest ever experienced in northern France. A little further practice will make it easy to read the climographs. Remember that the shading and the isopracts merely indicate the average healthfulness of months having the temperature and humidity indicated in the margins. Other circumstances cause a month to vary from the average, but the diagrams show what may be expected normally.

Now compare Figures 8 to 11. Each of them shows a small black dot where the temperature is 64° and the humidity 80 per cent. These conditions seem to be the best. They represent what may be called the optimum or ideal. In each of the climographs the dot lies not far from the center of the heaviest shading. Now turn to Figures 12 to 15, four climographs for the eastern and central parts of the United States. Here, too, the general aspect of the drawings is similar to the climographs for France and Italy, and the black dot lies not far from the middle of the darkest shading. Finally look at Figures 16 and 17 representing the Pacific Coast in the Puget Sound region, and Figures 18 and 19 representing deaths among white people and negroes respectively in the eastern part of the United States. In two of these the black dot comes close to the center of the darkest area, while in the other two it falls outside the darkest area and at a lower temperature. In these two exceptional cases, however, the climographs are based on relatively few deaths. Moreover, the failure of these two to conform to the rest amounts to only 6° in Figure 17 and 4° in Figure 19. In both it is due to special circumstances, for in California the breeziness of the hottest months makes them more favorable than the slightly cooler months, while in Figure 19 we are dealing with negroes whose ancestors come from a hot country.

These twelve climographs, representing nearly 9,000,000 deaths, agree with the results obtained from a less careful study of over 50,000,000 other deaths in Belgium, Finland, Sweden,

Japan, Russia, Scotland, Austria, and Germany. In a word, the human race seems to have the best health when the average temperature for day and night together is 64°F, that is, when the thermometer rises to about 70° at midday, and drops to perhaps 55° at night. One would suppose that the Swedes of the far north would have become wonted to a temperature colder than that which is best for the Sicilians of the sunny south, but such is not the case. Even the dusky American negroes, whose ancestors have lived for unnumbered ages in the tropical heat of Africa and who still live where it is fairly warm, are at their best in a temperature scarcely higher than that which is most favorable for the blond Finns under the shadow of the Arctic Circle. In fact, the poor Finns appear never to have a month warm enough to put them at their best physically. Their deathrate keeps declining as the temperature goes up, but might go still lower if the summer were a little warmer.

Thus far we have made no allowance for contagious diseases except in Figures 18 and 19. This makes no difference, however, for these two climographs are essentially the same as the others. Moreover, I have prepared the climograph for the deaths from contagious diseases which occurred in the same years and in the same places as the deaths from non-contagious diseases used in preparing Figure 18. This climograph is as regular as the others. It differs from them in only two respects: First, a departure from the optimum has a more pronounced effect with contagious diseases than with others. Second, at high temperatures the effect of low humidity is less harmful and of high humidity more harmful than with ordinary diseases. This last effect is quite marked. Nevertheless, the optimum is the same no matter which category is considered.

Such uniformity is most striking, but it is what the biologist would expect. Every species of plant and animal has its optimum temperature, the temperature at which its activities are greatest. It may happen, however, that one kind of activity is greatest at

Relative Humidity

50%   60%   70%   80%   90%

```
                                          Temperature F.
```

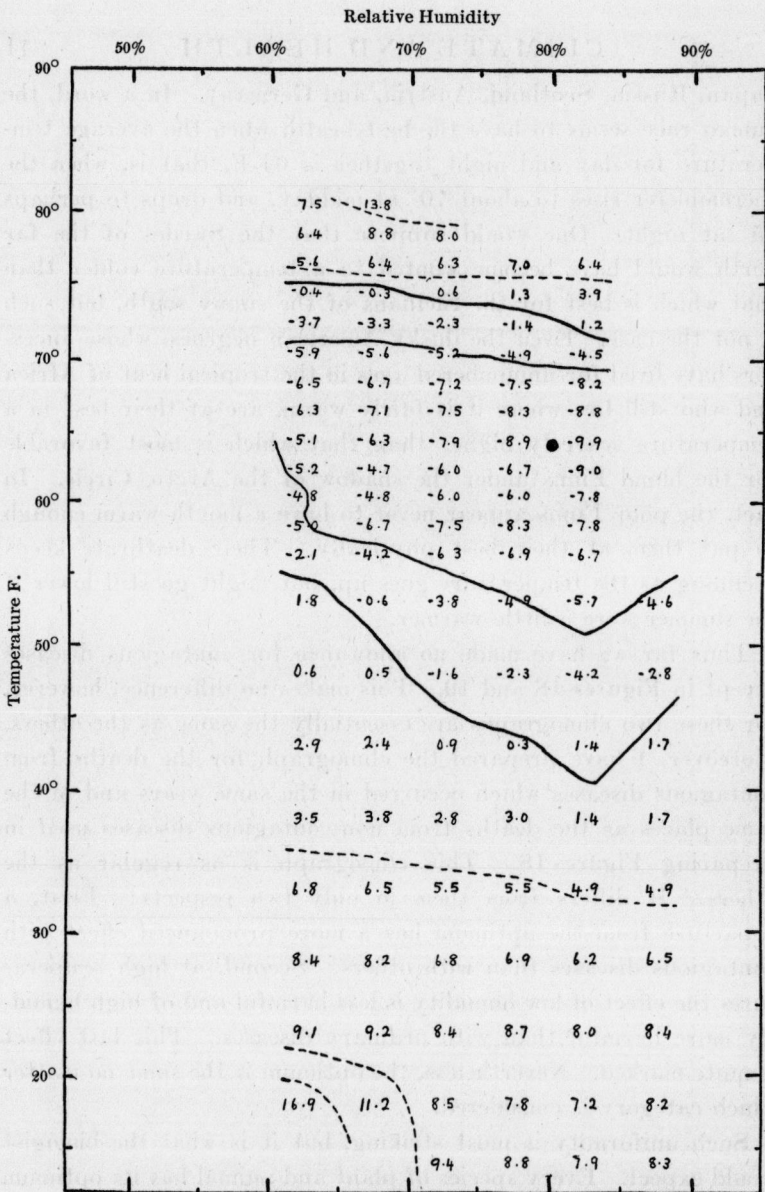

FIGURE 12 A.   Unsmoothed Climograph of the Northeastern
United States

The numeric data points within the climograph (arranged by temperature and relative humidity):

7.5	-13.8			
6.4	8.8	8.0		
-5.6	6.4	6.3	7.0	6.4
-0.4	-0.3	0.6	1.3	3.9
-3.7	-3.3	-2.3	-1.4	1.2
-5.9	-5.6	-5.2	-4.9	-4.5
-6.5	-6.7	-7.2	-7.5	-8.2
-6.3	-7.1	-7.5	-8.3	-8.8
-5.1	-6.3	-7.9	-8.9	-9.9
-5.2	-4.7	-6.0	-6.7	-9.0
-4.8	-4.8	-6.0	-6.0	-7.8
-5.0	-6.7	-7.5	-8.3	-7.8
-2.1	-4.2	-6.3	-6.9	-6.7
1.8	-0.6	-3.8	-4.9	-5.7	4.6
0.6	0.5	-1.6	-2.3	-4.2	-2.8
2.9	2.4	0.9	0.3	1.4	1.7
3.5	3.8	2.8	3.0	1.4	1.7
6.8	6.5	5.5	5.5	-4.9	4.9
8.4	8.2	6.8	6.9	6.2	6.5
9.1	9.2	8.4	8.7	8.0	8.4
16.9	11.2	8.5	7.8	7.2	8.2
		9.4	8.8	7.9	8.3
```

Temperature axis: 90°, 80°, 70°, 60°, 50°, 40°, 30°, 20°
```

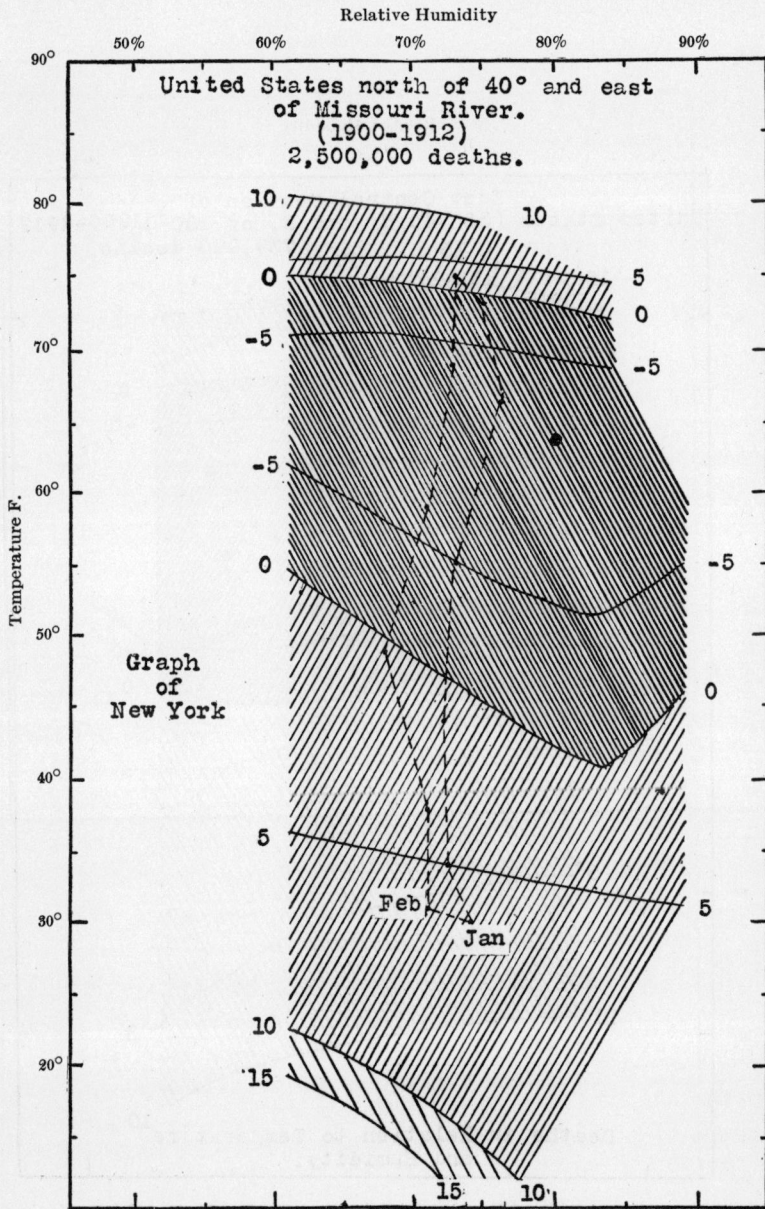

Relative Humidity

50% 60% 70% 80% 90%

United States north of 40° and east
of Missouri River.
(1900-1912)
2,500,000 deaths.

Temperature F.

Graph
of
New York

Feb   Jan

FIGURE 12 B.   Smoothed Climograph of the Northeastern United States

The dash-line in the center shows the conditions of temperature and humidity in
New York City for January, February and so on through the year. Note that 5
months lie in the heavy shading and 7 outside.

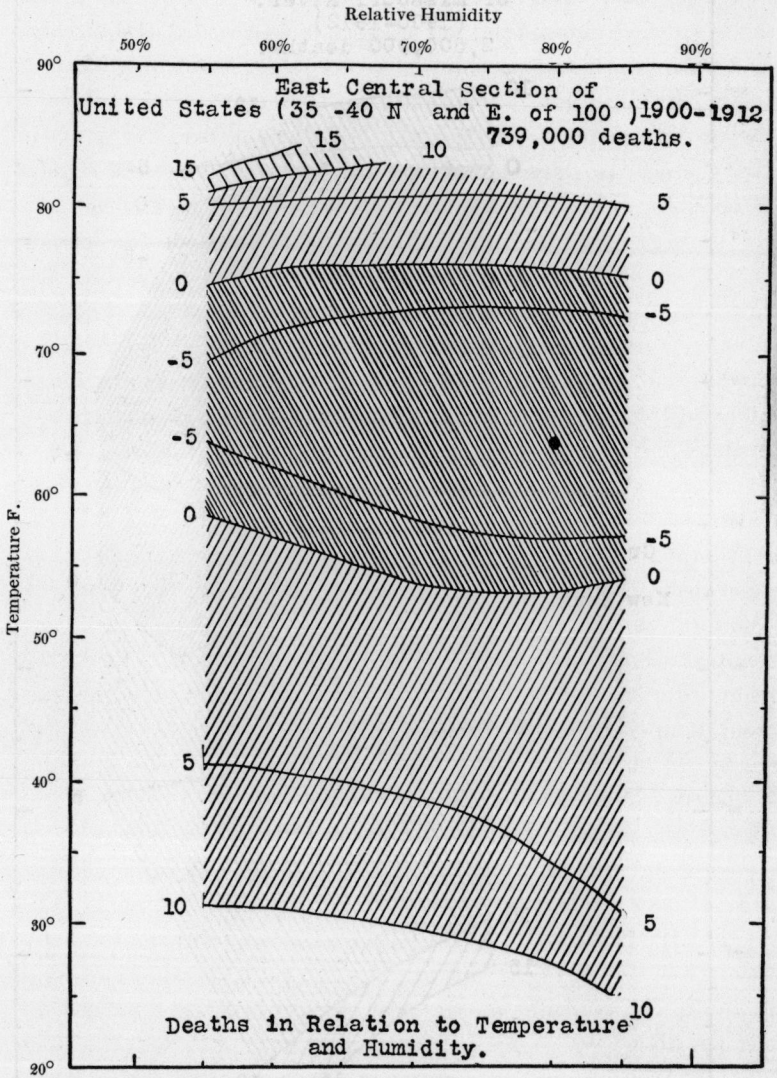

FIGURE 13.   Climograph of the East Central United States

one temperature and another at another.   Little one-celled
creatures called paramœcia and amœbas, cold-blooded crustaceans
such as the crayfish, amphibians like the frog, and warm-blooded
animals like mice, not to mention a host of plants, have all been
tested in this respect.   In each the best temperature for a given
activity seems to be constant for the species.   It seems highly
probable that when fuller data are available we shall find that
even the negro has the same optimum as the rest of the human
race.   Perhaps the temperature optimum is something like the
temperature of the blood which is the same for all races, and does
not vary from the tropics to the poles.   Indeed, it seems quite
probable that man's uniform response to the outside temperature
is due to the fact that his inside temperature remains always
the same.

If men of all races are physically at their best at a mean temperature of 64°, why are not the people of the Hawaiian Islands,
for example, who have lived for many generations in almost that
temperature, the strongest in the world?   Why are they not able
to endure as the white man endures?   Why have they not
developed a high civilization?   The answer is twofold.   First, the
optimum for mental activity is not the same as for physical, and
second, temperature is by no means the only factor.   As to mental
activity the matter has not yet been investigated so fully as could
be wished.   Nevertheless the investigations of Lehmann and
Pedersen on school children, the general results of observations
on mental activity in many countries, and my own study of the
marks of over 1,600 students at West Point and Annapolis indicate that the best mental work is done at a temperature decidedly
lower than the physical optimum.   At both West Point and
Annapolis the students do the best work when the temperature
averages about 40°.   As I have explained in "Civilization and
Climate," this happens in spite of the fact that the season when
this temperature prevails is different in the two places.   Whether
the true mental optimum is 40°, that is, when there are mild frosts

at night and a noon temperature approaching 50°; or whether it is a little higher, there seems to be little question that it is distinctly lower than the physical optimum.   A high civilization

Relative Humidity

30%   40%   50%   60%   70%   80%   90%

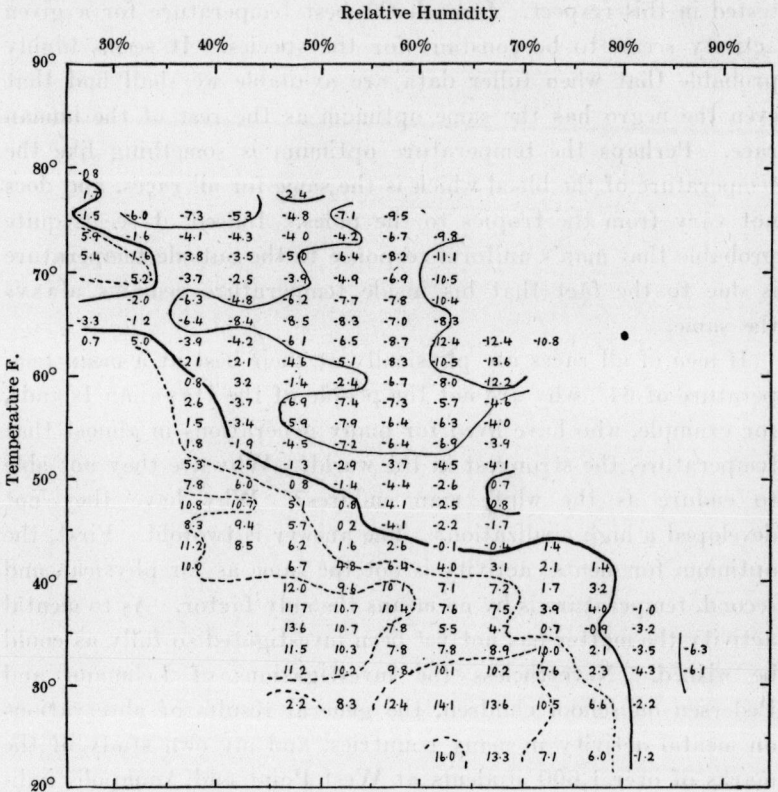

FIGURE 14 A.   Unsmoothed Climograph of the Dry Interior of the United States

cannot be based either upon physical well-being or mental well-being alone.   The two seem to be equally necessary.   Therefore the best climate would apparently be one in which the winters are cool enough so that there are several months with frost, while the

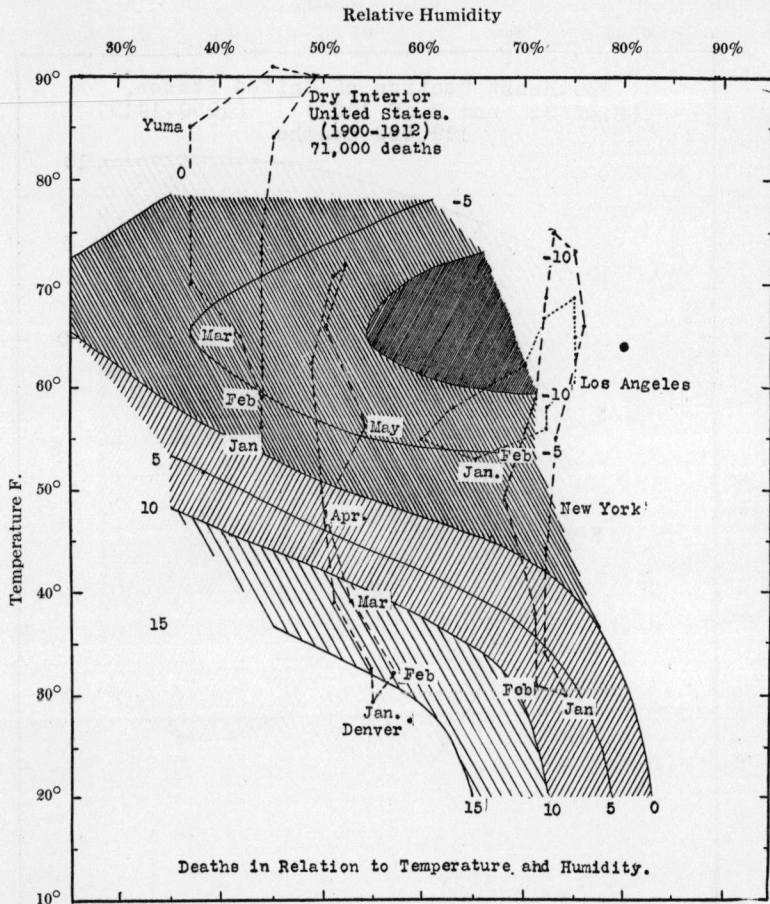

Relative Humidity

Dry Interior
United States.
(1900-1912)
71,000 deaths

Deaths in Relation to Temperature and Humidity.

FIGURE 14 B. Smoothed Climograph of the Dry Interior

For purposes of comparison, graphs showing the temperature and humidity month by month have been added. Notice how much too hot and dry the climate is at Yuma. Denver is also so dry that its cold weather has a very bad effect. Los Angeles appears better than New York at first sight, but as a matter of fact the reverse is the case, because New York has a stimulating variability which is lacking in Los Angeles. See Figures 12 B and 17.

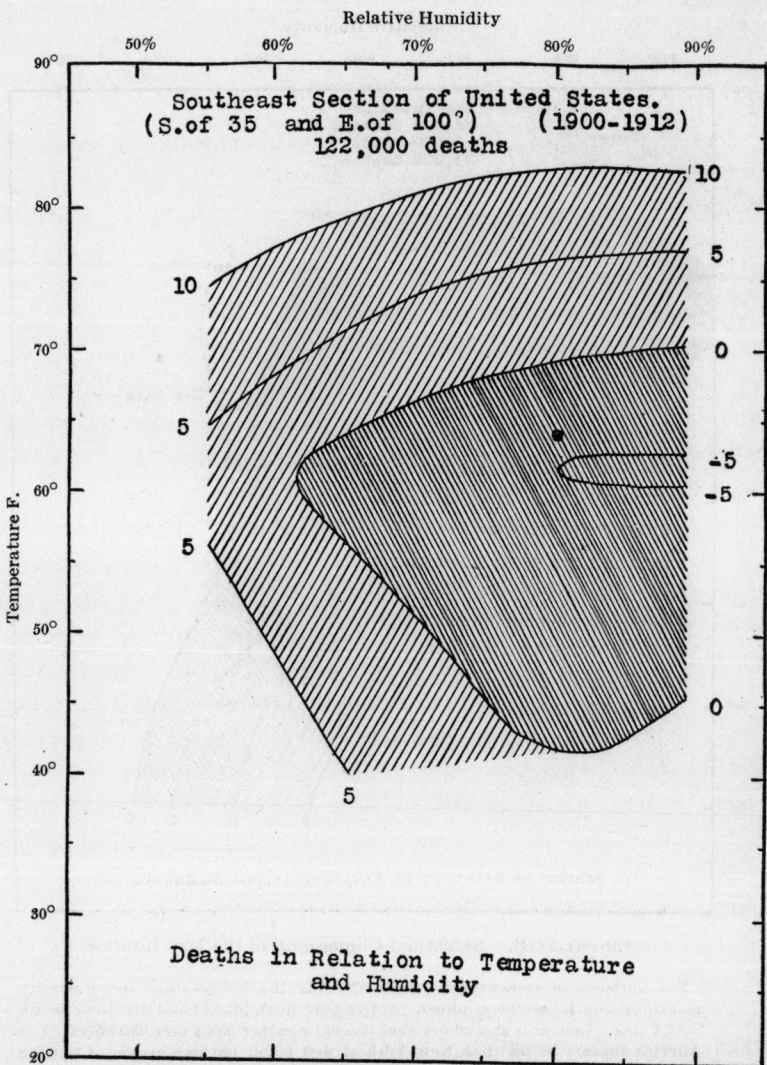

FIGURE 15. Climograph of the Southeastern United States

summers are warm enough so that there is a considerable period when the thermometer approaches 70° at noon. Such conditions apparently prevailed in the region where our ancestors acquired their present adaptation to climate.

In this connection a curious fact should be noted in respect to the negroes. For sixteen months Miss Ellen Cope, Mr. H. S. Williams, and some of the other teachers at Hampton Institute carried on a series of tests under the direction of the author. Eleven young men and eleven young women, all being negroes ranging from seventeen to twenty-five years of age, were given daily tests at a set hour under highly uniform conditions. Their physical strength was tested by pressing a dynamometer ten times. Their mental activity was tested by placing letters in the proper order on some prepared boards and by the common test of striking out letters on a printed sheet. The test with the boards proved much the more satisfactory. At the beginning of each test each scholar had before him a board with a series of compartments arranged in horizontal rows of seven. On the left of these the various letters of the alphabet were placed in piles arranged differently each day so that it was impossible to learn any particular arrangement. After the pupils had been called to attention, the teacher slowly read five letters, started a stop-watch and let it run a minute. The pupils had to remember the order of the letters, which proved to be a fairly severe memory test; find them among the piles on their left; and place them in the proper order in the little compartments as many times as possible. At the end of a minute the teacher called time, read a new set of letters, and the work was repeated. This was done five times each day.

These tests involved a physical factor, namely, the speed with which the pupils moved their hands, but they involved to an equal or higher degree the mental factors of attention and memory. Reason, however, was not involved. Hence I do not feel sure whether the results show a real mental difference between the

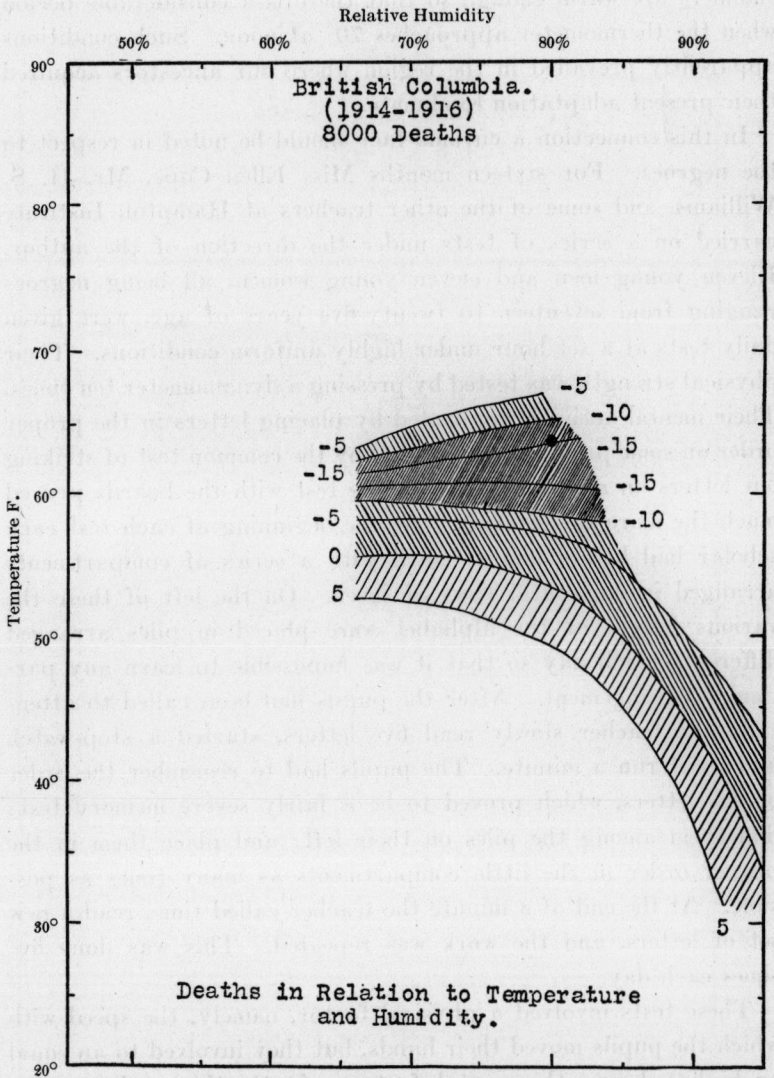

Relative Humidity

FIGURE 16.   Climograph of British Columbia

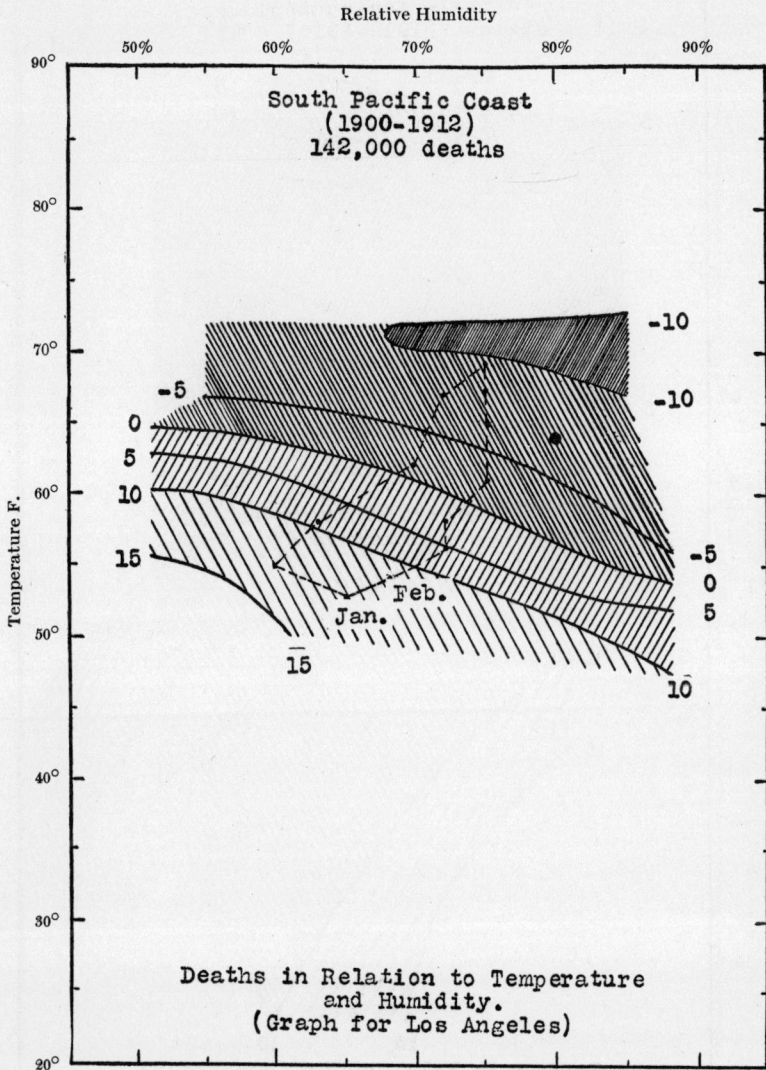

FIGURE 17.   Climograph of Southern California

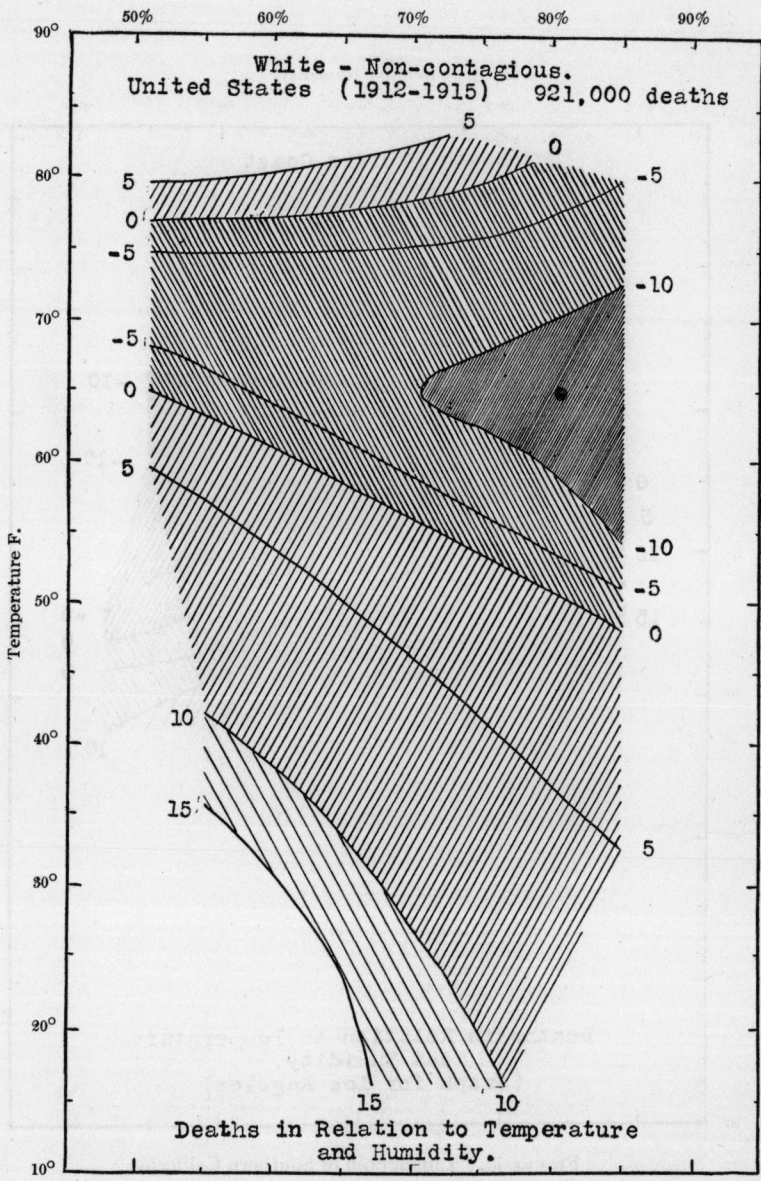

FIGURE 18. Climograph of the White Race in the Eastern United States

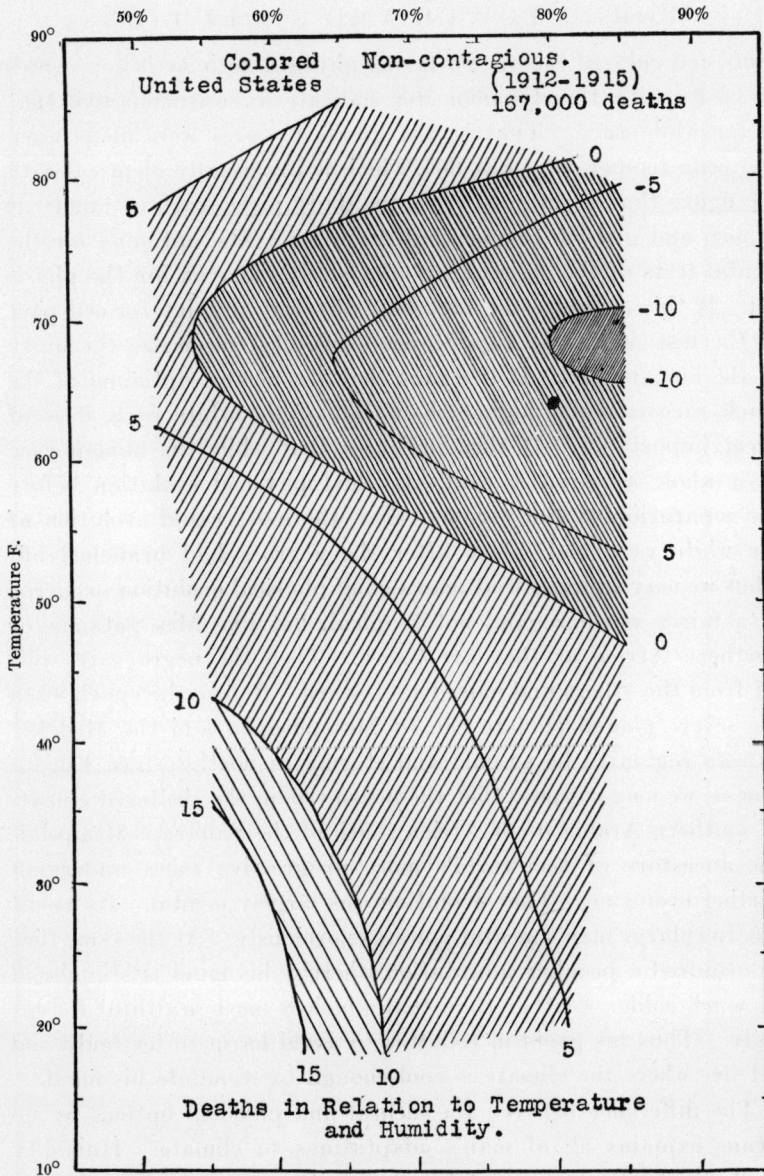

FIGURE 19.   Climograph of the Colored Race in the Eastern
United States

white and colored races. So far as physical activity is concerned,
the tests with the dynamometer indicate an optimum like that
of the white race. That is, the greatest scores were made when
the mean temperature was 60°, which is practically identical with
the figure that I obtained from the daily piece work of hundreds
of men and girls in Connecticut factories. The optimum for the
mental tests of the negroes was almost the same as for the physical. If this is due to the fact that physical activity formed part
of the test, it has no significance except to emphasize the unity
of the human race. If it means that the mental optimum of the
black race is really higher than that of the white race, it is of
great importance. It then indicates that while the human race
as a whole apparently made its chief physical evolution before
the separation of the various races, the most rapid evolution of
the white race took place after the negroes had branched off.
Thus we may suppose that man's chief physical evolution occurred
in a fairly warm region, not tropical, but like Mesopotamia or
northern Africa as they are today. Then the negro race split
off from the others and moved southward. Before the epoch when
the severe glacial climate caused Mesopotamia and the Mediterranean region to be as cold and stormy as northwestern Europe
now is, we may suppose that the negro was in the sheltered climate
of southern Arabia or of Africa south of the Sahara. Meanwhile
the ancestors of the world's more progressive races underwent
further evolution. That evolution was largely mental. Its result
was to enlarge man's mental powers enormously. At the same time
he acquired a peculiar adaptation whereby his mind is stimulated
by much colder weather than that which is most healthful for his
body. Thus his problem today is to avoid harm to his body and
yet live where the climate is cool enough to stimulate his mind.

The difference between the mental and physical optima by no
means explains all of man's adaptations to climate. Humidity
is of great importance. Glance over Figures 8 to 19. Notice
that in every case the curved lines or isopracts separating the

different health conditions converge somewhat toward the left. In eight cases out of twelve some of them are actually closed on the left at the level of the optimum temperature. This is important. It means that at the most favorable temperatures a fairly high degree of moisture, that is, a relative humidity of about 80 per cent for day and night together, is the most favorable. Moreover, dry weather increases the deathrate, as appears from the way in which the shading becomes lighter on the left side of many of the diagrams. Even at high temperatures very dry air is bad, as may be seen in Figures 10, 13, 18, and others. Damp, warm air is also harmful, as everyone knows, and as appears in Figures 11 and 12. It is surprising, however, to see how much less harm is done by warm damp air than by warm dry air. I confess that this does not seem reasonable; it seems to go counter to our ordinary experience. Yet it is scarcely possible to question the reliability of our diagrams for they are based on the official records of nearly 9,000,000 deaths and on the official figures of the weather bureaus of some of the greatest countries.

When we examine the lower parts of Figures 8 to 19, the bad effect of dry air becomes even more surprising. Notice how the lower isopracts curve downward on the right in almost every diagram. Take Figure 9 for example. At a mean temperature of 30° and a relative humidity of 70 per cent the deaths are 35 per cent more than the normal. At the same temperature, but with a humidity of 90 per cent, the deaths are only 15 per cent above the normal, a gain of 20 per cent. Notice the same feature in other diagrams, Figures 10, 14, 16, 18, and 19. In cold weather dry air seems to be exceedingly harmful. Only in southern Italy, as appears in Figure 11, does there seem to be little difference in the effect of moist and dry air in winter. Southern Japan likewise seems to show the same condition, for there dry winter weather does no more harm than moist. As I have shown elsewhere, the apparent effect of dryness cannot be due to the season at which the weather happens to be dry. If we compare the dry Januaries with the wet Januaries of the same temperature at specific places such as New York, Chicago, San Francisco, or elsewhere, we find that the dry are systematically less healthful. The same is true if we compare the wet and dry Februaries or Marches. Neither can the wind be the cause of the many deaths, for when we compare the most windy Januaries or Februaries and so forth with the least windy, we find by no means such a difference as when we compare wet and dry.

The only satisfactory explanation of the harmful effect of dry air in winter seems to be that our houses are heated. Southern Italy and southern Japan, the two places where dry winter air does no harm, are also the only two where the houses are not heated in winter. At temperatures from 65° to 70° such as prevail in our houses in winter, dry air is harmful, as is clearly evident in most of the diagrams. In Figure 14, which represents the dry interior of the United States, a relative humidity of less than 30 per cent increases the deathrate by at least 10 per cent above what prevails when the relative humidity is 70 per cent or higher. In winter, when we heat the outside air from near the freezing point to about 70°, we give our houses a climate as dry as that of the driest parts of the continental interior. Such dryness there in summer causes an increase of at least 10 per cent in the deathrate, as appears in Figure 14. It causes similar harm to health elsewhere in winter, as appears in the lower parts of most of our climographs. Apparently during the long processes of man's evolution he has become adapted not only to certain strictly limited conditions of temperature, but also to a relatively high degree of humidity. This does not complete the tale of climatic adjustments, but it shows how extraordinarily delicate is man's adjustment to the air in which he lives. It proves that "air is the first necessity of life," and also that changes in the air must be the most potent causes of changes in human health.

CHAPTER VI

THE IMPORTANCE OF VARIABILITY

IT is not enough to understand man's extremely sensitive adjustment to temperature and humidity. We must understand the effect of changes. A *variable* climate has utterly different effects from a uniform climate even though both have the same *average* temperature and humidity. Changes in the atmosphere appear not only to cause the fluctuations of business which we have been studying, but to be among the most potent forces in making some nations strong and others weak. When I began the present investigation and discovered how much harm is done by our cold northern winters I reasoned that in places with uniform climates like southern Italy and California, where the winters differ only a little from the summers, the conditions of health at the two seasons must be nearly the same. The difference between summer and winter, however, is relatively far greater in the mild climates than in those that are more rigorous. In northern France, Figure 8, for example, the range from the lowest death-rate to the highest is only about 25 per cent; in southern Italy, Figure 11, it amounts to 45 per cent. In the United States similar contrasts prevail. The rigorous northeastern section, Figure 12, where the temperature for a month at a time may average 20°, shows a difference of only 20 per cent between the best months and the worst. On the other hand, southern California, Figure 17, where the coldest month does not average below 50°, shows a difference of over 25 per cent between summer and winter. A comparison of individual cities, such as Boston and Los Angeles, or New York and San Francisco, emphasizes this contrast still more strongly. So, too, does a comparison of the French diagrams,

Figures 8 and 9, with those of the eastern and central United States, Figures 12 to 14. In the milder French climate the lines of the diagrams are closer together and the contrast between the health of summer and winter much greater than in the more rigorous climate of the northern United States. If southern Italy were the only place to show a high deathrate in winter, we might attribute it to lack of care and to poor medical service. When Los Angeles, San Francisco, and Seattle follow suit, however, such an explanation is untenable.

The real explanation of the unexpectedly favorable conditions in rigorous climates seems to be that the rigorous climates are also highly variable. In "Civilization and Climate" I have described a series of studies of factory operatives and students which bear on this point. Both mental and physical work appear to be stimulated by changes in temperature. In general, if today's temperature is the same as yesterday's, people do not work so well as when there is a change. When winter and summer are averaged together a rise of temperature seems to be slightly stimulating to physical activity, although it is distinctly harmful to mental. A fall of temperature, on the contrary, appears to be stimulating under all conditions, although an extreme fall is not so good as one of more moderate dimensions.

I have now tested this conclusion by means of the records of daily deaths in New York City from 1877 to 1884. These deaths number approximately 300,000, and the number of days concerned is approximately 3,000. Hence the body of data on which we shall base our conclusions is large enough to give thoroughly reliable results. These results agree with those obtained from the study of students, but fail to show any favorable effect corresponding to the slight stimulus which a rise of temperature seems to exert upon factory operatives. All three types of investigation, however, namely, studies of deaths, factory operatives, and students, agree in indicating that changes of temperature are, in general, a stimulus, and this is the main point.

The years 1877 to 1884 were chosen for investigation because, extraordinary as it may seem, those eight years with the four that followed them are the only ones for which accurate daily records of deaths appear to be available in any American city. At present not even the weekly records in most places are accurate. Instead of tabulating and publishing the *actual* deaths during a given week or month, the *reported* deaths are given. In New York City, for example, the physicians who send in the reports are allowed by law an interval of thirty-six hours between the hour of death and the hour of filing the reports. In practice this is extended to three or four days. No record of daily deaths is kept, and the deaths which are published as those of a given week really belong in part to that week and in part to the last half of the preceding week. It is much to be regretted that exact records of the deaths each day are not available for all parts of the country, for, as we shall soon see, such records are of the highest importance. With the counting machines that are now used in large cities it would take a clerk only three or four days to get out a year's daily record even in New York.

Some of the results of a study of the daily deaths in New York City from 1877 to 1884 appear in Figure 20. The figures at the top indicate the number of degrees by which the temperature of a given day differed from that of the day before. Thus the left-hand side of the diagram pertains to days when there was a sharp drop of temperature and the right side to those when warm waves occurred. The figures on the right and left margins indicate the amount by which the deaths on a given day exceeded or fell short of those occurring on the previous day. The figures have been inverted so that good conditions of health may be represented by high positions and bad health by low. Since the average number of deaths per day was not far from 100, the figures in the margins are almost equivalent to percentages. The four dotted lines represent the conditions during the four seasons, beginning with the

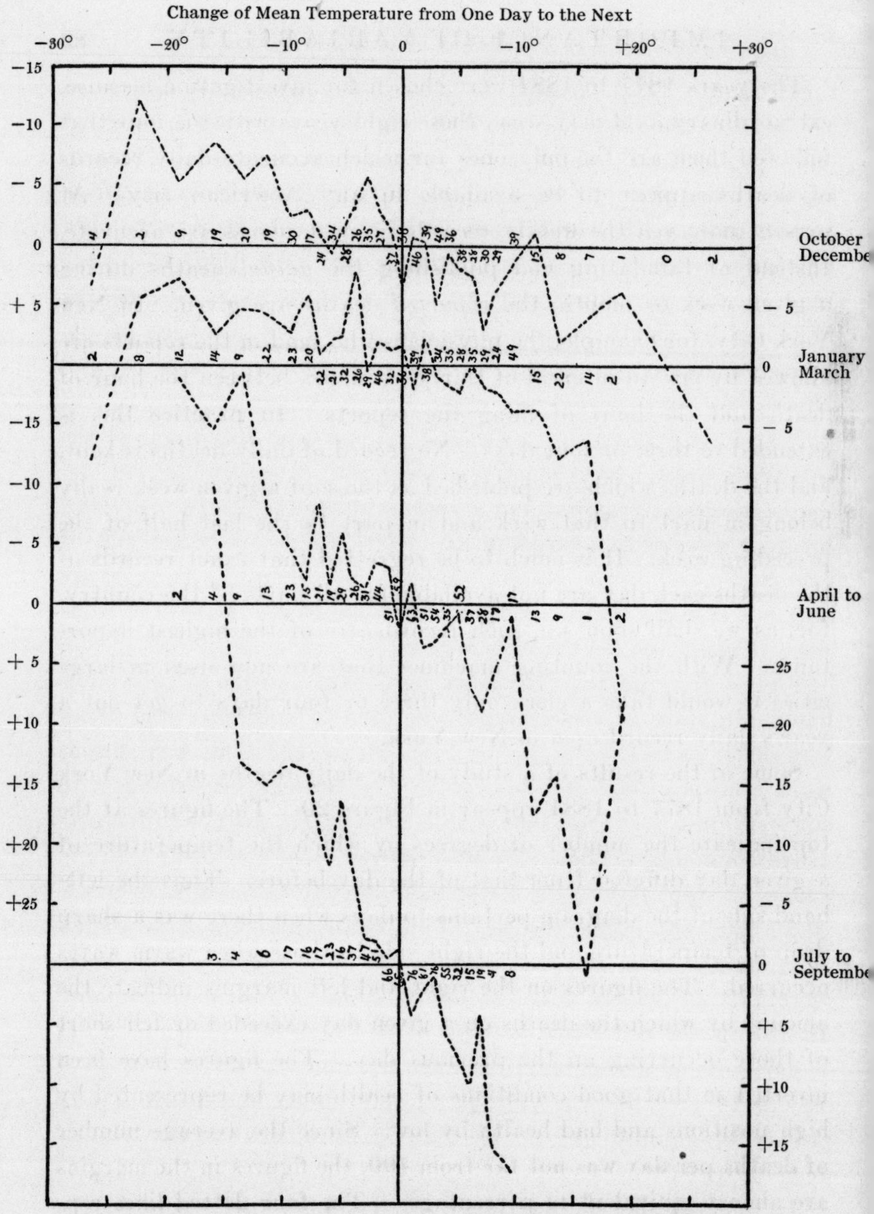

FIGURE 20. Daily Changes in Health compared with Changes of Mean Temperature at New York City, 1877 to 1884

three months from October to December. The little figures in the body of the diagram near the zero lines show the number of days on which each point in the various lines is based. Thus, to begin in the upper left-hand corner, during the months of October to December in the eight years under discussion there were only four days when the mean temperature was more than 25° lower than on the preceding day. On those four days the deaths increased by about 3.5 per cent over what they had been on the preceding days. So extreme a drop in temperature is not good. During the same period two days showed a drop of from 21° to 25°, and their deathrate averaged 12 per cent less than on the preceding days. Next come nine days with a drop of 18° to 20° and a decline of more than 5 per cent in the deathrate; then nineteen days with a drop of 15° to 17° in temperature and of over 8 per cent in the deaths. Notice that when the temperature does not change, there is almost no change in the deathrate, while when it rises, the deaths also increase.

Figure 20 is perhaps the most significant feature of this whole book. In spite of some irregularity due to epidemics and other accidental causes, each of the four curves has a marked downward tendency from left to right. The tendency is strongest in summer when the three days with a drop of 15° to 17° in temperature showed a decline of about 40 per cent in the deathrate, while the eight days with a rise of 9° to 10° suffered an increase of 17 per cent in the deaths. This means that there were only sixty deaths when the temperature fell most rapidly, while there were 117, or nearly twice as many, when it rose most rapidly. In spring the difference between a rise and fall of temperature is not quite so great, but if we take the nine days with a drop of 13° to 14°, we find an average of only eighty-one deaths (−19 per cent) against 114 on the nine days with a similar rise of temperature.

In general the average slope of the four lines diminishes in proportion to the temperature. That is, changes of temperature produce the most marked effect in summer, a very strong but less marked effect in the spring, somewhat less in autumn, and least in winter. As yet we cannot say positively what this means. Two possibilities suggest themselves. One is that people have less power of resistance in summer, just as we have found to be the case in mild climates when these are compared with those where changes are abundant. It is a well-known fact that the variability of the temperature from day to day is much less in summer than in winter. The other possibility is that change of temperature has less effect in winter than in summer because in cold weather we protect ourselves from the outside air by means of our houses. The fact that we are dealing with sick people and not with those in good health makes our results all the more remarkable. Remember that sick people do not go out of doors, and that the deaths which we are studying occurred before the value of fresh air had begun to be realized as it is today. Nevertheless these sick people felt at once the effect of a change of even a single degree in the mean temperature. They felt it in winter as well as in summer. Perhaps this means that a change in temperature is accompanied by some other change, perhaps electrical, and that the other change is the important factor. However that may be, there seems no escape from the conclusion that the slightest change of temperature finds its immediate reflection in man's health.

Many of us have wondered why we have "spring fever" when the first warm days arrive. We know that at such times the temperature is much more favorable than formerly. Why, then, should we feel a sense of lassitude? The answer is that the effect of a *constant* temperature is very different from the effect of a *change* to that temperature. An average of 64° for day and night together is the most favorable, but a drop from 75° to 64° is highly stimulating and causes a decline of perhaps 10 per cent in the deathrate. A similar rise, on the other hand, from 53° to 64°, causes a corresponding increase in the deathrate.

The reader cannot too sharply distinguish between the effect of *mean* temperature and the effect of *change* of temperature. The conditions seem to be closely analogous to those of baths. The first plunge into a cold bath is highly stimulating. Almost everyone is benefited. But what happens if the bath is prolonged? Unless people take vigorous exercise there is a prompt reaction which soon brings on a chill, and may end seriously. With a hot bath the effect is the reverse. The first plunge brings on a sense of lassitude, a desire to lie still and do nothing. So long as the bath remains hot this feeling persists, and if the bath is prolonged one finds one's will power declining. It becomes harder and harder to summon up the decision to take a cold douche. Thus it happens that even in winter a drop in the temperature of the air is stimulating even to sick people. If the temperature remains low, however, the good effect speedily passes and the deathrate rises.

In studying Figure 20 one is led to inquire whether the total effect of falling temperature is more beneficial than the total harm done by a rise. The answer is that the two are bound to be equal. Otherwise the deathrate would keep declining until it fell to zero, or would keep rising till everyone died. This sounds at first as if the good and the harm of a variable climate balanced each other, thus leaving people in the same condition that would prevail if the temperature remained constant. This is by no means the case, however, as appears from the following table, based on the daily deaths in New York City from 1877 to 1884. In preparing these figures we have first largely gotten rid of the effect of daily changes by taking the average number of deaths for overlapping periods of five days, that is, the first to the fifth of the month, the second to the sixth, the third to the seventh, and so forth. Generally such a five-day period contains some days with a rise of temperature and some with a fall, so that the two tend to balance each other. Then we have divided each month into two halves, and from each half have selected the five successive days showing the best health and the five showing the worst. Finally we have calculated the average amount by which the temperature changed from day to day in the ten days ending with the middle day of each five-day period. This sounds complicated, but all that the reader need do is to notice whether the figures in the table are plus or minus. If they are plus it means that periods of unusually variable temperature preceded those of unusually good health. If they are minus, it means that the variability of the weather was less than usual before the periods of good health.

PERCENTAGES BY WHICH THE VARIABILITY OF THE TEMPERATURE FROM DAY TO DAY IN TEN-DAY PERIODS PRECEDING THE BEST HEALTH DIFFERS FROM THE VARIABILITY IN SIMILAR PERIODS PRECEDING THE WORST HEALTH. (*Smoothed.*)

January	1-15	+2.3%	April	1-15	+3.7%
January	16-31	+3.2%	April	16-30	+5.1%
February	1-14	+2.7%	May	1-15	+5.8%
February	15-29	+2.8%	May	16-31	+6.0%
March	1-15	+3.4%	June	1-15	+4.9%
March	16-31	+4.0%	June	16-30	+3.6%
Average		+3.1%	Average		+4.9%
July	1-15	+3.4%	October	1-15	+0.1%
July	16-31	+4.3%	October	16-31	—0.2%
August	1-15	+7.2%	November	1-15	—0.2%
August	16-31	+6.8%	November	16-30	—1.0%
September	1-15	+4.7%	December	1-15	—0.8%
September	16-30	+0.7%	December	16-31	+1.1%
Average		+4.5%	Average		—0.2%
Grand average			+3.1%		

The table indicates that on the whole, variability of temperature is a decided stimulus.

Follow the figures through from January to December. From January to the last of May there is an almost steady rise from 2.3 per cent to 6.0 per cent. Periods of good health evidently follow times when the variability is above the normal for the season, while the worst health follows times when the variability is less than the normal. This tendency increases until the end of May. That is, it is at a maximum when the temperature is close to the optimum. Then during June and July the value of changes in the weather declines. This is natural, for although there is much less variation from day to day in hot weather than in cold, the hottest days are included in the periods when the weather is subject to the greatest changes. Nevertheless, even in hot weather people's health is better when there is much change from day to day than when there is little. Of course in the New York climate there are never any long periods with practically no changes of temperature, so we cannot tell how much greater the value of variability would appear if we could compare people who live where there are no daily changes with those who live where there are many.

Passing on to August we find that as soon as the hottest weather is past, the value of daily changes increases to the maximum for the whole year. That is because the variable periods are the ones in which cool waves begin to be prominent. Then during September the value of variability appears to decline, and from the middle of October to the middle of December the most variable weather is not quite so favorable as that which is more nearly uniform. The reason is not apparent. It should be noted, however, that this is the time when people's health is at its best, as is evident from the New York curve in Figure 7. Perhaps when other causes combine to produce good health, variability ceases for a while to be of so much importance. The figures with the minus sign in the table are so small that they might almost as well be zeros. However this may be, there seems to be strong evidence that for ten months out of twelve the health of New York is better after periods of high variability than after those of relative uniformity. When people become accustomed to a mild, uniform climate such as that of southern Italy or southern California, their power to resist variations in the weather declines, and they suffer from slight changes much more than the people of variable climates suffer from large ones.

The practical applications of the preceding discussion are almost innumerable. I shall content myself with two or three samples. The study of the daily deaths in New York suggests that our medical practice may well be radically revised. Many physicians have of late recognized the value of open-air treatment. Its potency in cases of tuberculosis is universally recognized. Freeman goes so far as to say that low temperature is the most effective cure for a large number of diseases and perhaps for almost all. He cites cases where soldiers with infected and putrifying wounds were placed out of doors in cold weather with only thin sheets of gauze over the raw flesh. A phenomenally rapid recovery followed in many cases. In his own practice, Freeman states that in cases of puerperal septicæmia he has succeeded in reducing the mortality 50 per cent by placing his patients in the open air in winter. Many other similar cases might be cited. Yet the general medical practice is still to keep patients in a relatively high temperature and not to expose them to sudden changes.

A comparison of our results in New York with those obtained by Freeman and with the general practice in respect to tuberculosis raises the query whether *changes* rather than low temperature may not be the effective agent. An ordinary tuberculosis patient sleeps out of doors, comes into the house to dress and have breakfast. After perhaps two hours in the house the patient goes out again to stay till noon. Then he comes in again for luncheon, goes out once more, comes in for supper, and again goes out. In addition to this most patients go back and forth at other times. Moreover, the mere fact of being out of doors means that the patient not only has good air, a fact of the highest importance, but is subjected to far greater changes of temperature than would be the case if the same amount of time were spent in the house. Even the modern practice of "heliotherapy" where the patients are exposed to the sunlight and are gradually toughened until they can be comfortable out of doors with practically no clothing even in winter may owe much of its efficacy to changes of temperature. Certainly the sun falling on the skin causes rapid changes of temperature, for its effect is very different from that which is produced as soon as the patient turns and brings his body into the shade. Moreover, it is noteworthy that the supposed healing effect of sunlight is at a maximum when the skin is tanned to the color of leather and has thus acquired the power to keep out the actinic or chemical rays of the sun which are usually taken to be the effective agent. At such times, however, the patient has become so hardened to the air that he can and does endure the most extreme and rapid changes of temperature without discomfort. Perhaps these changes are as effective as the sunlight.

Apparently one of the best possible safeguards of health is constant changes of temperature. We need to return to the conditions under which the evolution of our unclothed ancestors took place. In places where healthy people work, as well as in hospitals, the ideal practice would seem to be to keep the temperature constantly varying. The extent of the variations must of course depend upon the circumstances, but even patients who are very sick can usually stand a sudden, sharp drop provided the return to warm conditions is speedy enough. If we have rightly interpreted the New York figures such variability will strengthen most patients throughout their illness. Then when the actual crisis of the disease arrives it would seem as if the patient should be subjected to a sudden drop of temperature at just the time when he most needs a stimulant. I know that this sounds extreme. Yet what else can be the meaning of the fact that the days when the temperature falls most in New York are accompanied by an improvement of 10 per cent, 20 per cent, and even 40 per cent in the deathrate? I know, too, that different diseases may act differently, and that this whole matter needs far more thorough investigation than has yet been possible. Physicians are the ones to carry on this investigation, and already some of them are at work on it.

The principles discussed in this chapter enable us to answer another important practical question: What climate is really the best? I have discussed this question in "Civilization and Climate," and the answer there given is strongly reënforced by our studies of the deathrate. We have seen that a mean temperature of 64°, a mean humidity of about 80 per cent, and frequent changes of temperature are the most desirable conditions for purely physical health. We have seen that in factory work where physical effort is the chief item, but where mental activity takes a certain share, the best conditions seem to be the same except that the optimum temperature should apparently average about 60°F for day and night together instead of 64°. Finally for purely mental work the conditions of humidity and variability should apparently be about the same as in the other cases, but the mean temperature should be much lower, perhaps 40°. The only way to get all these conditions is to live in a climate which has several frosty but not cold months in winter, several warm but not hot months in summer, and a constant succession of storms at all seasons. No part of the world fulfills all these conditions. England is admirable in temperature and has a great deal of variety although not quite enough. New Zealand in many ways rivals England as a candidate for first place. The northeastern United States is variable enough, but its winters are too cold and its summers too hot. Germany falls in the same class with the United States, but in both regions the nervous stimulus seems to be too great. The Pacific Coast of the United States, especially in the northern portions, has an admirable range of temperature, but not enough variety. Further discussion of this point is unnecessary. The reader can apply the principles for himself.

Since mankind is obliged to live in all sorts of climates, one of the greatest problems of civilization is to provide an artificial climate that shall be as nearly ideal as possible. I cannot illustrate this point better than by discussing two experiments which form part of one of the largest and most careful attempts that has yet been made to discover just what kind of artificial climate is most favorable. The experiments were carried on by the New York State Ventilation Commission under the chairmanship of Professor C. E. A. Winslow. They were planned by a group of the most competent experts to be found in the American metropolis. They were conducted with the utmost accuracy, and without any prepossessions as to what results ought to be found.

In one of the experiments a class of forty-three school children was divided into two groups of approximately the same size. The greatest pains were taken to see that the average mental ability of the groups was equal. Then from December to March one group was kept in a school room where the conditions of ventilation and temperature were as perfect as possible, but where the air had the ordinary dryness characteristic of our winters. The relative humidity averaged 28.7 per cent. The other group was kept in a similar room except that the air was humidified and the relative humidity averaged 42.2 per cent. In both rooms the temperature averaged about 67°. Two teachers divided the care of the two groups, each teaching certain subjects to both groups. At the end of each month the rooms were interchanged; the pupils who had been in the dry room went to what had been the damp room, which now became the dry room. Thus while the conditions of the air remained unchanged for each group, the rooms were interchanged so that there was no chance for one set of pupils to have an advantage because of being in a room with a better outlook.

The two groups were tested at the beginning and end of the experimental period by examinations, lasting in all seven hours, but covering several days. The children's progress was measured by the difference between the score made by each pupil in a given test the first and second times. Measured by this standard the children in the drier room, contrary to what would be expected, made a very slightly better showing than the others, although their superiority was not enough to be significant. Thus there seemed good ground for the conclusion that a difference of about 13 per cent in relative humidity does not make any appreciable difference in the mental activity of school children. The obvious inference is that it will not pay to attempt to improve the health of the community by dampening the air in our dry winter houses.

This conclusion is at variance with the lesson taught by our study of millions of deaths. In trying to find some explanation of this anomaly it occurred to me that there may have been a real but unnoticed difference in the two rooms because dry air loses its heat faster than moist air. Hence the dry room may have been more variable than the other. Through the courtesy of the chairman of the Ventilation Commission I was able to test this by means of the original thermograph sheets from the two rooms. Dividing the sixty available sheets into four consecutive sections of fifteen days each, I found that the actual temperature and the variability were as follows:

			Actual Temperature	Excess of Dry over Wet	Average Change of Temperature per Hour	Excess of Dry over Wet
(A)	Dec. 4-22	Dry	66.6°	0.1°	1.40°	—18%
		Wet	66.5°		1.71°	
(B)	Jan. 2-23	Dry	66.8°	—0.4°	2.51°	15%
		Wet	67.2°		2.18°	
(C)	Jan. 24-Feb. 13	Dry	67.0°	0.3°	2.55°	29%
		Wet	66.7°		1.97°	
(D)	Feb. 14-Mar. 19	Dry	68.0°	2.1°	2.15°	54%
		Wet	65.9°		1.40°	

This little table shows that at the beginning of the experiment the average temperature of the two rooms was the same. As the experiment progressed the temperature of the two rooms became more different, until in the last period the dry room was 2.1° warmer than the wet. Thus, judging by the results obtained from a study of deaths and of factory operatives, the dry room had two disadvantages: it was too dry, and its temperature was too high. The variability of its temperature, however, grew steadily more favorable. From having a variability 18 per cent *less* than that of the wet room at the beginning of the experiment it changed to a variability 15 per cent *greater* in the second period, 29 per cent in the third, and 54 per cent in the final. Thus the greater variability seems to have overcome the handicap both of dryness and of too high a temperature. Hence we conclude that this experiment is inconclusive so far as humidity is concerned, but furnishes weighty evidence as to the value of a variable temperature.

It is to be hoped that further experiments as to the air of school rooms may be carried on. If this is done strict attention should be paid to variability, and the humidity in the wet room should be much greater and the temperature lower than in the experiment described above. In that case I feel confident that humidity will be found to have a real effect on mental activity.

The importance both of the mean temperature and of the variability is shown by another experiment carried on by the Ventilation Commission in coöperation with the Bureau of Child Hygiene of the Department of Health of New York City. During the period from February 19 to April 8, 1916, records of respiratory diseases were kept in eight New York schools having fifty-eight classrooms and 2,541 children, while from November 4, 1916, to January 27, 1917, similar records were kept in twelve schools having seventy-six rooms and 2,992 children. A corps of trained nurses under the supervision of physicians examined the children daily and looked up those who were absent. The rooms were divided into three groups: (I) cool rooms where the windows were kept open as much as possible and the temperature averaged below 60° most of the time; (II) moderately warm rooms having no ventilation except by means of windows; (III) moderately warm rooms provided with artificial ventilation by means of fans. When we divide these rooms into three groups according to temperature, as has been done by Miss Baker in her report on the experiment, we get the following result:

	Average Temperature	Absences Due to Respiratory Diseases per Thousand Possible Attendances	Respiratory Diseases per Thousand among Children in Attendance
(A) 46 coldest rooms	59.4°	10.2	58.1
(B) Next 44 rooms	66.6°	8.8	47.4
(C) 44 warmest rooms	69.4°	15.6	88.4

Evidently the warm rooms were much worse than the cooler rooms. In fact, the amount of sickness in group C was almost twice as great as in the rooms that averaged 66.6°, that is, group B. The cooler rooms, group A, were not quite so favorable as the middle group (B), but children are clearly much better off in such rooms than in the ones averaging 69° or more. It is striking to see that the best health is found in the group of rooms where the temperature comes nearest to the ideal, that is to 64°.

Another comparison of these rooms is still more significant. Miss Baker groups them as follows:

	Absences Due to Respiratory Diseases per Thousand Possible Attendances	Respiratory Diseases per Thousand among Pupils in Attendance
(I) Cool rooms with window ventilation	9.6	59.4
(II) Moderate rooms with *window* ventilation	10.4	37.5
(III) Moderate rooms with *fan* ventilation	13.5	88.8

The rooms of group I had an average temperature below 60°, and were apparently a little too cool for children dressed in the ordinary fashion. Yet their record is far better than that of group III,—the warmer rooms with the most approved system of fan ventilation. It should be noted here that no attention was paid to the dress of the children. That is, in selecting rooms for the different types of ventilation, the dress and social or physical condition of the children played no part. In all three groups of rooms the children were simply the ordinary type found in the average sections of New York. This facts lends added importance to the contrast between groups II and III. In both of these the temperature averaged the same, approximately 68°. The only difference was in the system of ventilation. In both groups the air was perfectly fresh. In one case, however, it came in through the windows. During the first year no attempt was made even to prevent drafts, but in the second year boards were placed at the bases of the windows so that the air did not blow directly on the children. Yet in both years this kind of ventilation proved much better than the other. In the rooms of group III fresh air was taken from outside just as in group II, but instead of entering the rooms directly it was heated and then blown in by means of fans. In fact, the system of ventilation was what is commonly supposed to be ideal,—no drafts, no sudden changes, no chance for the air to stagnate. Yet there were 30 per cent more absences from respiratory diseases than in the rooms with window ventilation, and over twice as many of the children in attendance had colds or similar ailments. This striking difference cannot have been due to the quality of the air, to its mean temperature, or to its humidity. It must apparently have been due to its variability. We try to keep our winter temperature as uniform as possible. In so doing we commit a great folly. What we want is not uniformity, but variability. If we could live all the time in air with the right variability as well as the right temperature and humidity, who knows what we might accomplish? Our bodies, our judgment, and our wills would all be stronger than now. Our death-rate would diminish, and our happiness be correspondingly increased. Moreover, the ebb and flow of business and the stress and strain of social life might become less wearing and harmful. Who can tell what more might be accomplished? Our best moments are those when our bodies feel strong and our wills courageous.

(NOTE. For a further discussion of the air in our houses in winter, and of the methods of obtaining ideal conditions, see Appendices E and F.)

CHAPTER VII

THE VOYAGE OF EVOLUTION

FOOD, drink, air. These, as we have seen, are the three primary needs of life. Probably three fourths of all man's efforts are directed toward obtaining food. That is why food figures so largely in all discussions of health and economics. Effort is also required in order that the right kind of drink may be available in proper quantities. Therefore we spend vast sums for waterworks, and count the liquor question as one of our greatest problems. But air, we have been wont to say, is different. If food were "free as air," most of mankind would sit around and do nothing a large part of the time. Hitherto the vast majority of mankind have thought of air chiefly as something against which we require protection. For this protection we have gone to vast labor in order that we may have clothes and shelter. As civilization has advanced these items have become of growing importance. Although the world as a whole may devote three fourths of its energy to obtaining food, Mrs. Richards, in her little book, "The Cost of Living," estimates that among sensible people in comfortable but not affluent circumstances about 20 per cent of the income is spent for rent, 3 to 5 per cent for fuel, and 15 per cent for clothing. Food, on the other hand, should require 25 per cent of the total income. Thus today among people of the kind who will read this book the amount spent for protection against the air averages about one and one-half times as much as is spent for food. But remember that in ordinary discussions of domestic economy, drink is counted with food. Our bills for water do not amount to 1 per cent of an ordinary income, and all other drinks are reckoned as part of our food bills. Thus it appears that intelligent people are spending 50 per cent more for protection from the air than for both food and drink together. The fact that the most expensive dresses often afford the least protection is neither here nor there. Neither does champagne at five dollars a bottle, or a fancy dessert at a dollar a plate supply as much drink or food as could be obtained for a cent in the form of water or potatoes.

The fact is that as man advances in civilization the percentage of effort which he spends upon food and drink steadily diminishes, while what he spends on air increases. If the reader is inclined to doubt this, let him ask himself why people spend large sums to go South in winter, or to the seashore and mountains in summer. Is it not for the air? How few people would even consider the plan of going to a summer or winter resort, no matter how fine the scenery, if the air was exactly the same as at home. Why do we do this? Because at last we are realizing that air is not merely something against which we require protection, but something which has a most far-reaching effect upon health and upon all kinds of success in the work of life. And now, in this book, we have seen that air is *the* great variable in man's environment. Its variations, not only from place to place and season to season, but also from day to day, have far more effect upon his health and work than any other factor or perhaps than all other factors combined. These variations are at the root of all sorts of differences in the capacity of different countries, and also of all sorts of changes in the course of business and hence in politics and other great affairs.

In view of the extreme importance of the air, it will pay us to turn back to the past and inquire how man happened to become so delicately adapted to one particular kind of climatic environment. How did the air come to control his health to an even greater degree than do food and drink? Why do his attempts to adjust himself to the air become of ever increasing importance as he rises in the scale of evolution and of civilization? In order to answer these questions let us go back to early geological times and review man's voyage of evolution.

Long before man's earliest ancestors had become different from the beasts the whole world of life had realized the necessity of air. Even the creatures that inhabit the water can live only by taking from it the dissolved air. Otherwise the chemical activities which are the basis of all life come promptly to an end. Before these primitive animals could give rise to higher forms, however, it was necessary that they should pass through a series of crises. Each of these crises was a step forward toward the estate of man. Each has left its impress not only upon the animal world but upon the human race. A few of these crises, such as the development of vertebrates from invertebrates, were due to causes other than climate, but most arose directly from the conditions of the air which we call climate. Let us consider three of the chief crises. The first was the emergence of the earliest vertebrates from the water. This was a most momentous step, for only in the highly varied environment of the land does brain power develop rapidly. Creatures like the seal, the whale, and the manatee, which have gone back to the water from the land, fall behind in the mental race, for they are not sufficiently stimulated. The second great crisis was the change which caused certain forms of life to become warm-blooded. This not only enabled man's animal ancestors to continue their vital activities at all seasons and in almost all parts of the world, but it gave rise to the close bond between mother and child which has been the greatest of all factors in promoting the higher qualities of love and altruism. The third great crisis was the separation of man— the two-handed, two-footed, big-brained creature—from his four-handed and smaller-brained relatives. This was the time when mental qualities evolved most rapidly. Therefore it interests us most of all because the conditions which fostered the evolution of our minds are those which today stimulate them most strongly.

It is perhaps a misnomer to speak of these as crises, for each of these three steps in evolution required a long time for its consummation. Yet as we look backward into the dim vistas of the past, the steps are so foreshortened that they appear like genuine crises. They are, as it were, great slopes in a terraced plain. For long periods the life of the world was confined to the waters. Then during a relatively brief period, as geology counts time, there came a transformation. The highest forms that inhabited those ancient seas, that is, the fishes, gave rise to a stock which left the water and made its home on the land. Then our ancestors, for such they were, moved on once more across the vast plain, rising here and there over smaller terraces, until at last they began to climb to the warm-blooded condition. Another vast stretch of plain and minor terraces brought them to the final steep upward slope. At its base our ancestors were animals; at its top they were men. But have we yet reached the top? More likely we are now upon the very steepest part of the terrace. Hitherto we have climbed upward because some unknown force kept driving us. Now we are conscious of ourselves, and are able to direct our movements. It is for us to say whether we will climb straight upward, or whether, like many of the creatures of the past, we will wander this way and that, and perhaps fail to be among the chosen few who finally emerge at the highest level.

Let us consider how each of these three great crises impressed upon our ancestors the supreme importance of the air. Each, as has been implied, was associated with profound climatic changes. It was drought, for instance, which apparently drove our fishlike ancestors out from the water upon the land and into the air. There are today examples of types that are undergoing just such a transformation. For example, the so-called lung fishes live in tropical regions where a long dry season causes many of the pools and streams to dry up. When this happens the lung fish burrows into the mud and makes for itself a slimy chamber where it lies coiled up for half the year. Like all other forms of life it must have air. As it cannot get this from the water, it builds a little tube from its mouth to the door of its chamber. Thus it actually breathes. Dry balls of mud containing such fish have often been brought to Europe. When soaked in water the fish emerge as lively as ever.

Such fishes make their first appearance in the early geological era known as the Devonian. How far back this was may be judged by a reference to Figure 21 which shows the names of the geological periods, the conditions of climate, and some of the chief crises in the evolution of life. In the Devonian Period the former moist climate gave place to aridity. Throughout large parts of the earth vast deserts prevailed, as is evident from great deposits of red sandstone. In the early stages of this desiccation a great advantage was possessed by those fresh-water fish which were able to act like the modern lung fish. As the climate became drier, forms which were highly developed in this direction were the only ones that were able to survive in many regions. Moreover, those fish which could crawl to new pools also had a great advantage, for when a stream became low they could move down its bed from their own diminished pool to a larger one. Today in Ceylon the climbing perch is able to use its fins in this way. Thus the dryness of the Devonian Period caused the evolution of legs as well as lungs, and there arose the class of animals known as amphibians.

For millions of years amphibians were the highest type of life. Little by little their lungs and legs became better developed until the creatures seemed to belong wholly to the land. Nevertheless they still returned to the water to lay their eggs. Their young passed through a fishlike stage such as we see not only in tadpoles but in the embryos of man and the higher animals. They had not yet taken the final step to the top of the great terrace where the land animals dwell. Finally, however, in the latter part of the period known as the Mississippian there came another time of climatic stress. Aridity once more became so pronounced

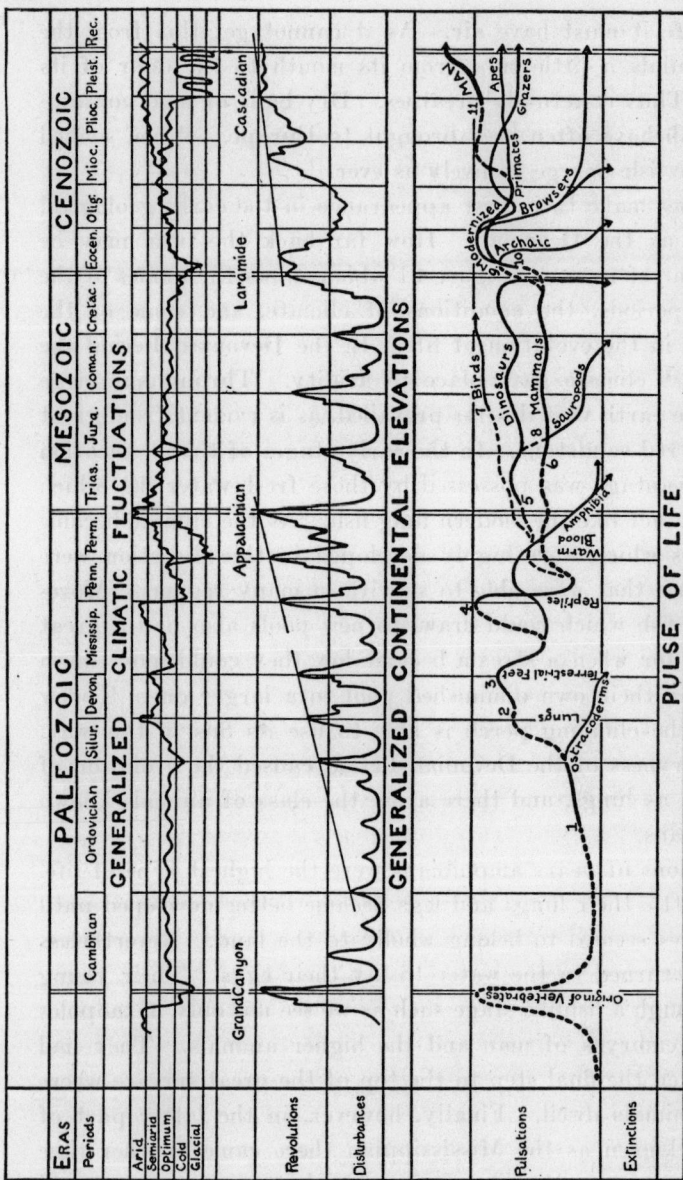

FIGURE 21. The March of Geological Time. After Lull.

THE upper line represents changes of climate during geological times. Minor jogs represent the smaller changes constantly in progress. Depressions below the optimum or most favorable conditions represent cold or glacial periods, while elevations above the optimum indicate dry periods. Note that aridity and low temperature may occur together. The second wavy line indicates movements of the earth's crust, small movements being called disturbances and great ones revolutions. Note that revolutions or periods of great mountain building and of continental upheaval generally coincide with glacial periods or with times of great aridity. The lower series of lines indicates the way in which different types of vertebrate animals have branched from the parent stem and risen or fallen in the scale of importance. The occurrence of crises in evolution, such as the development of lungs, is also indicated.

that in large areas the amphibians could not return to the water to lay their eggs. Hence many types perished. Only those persisted which became true reptiles whose eggs are able to hatch upon the land. The crisis had at last been weathered.

Not till millions of years later did the next great step in evolution occur. That step was the rise of the warm-blooded mammals. We do not find their fossil record until the time known as Upper Triassic, but they must have originated farther back, apparently in the Permian. The date of the Permian Period is estimated as anywhere from ten million to two hundred million years ago. The break between the types of life before and after this great crisis is the most profound in the history of evolution. It is therefore highly important to find that this was also the time of the greatest changes of climate. Vast glaciers descended to sea level within thirty degrees of the equator. Perhaps at no other time during the evolution of man's ancestors has there been such a succession of cold, stormy glacial epochs alternating sharply with mild, interglacial epochs.

Let us consider the effect of such climatic stress upon other forms of life as well as upon our ancestors. Previous to the Permian Period the vegetation of all parts of the earth's surface, including even the far north, was much alike. In general the lands were covered with forests, averaging perhaps forty feet in height but with some trees towering a hundred feet. Schuchert describes it as a forest of rapid growth, of soft and even spongy woods, in which evergreen trees with comparatively small, needle-like leaves were prominent. Associated with these were thickets of rushes, also of very rapid growth, which in habit resembled modern cane brakes and bamboo thickets. Here and there stood majestic treelike ferns, while many smaller ferns and similar plants thrived in the shady places or climbed among the trees. Flowers of a certain sort were sparingly present, but of insignificant size and unattractive color. Spores took the place of seeds to such a degree that when the trees and ferns were liberating them the entire forest was covered with a greenish yellow or brown dust. During the Permian Period the sharp transitions from cold to warm, or from moist to dry caused these ancient forests to die out. Conifers much like those of today came into existence. Seeds largely took the place of spores. These changes were accompanied by a general reduction in the size and variety of the plants, and by a tendency for them to become hardier and to have thicker and less ornate leaves.

During the great climatic changes of the Permian, animal life suffered an even greater transformation than plant life. For example, previous to that time the insects had been of truly astonishing size. Out of the 400 forms known in the early and middle parts of the Pennsylvanian Period which preceded the Permian, the smallest had wings over a third of an inch long. The wings of more than twenty species were six inches long, six attained to nearly eight inches, and three were giants of twelve inches! Imagine a spore-dusted forest full of insects as large as crows! The cold and changeable climate of Permian times apparently caused the extinction of all these forms. Their place was taken by small species resembling those of today. Moreover, the very nature of insects was profoundly modified by the introduction of metamorphosis. That is, where there had formerly been merely a gradual growth from the egg to the adult, there was now a growth from egg to maggot or caterpillar, then a resting period, and finally a transformation from maggot to fly or from caterpillar to butterfly. At the same time the insects acquired the power to become dormant and thus persist for months at a time. All these changes apparently were due to the necessity for adapting themselves to sudden periods of drought or cold during the time of growth in summer, or to the necessity for enduring long, severe winters. Thus the climatic variability of the Permian Period not only caused a remodelling of the earth's garment of vegetation, but introduced a unique stage into the life history of insects.

For our present purpose another change is far more important. At this time apparently there occurred one of the most vital steps in the evolution of our direct ancestors, the mammals. Extreme aridity and low temperature were both characteristic of certain epochs of the Permian Period. Among the more progressive types of land animals aridity has a tendency to accelerate development. It places a premium upon the power to travel, and especially upon speed. As Lull puts it: "Not only are food and water scarce and far between, but the strife between pursuer and pursued becomes intensified—neither can afford to be out-distanced by the other. This means increased metabolism, which in turn generally implies not only greater motive powers but higher temperature. With increasing cold a premium would be placed upon such creatures as could maintain their activity beyond the limits of shortening summers, and this could be accomplished only by the development of some mechanism whereby a relatively constant temperature could be maintained within the animal regardless of external conditions." In other words, there arose warm-blooded animals whose temperature was more or less independent of the surrounding air instead of varying with it as is the case in cold-blooded animals. Among mammals this led to the production of the young within the body of the mother instead of from eggs in which the mother took little or no interest after they were laid. Among birds it forced the mother to care for the eggs if they were to be hatched. Thus the relation of mother and child became firmly established. The later development of this relation has been the chief source of all that is best in mankind.

We must not suppose that during the climatic stress of the Permian the mammals emerged full-fledged. The first warm-blooded creatures were not warm in the sense that we are. Their temperature varied through wide limits, just as now is still true of infants even when they are perfectly healthy. Nor were the young born alive at first, for eggs continued to be laid as is today the case with some of the most primitive mammals of

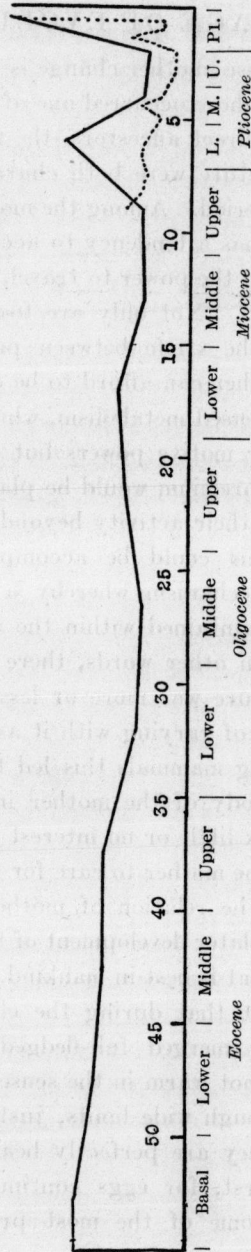

FIGURE 22. The Extinction of Mammalian Genera in North America and Europe

Australia. Moreover, the early mammals were but a feeble folk. The reptiles were the great lords of creation, while the mammals were tiny little beasts skulking in out-of-the-way corners. Not for long ages did they rise to dominance in the lowland regions where the great reptiles lorded it. Among the hills, however, or elsewhere in safe retreats they were slowly evolving two of their vital characteristics, namely, a uniform temperature and a large brain.

Once more we must skip millions of years. The mammals have grown in size and variety until they range from the mouse to the mammoth. They have ousted the reptiles from the best parts of the earth. They have taken to the air with the wings of the bat, they have gone back to the sea with the whale, they have learned to run like the antelope, to burrow like the mole, and to climb trees like the squirrel. Their limbs have become hoofs, claws, wings, flippers, and hands. The Age of Mammals has come to its epiphany. Then, as in Permian times, there once more comes a widespread period of climatic stress, the last Glacial Period. A new element enters into evolution, for at last man appears, and intelligence becomes dominant.

Before we consider man let us pause for a moment to estimate how great was the change in life wrought by the Glacial Period. For this purpose I have taken the table of mammalian genera in Osborn's "Age of Mammals." It includes every known genus whether living or dead. From this table I have ascertained the number of genera which were alive during the geological periods preceding the Glacial Period. The number of genera has been counted for Europe and North America separately. I have also ascertained the total number extinguished in each period and the percentage that were extinguished on an average during each hundred thousand years. The method by which this has been done is explained in the Appendix.

The results of this tabulation of mammals are shown graphically in Figure 22. There the names of the geological periods appear at the bottom, reading from the oldest on the left to the latest on the right. The figures in the body of the diagram show the lapse of time in millions of years according to Barrell's scale. Thus the diagram begins about fifty-five million years ago. The numbers on the right show the percentage of mammalian genera that were extinguished per hundred thousand years. Of course new forms keep coming in to replace the old ones, so that the total number tends on the whole to increase. The rate of extinction is indicated by the solid line. If our knowledge of the past were fuller the line would lie lower in its earlier portions. The striking fact about the line as a whole is the sudden way in which it rises at the right-hand end. This means that during the Glacial Period (marked Pl.), the mammals were extinguished at least three times as rapidly as during most of the millions of years that preceded. When the mammals had reached a condition of complete dominance they suddenly were wiped out wholesale. In North America the whole family of horses was destroyed; the elephant tribe including the mammoth and mastodon disappeared; the camel which had formerly been abundant passed away leaving no trace save his bones. Still other great families such as the giant beaver, the sloth, the tapirs, and the so-called glyptodonts were likewise exterminated. In Europe there was a similar appalling destruction of life.

Directly or indirectly all this destruction arose from the severe climatic oscillations of the Glacial Period, for this one period included four great "epochs." Indeed, if we include all the indirect effects of that period we must include man's part in destroying living creatures. It was apparently the Glacial Period which chiefly stimulated man's mental development and caused his intelligence to dominate the earth. In recent times his activities during a period which is but a day geologically are causing the wholesale extinction of all sorts of animals such as bears, wolves, foxes, lynxes, weasels, buffaloes, mountain sheep, and the like. Not all the larger wild animals are gone yet, but they are fast disappearing. Even without man's help, however, the extinction has gone on to such a degree that we may well hold up our hands in astonishment. If nature by the simple expedient of a cold, stormy period can destroy life so rapidly, can she at the same time produce new forms with equal rapidity? That is what she seems to have done in the Permian and in the earlier crisis when animals left the water. That is what she also did in the last Glacial Period. This time, however, her infinite resourcefulness directed itself toward the evolution of intelligence, and man appeared upon the scene. Yet though her end was so different, this time as formerly, the chief agency that she employed was climate.

Let us consider briefly the great outstanding fact of the last Glacial Period, that is, the development of the human mind. The history of early man and the climatic changes of this period are summed up in Figure 23. At the beginning of the great climatic pulsations shown in this diagram, we do not know whether there was any such creature as man. In Java, to be sure, there has been found the top of a skull, two teeth, and a thigh bone of an animal too advanced to be an ape, too low to be a man. Volumes have been written about these few bones of the "missing link." The brain of Pithecanthropus erectus, or the "erect apeman" as he is called, was only half as large as that of modern man. His forehead, with its great projecting ridges above the eyes, was so low that there was little room for the frontal lobes where self-control, attention, and the higher mental faculties have their seat. We do not even know whether his powers of consecutive thought enabled him to fashion any implements. He had indeed progressed much beyond the apes in intelligence, but his life was still essentially the same as that of the beasts.

Not for hundreds of thousands of years was man to rise to the point where brain triumphed over brawn. On the road to that goal one of the chief time-markers is the Heidelberg jaw. This is the jaw of an apelike, chinless man, but man he surely was. On this one jaw a whole "race" of primitive men has been built up.

Perhaps these early Heidelberg men possessed the power of articulate speech, but this is doubtful.   The jaw is too narrow to allow free play to the tongue.   Probably the Heidelberg race fashioned some kind of crude implements from sticks and stones, but even of this there is thus far no real proof.   Yet this primitive man lived after half the Glacial Period had run its course.   He hunted the deer, the horse, the elephant, the rhinoceros, the wild boar, the moose, the bison, the wild ox, the bear, and the beaver.   He fled from the lion, and hated the wolf and the wildcat.   All these animals of Asiatic and African as well as European types lived together near Heidelberg in the valley of the Rhine.   They, as well as many others, including man himself, had been driven from their former homes by repeated changes of climate.   The time when they lived was apparently the Second Interglacial Epoch, that is, the epoch of mild climate after the second of the great glacial epochs when the ice expanded from Scandinavia and from the Alps.   According to Osborn's chronology this was about 250,000 years ago.   Others lengthen the time to half a million years, but at any rate the Heidelberg man seems to have lived only about half as long ago as the ape-man of Java.   During that long interval there had been a great and unquestionable evolution in the size of the human brain, but there is no evidence of any appreciable change in the mode of life.

After the days of the Heidelberg man there is another long interval during which the book of human history is blank.   The next record on the pages is the "dawn man" found at Piltdown in southeastern England.   Osborn's summary of the reasons for putting him after the third great advance of the ice seems conclusive.   This brings us down to a period which Penck estimates as about 100,000 years ago, but which may be 150,000.   This seems very long as men count years, but geologically it is almost the present time.   Previous to the Glacial Period the brain of man's animal ancestors had been evolving very slowly for hundreds of millions of years.   During the half million years more or less

of the Glacial Period previous to the time that we have now
reached, that is, previous to the last Interglacial Epoch, it had
been increasing at a rate vastly faster than formerly. Yet at the
time of the Piltdown Man the human animal, as we may perhaps
still call him, had made almost no advance in the use of material
resources. His weapons were probably nothing but stones, bones,
and sticks that he broke with his hands. His most elaborate
manufactured implements were flints of the rudest sort. These
were merely thick chips roughly flaked a little to increase their
cutting power. So far as we yet know, man was still ignorant
of the use of fire.

In those days the climate of central Europe was apparently
somewhat milder than at present. This mild climate continued
for a long time, approximately 50,000 years according to Osborn's
chronology which we are now following. During this time the
region from northern Spain and Italy to southern England and
western Austria, whence our knowledge of early man is chiefly
derived, was peopled by the Neanderthal race. These people
appear to have been a little more advanced than the Piltdown
type, but their brains were distinctly smaller than those of the
Europeans of today. Little by little their skill and power increased. Yet even at the end of the period of mild interglacial
climate, they were still extremely primitive. They had no
æsthetic art so far as we know. Their greatest exhibition of skill
was in "flaking" the edges of flints to produce sharp cutting
edges. This they did with great skill, producing implements of
beautiful symmetry and of considerable utility. Doubtless they
had other arts, such as the dressing of skins, the building of huts,
and the making of wooden clubs. Yet how little this represents
in proportion to the hundreds of thousands of years since man
first began to chip the flints that he picked up from the ground!
Only at the end of this last Interglacial Epoch do we find the first
positive evidence that man had learned to use fire.

We now come to a strange and most significant fact. Man had

lived through three great glacial epochs, but he had never been subjected to a really severe climate. Now for the first time he endured one, for the last epoch was much more rigorous than its predecessors. At the same time his evolution proceeded much more rapidly than ever before. Let us try to get at the meaning of these facts. In the first place are we sure of them? The proof lies in the animals whose fossil bones are found in large numbers in connection with the remains of early man. In this respect, as in most questions concerning primitive man, we must rely on evidence from central and western Europe, for only there has any abundant evidence of our remote ancestors yet come to light. "Until the close of Third Interglacial times," says Osborn, that is, until the approach of the last glacial epoch, "no traces of northern, much less of arctic forests and animals are discovered anywhere, except along the borders of the ice-fields. It would appear as if the animal and plant life of Europe were, in the main, but slightly affected by the first three glaciations. We cannot entertain for a moment the belief that in glacial times all the warm flora and fauna migrated southward and then returned, because there is not a shred of evidence for this theory. It is far more in accord with the known facts to believe that all the southern and eastern forms of life had become very hardy, for we know how readily animals now living in the warm earth belts are acclimatized to northern conditions" (page 108). The tiger, for example, thrives today in Manchuria, where temperatures of 20°F below zero are not uncommon.

The meaning of this seems to be that during the earlier glacial epochs such regions as southern France, for example, became colder and stormier than now, but not cold enough to exterminate such animals as the horse and rhinoceros. During the last Glacial Epoch, however, although the ice-covered areas in western Europe and Britain were far more limited than during the Third Glacial Epoch, "the climate appears to have been more severe than at any previous period." (Osborn.)

The approach of this severe climate was gradual. First there was a long period of relatively cool, dry conditions. Central France, for example, may have been something like what south-eastern Russia now is. This caused the disappearance of two rather sensitive Asiatic mammals, the hippopotamus and the southern mammoth. Then, as the Scandinavian ice-sheet accumulated farther north, the climate became more severe. Men repaired to the shelter of grottos and caverns as they had not for tens of thousands of years. The hardy broad-nosed rhinoceros and straight-tusked elephant both disappeared, while animals of the cold Arctic tundra, such as the reindeer, the woolly mammoth, the woolly rhinoceros, and the Arctic lemming, migrated all over southern Britain, Belgium, France, Germany, and Austria. This condition was too severe for early man. The stage of human development, which coincides with the *beginning* of refrigeration, "is seen to present the climax of a gradual and unbroken development" not only in industries but in ideas. The next industrial stage, which certainly presents the closing workmanship of the same Neanderthal race, and which coincides with the main cold period of the Fourth Glaciation, "shows a marked retrogression of technique in contrast to the steady progression which we have observed up to this time." (Osborn, page 180.)

The climatic conditions which were unfavorable to development in central Europe seem to have been highly favorable in other places where they were not quite so severe. Thus somewhere in central Asia there appears to have developed during this period the great Cro-Magnon race. These highly gifted people had brains as large as those of modern Europeans. They invaded southern Europe after the most severe part of the Fourth Glacial Epoch had passed away. "After prolonged study of the works of the Cro-Magnons one cannot avoid the conclusions that their capacity was nearly if not quite as high as our own; that they were capable of advanced education; that they had a strongly developed æsthetic as well as a religious sense; that their society was quite highly differentiated along the lines of talent for work of different kinds." (Osborn, pages 274-5.) The civilization, such as it was, of the time of the Cro-Magnons "was very widely extended. This marks an important social characteristic, namely, the readiness and willingness to take advantage of every step in human progress, wherever it may have originated."

These fine people lived in Europe from about 25,000 years ago until 7,000 years ago. Their art was perhaps their greatest claim to fame, for their drawings and paintings on the walls and roofs of caverns are wonderful considering the primitiveness of the tools employed. Why they disappeared we do not know. They were not the ancestors of most of the modern Europeans. They may have been fair-haired like the Nordics, but they had peculiarly broad faces and relatively narrow heads unlike any of the present great races. They were displaced by other races, the long-headed, dark Mediterraneans, the broad-headed, brown-haired Alpine people, and the tall, fair-haired, blue-eyed, long-headed Nordics. These later races, which have carried civilization forward by leaps and bounds, appear to have risen to their present mental power during this same last Glacial Epoch. The place of their origin is not certain, but their common center was quite surely in central Asia not far from where the Cro-Magnons developed. In that same region dwelt the ancestors of the races that evolved the early civilizations of India, China, and Asia Minor, and at least a part of the Mesopotamian civilization. There in an environment not quite so severe as that of central Europe, these early people developed the art of smoothing stone implements and evolved other capacities which enabled them to conquer the artistic Cro-Magnons. There, too, or else in the not greatly dissimilar climate which then prevailed in North Africa, the art of smelting copper was invented. A little later, in essentially the same Asiatic regions, the far greater art of making iron tools was developed, and man took still another of the great steps which mark his advance toward civilization.

In view of these facts and many others it is hard to avoid the conclusion that the last Glacial Epoch and the succeeding period of less pronounced climatic changes were peculiarly stimulating to mental development. The coldest places were not favorable, but on their borders where the climate was severe enough to be highly bracing, but not benumbing, there occurred an extraordinary development of brain power. As evolution counts the years we are still too near to see this development in its true light. Yet it can scarcely be mere chance that man rose above the animals during a great glacial period such as that which directed the wonderful evolutionary changes of the far earlier Permian Period. Still less is it likely to be mere chance that the evolution of the powers of the human brain was relatively slow until the last of the four great epochs into which the Glacial Period is divided. That last epoch was colder and more severe than any of the others. Close to the ice-sheets it was apparently so severe that it caused retrogression, but farther away it somehow provided conditions such that man changed a thousand times faster than the animals had changed during the vast periods of relatively uniform climate in earlier geological times. Moreover, it was this last cold epoch which caused most of the change in the mammals of Europe and North America. So even among the higher animals we may well say that the last Glacial Epoch of 50,000 years or less produced most of the change which in Figure 22 has been ascribed to a million years. In that case the change in animal life was at least fifty times as rapid as the average during the preceding geological epochs. Clearly a severe climate is wonderfully potent in hastening the course of evolution.

CHAPTER VIII

THE ENVIRONMENT OF MENTAL EVOLUTION

EVEN yet we have not seen the full importance of air, that is, of climate, upon man's evolution. We have seen how it influenced his body, but why should his mind be even more sensitive than his body? Why should the mental optimum be lower than the physical? Why should variable weather and cold waves stimulate business and invention as much or more than they stimulate health? The answer seems to be found in the climatic conditions under which man's mind made its most rapid evolution. We have seen that the greatest crises in the evolution of the human body were associated with epochs of severe climate. Other factors have indeed played a part, but as Lull puts it: "Changing environmental conditions stimulate the sluggish evolutionary stream to quickened movement. Whenever it has been possible to connect cause and effect, the immediate influence is found to be generally one of climate."

This is preëminently true of mental evolution. Throughout the Glacial Period the form of the lands was essentially the same as now. The one thing that was profoundly different was the climate. It must have worked in two ways. First, it must have weeded out those members of the human race who could not endure its rigors, or who did not migrate to milder climates. Second, as we shall see in the next chapter, it probably was the actual cause of what the biologist calls mutations, so that new human types arose.

In order to appreciate the part played by climate in the evolution of man's mind and hence in our own activities at present, we must first find out what kind of climate prevailed in the Glacial Period. Within recent years our ideas of the climate of the past have changed greatly.

A few generations ago the earth's atmosphere was supposed to have grown gradually clearer, drier, and cooler for millions of years. Then it was discovered that glaciation again and again recurred in relatively low latitudes. This means that since the earliest geological times there have been repeated periods when the earth's climate has grown cold and then warm again time after time. There have also been prolonged dry periods and wet periods as is suggested in Figure 21. Coincident with the discovery of the complexity of the earth's climatic history went the further discovery that minor variations are constantly taking place. Each glacial *period* is divided into *epochs;* each epoch into *stages;* and each stage into *minor cycles.* This is illustrated by Figure 23, which shows the climatic pulsations of the Glacial Period, and by Figure 24, which shows the minor fluctuations of the last 3,000 years. If we knew the past as well as we know the present, we should doubtless find that every glacial period is a time not only of great climatic changes lasting hundreds of thousands of years, but of innumerable shorter, more rapid changes.

The inquiring mind naturally asks the cause of these changes. Four chief hypotheses have been advanced, but three of them seem incompetent to explain the known facts. One of these is Croll's idea that glaciation arises because once in about 24,000 years the earth is farthest from the sun in winter instead of in summer as is now the case. Alluring as it sounds, this hypothesis has been entirely discarded by geologists. This is partly because the variations in the sun's distance from the earth are apparently not enough to cause the supposed effect. A much stronger argument is that Croll's hypothesis demands a glacial epoch every 24,000 years, which is wholly at variance with the facts. A second hypothesis holds that glaciation is due to the uplifting

Climatic			
Geological Epochs	Epochs	Human Epochs	Animal Epochs

CORRELATION OF CLIMATIC, RACIAL, CULTURE & LIFE STAGES 1914

Geological Epochs	Climatic Epochs	Time	Human Epochs	Animal Epochs
POST GLACIAL "Newer Loess"	DAUN GSCHNITZ BÜHL	PREHISTORIC NEOLITHIC 8 AZILIAN-TARDENOISIAN 7 MAGDALENIAN 6 SOLUTREAN 5 AURIGNACIAN 25000 YEARS — UPPER PALAEO-LITHIC	GRENELLE CRO-MAGNON GRIMALDI	RECENT FOREST, MEADOW, ALPINE
IV. GLACIAL WÜRM, WISCONSIN "Upper Drift" "Lowest Terraces"	LAUREN	4 MOUSTERIAN 2·50000 YEARS	NEANDERTHAL " " " "	REINDEER PERIOD, ARCTIC TUNDRA, STEPPE, ALPINE FOREST, MEADOW COLD FAUNA ARRIVAL: STEPPE, TUNDRA, FAUNA
3. INTER-GLACIAL RISS—WÜRM SANGAMON "Middle Loess"		3 ACHEULEAN 3·75000 YEARS 2 CHELLEAN 4·100000 YEARS 1 PRE-CHELLEAN 5·125000 YEARS — LOWER PALAEO-LITHIC	" (KRAPINA) PILTDOWN	LAST WARM AFRICAN-ASIATIC FAUNA E. ANTIQUUS, HIPPOPOTAMUS D. MERCKII, E. TROGONTHERII ALSO FOREST, MEADOW EURASIATIC FAUNA
III. GLACIAL RISS, POLANDIAN "Middle Drift" ILLINOIAN		6·150000 7		COLD TUNDRA FAUNA WOOLLY MAMMOTH & RHINOCEROS. FIRST STEPPE & REINDEER
2. INTER-GLACIAL MINDEL-RISS HELVETIAN YARMOUTH Long Warm Stage "Older Loess"		8·200000 YEARS 9·225000 " 10·250000 " 11·275000 " 12·300000 " 13·325000 " 14·350000 "	HEIDELBERG	WARM AFRICAN ASIATIC FAUNA E. ANTIQUUS, E. TROGONTH-ERII, D. MERCKII, HIPPO-POTAMUS
II. GLACIAL MINDEL, SAXONIAN KANSAN "Old Drift"		15· 16·400000 YEARS		FIRST COLD FAUNA
1. INTER-GLACIAL NORFOLKIAN GÜNZ-MINDEL		17·425000 " 18·450000 "		WARM AFRICAN-ASIATIC FAUNA E. MERIDIONALIS — TROGON-THERII, D ETRUSCUS, HIPPOPOTAMUS MACHÆRODUS
I. GLACIAL GÜNZ, SCANIAN NEBRASKAN "Old Terraces"		19·475000 " 20·500000 YEARS	PITHECAN-THROPUS (TRINIL)	COLD FOREST BED FAUNA IN S. BRITAIN
PLIOCENE		525000 "		PLIOCENE WARM FOREST
GLACIAL AND INTERGLACIAL	METERS 300 200 100 — TIME RATIOS		STONE CULTURES AND COLD FAUNAS	HUMAN RACES	STAGES OF MAMMALIAN AND PLANT LIFE

FIGURE 23.   Climate and Life during the Glacial Period.   After Osborn

The top line indicates the present and the bottom line a period about 550,000 years ago, near the beginning of the Glacial Period.

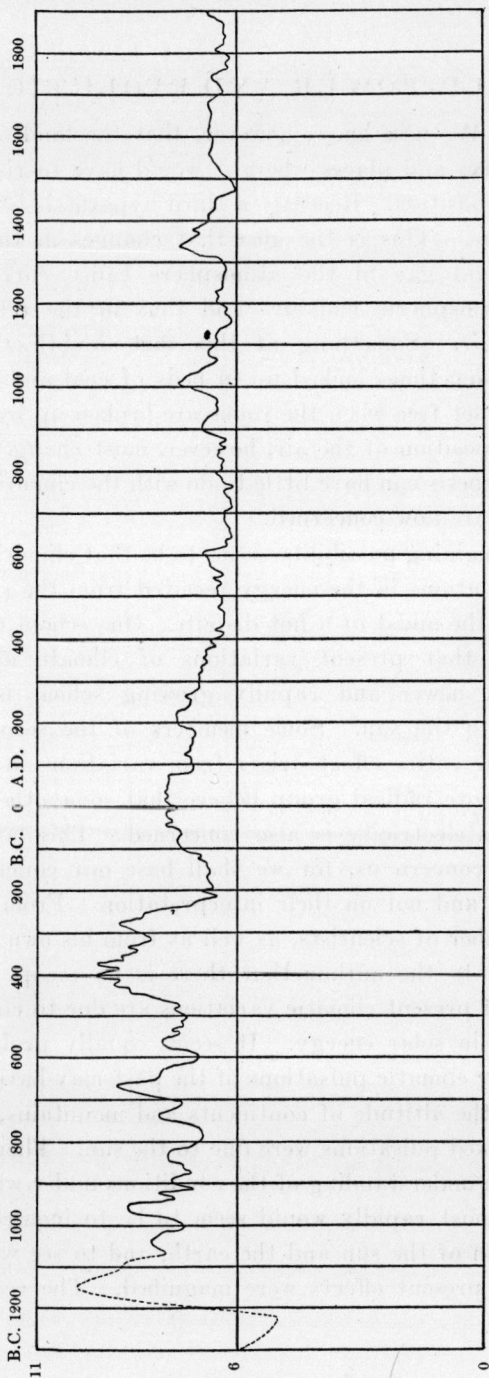

Figure 24. Climatic Pulsations of Historic Times

of the lands. We now know, however, that the land often sank
at the very times and places where it would have to rise according to this supposition. Recently a third hypothesis has received
wide acceptance. This is the idea that changes in the amount
of carbonic acid gas in the atmosphere cause corresponding
changes in atmospheric moisture and thus in the retention of
heat by the air. Something of this sort doubtless happens,
for carbon is sometimes locked up in beds of coal and limestone,
and sometimes set free when the rocks are broken up by weather-
ing. The composition of the air, however, must change so slowly
that this hypothesis can have little to do with the climatic changes
with which we are now concerned.

The only remaining possibility seems to be that climatic changes
are due to variations in the energy received from the sun. This
brings us into the midst of a hot dispute. One school of meteor-
ologists holds that present variations of climate are purely
accidental. A newer and rapidly growing school holds that
they are due to the sun. Some members of the second school
believe that the entire effect arises from variations in the sun's
heat, while a more radical group believe that some other form of
energy such as electricity is also concerned. This latter point
need not now concern us, for we shall base our conclusions on
observed facts and not on their interpretation. From the work
of a large number of scientists, as well as from his own investigations, it seems to the author that there is no escape from the
conclusion that present climatic variations are due to corresponding variations in solar energy. It seems equally probable that
while the slower climatic pulsations of the past may have been due
to changes in the altitude of continents and mountains, the more
rapid and marked pulsations were due to the sun. Therefore, the
best road to an understanding of the conditions under which man's
mind evolved most rapidly would seem to be to inquire into the
present relation of the sun and the earth, and to see what would
happen if the present effects were magnified. The reader must

remember, however, that a considerable body of thoughtful investigators do not yet accept the view here presented.

One of the most firmly established of all facts about the earth and the sun is that when the sun is especially active, as indicated by sunspots, the average temperature of the earth is *lower* than usual. This conclusion is based chiefly on the work of Köppen, who tabulated the results of over twenty million meteorological observations covering all available parts of the earth and distributed through a century. With it must be coupled another fact. Although the sun as a whole probably changes its temperature very slowly, the temperature of the surface may change rapidly. Superheated gases appear to be shot up from below, much as the earth pours out lavas. Thus the amount of heat received by the earth changes constantly. Abbot's measurements show that when sunspots are numerous the sun gives out more than the usual amount of heat. Thus we have the strange anomaly of a hotter sun and a cooler earth.

How is this possible? The answer is apparently found in the movements of the earth's atmosphere. When the sun's surface is disturbed by eruptions from below, some force, perhaps electrical, causes the earth's atmosphere to be correspondingly disturbed. The terrestrial disturbances take the form of changes of atmospheric pressure which give rise to stronger winds and more intense storms. All storms are more or less cyclonic in nature. That is, they may be compared with inverted whirlpools. From every side the winds blow spirally inward toward the center of the storm. In the center the air moves upward. The area of the upward movement may have a diameter of only a few hundred yards as in a summer dust-whirl, or of hundreds of miles as in an ordinary storm. The rate of upward movement may be so rapid that roofs are lifted bodily as in a tornado, or so gentle that it is not noticed except through the cooling of the air. Everyone knows that a warm wave commonly precedes a storm, especially in winter. The wind blows from a southerly direction, and brings air from lower latitudes. When the air rises, heat is removed from the earth's surface. As the air stays aloft a long time before coming down again, the heat is radiated into space and lost. When the air finally descends in clear areas of high pressure, it has become decidedly cold. Because this cold air is heavy it flows under the warm air in the storm center and raises it. Thus cold waves follow warm waves. When the sun is active this process takes place more rapidly than when the sun's surface is at rest. Hence, even though the sun gives out more heat than usual, the increased storminess causes the earth's surface to become cool. The amount of cooling is greatest at the equator, and least in high latitudes.

Still another point deserves special study. It bears not only on the problem of the kind of climate under which man's mental evolution took place, but on his historic activities and the conditions of such modern matters as financial crises. When sunspots are abundant, the ordinary cyclonic storms which bring our frequent changes of weather tend to become concentrated in certain belts. The main belt, both in the United States and Europe, lies well to the north. At present, during times of the greatest solar activity, its center lies in southern Canada and southern Scandinavia. With greater solar activity the belt would apparently lie still farther north. South of the northern storm belt, that is, in the central parts of the United States and Europe, the storminess declines when sunspots are numerous. Hence these regions tend toward aridity when those farther north are moist. Still farther south lies a second belt of increased storminess at times of solar activity. This belt extends from the southwestern United States to the Gulf of Mexico, and reappears east of the Atlantic where it embraces the Mediterranean region, Syria, Persia, northern India, and other parts of central Asia. Here the increase in storminess is like that of the northern belt, although much less intense.

Having seen what happens at present during times of increased sunspots, let us go back to the fourteenth century. Many lines of evidence indicate that this was a period of unusual climatic stress. (See Figure 24.) It was like a glacial period on a small scale, and like present periods of solar activity on a large scale. This was especially evident in the two storm belts. In the southern belt during the early part of the fourteenth century the Big Trees of California, as we know from the rings of their stumps, suddenly increased their rate of growth. They grew with a vigor unequalled at any other time since about 1000 A. D. This means that the rainfall, especially in the late winter and spring, was at a maximum. Not far from the Big Trees, but on the opposite or eastern side of the Sierra Mountains, lies Owens Lake. This body of salt water now has no outlet, but formerly it overflowed. When the Owens River was diverted into the Los Angeles aqueduct to be carried two hundred and fifty miles across the mountains, both the lake and the river were most carefully measured and analysed. From the amount of salt in the two, Gale has calculated the length of time since the lake overflowed. This must have happened not long before the time of Christ. The climate must then have been so moist that the lake was two and a half times as large as at present. From this fact and from our knowledge of the Big Trees we can determine which of the various elevated beaches surrounding the lake belongs to the fourteenth century. The beach thus determined appears to have been formed by waves of unusual intensity. This means that the storms of the early part of the fourteenth century were very violent. Far away in western Asia historic records show that at this same time the Caspian Sea rose rapidly to a level many feet above that of today and above the position it had previously held for several centuries. Still farther to the east in the very heart of Asia the desert lake of Lop-Nor in Chinese Turkestan likewise rose, and overwhelmed the "Dragon Town." Thus at both ends of the southern storm belt we find signs of unusual storminess culminating about 1325 A. D., while other evidence indicates that similar conditions prevailed in the intervening portions.

Let us turn now to the northern belt. During the fourteenth century abundant storms and low temperature seem to have increased the ice-pack on the coasts of southern Greenland so that communication with Norway became extremely difficult.   The same causes, according to Pettersson, impoverished the settlers, and diminished their numbers.   Hence they were finally exterminated by the Eskimos, and the New World was lost for a while to the white man.   Previously the Eskimos appear to have been a quiet folk living far to the north.   The cold and storms of the fourteenth century, however, apparently deprived them of the means of livelihood.   Thus they were driven south as raiders.

In northwestern Europe similar untoward circumstances prevailed.   In Norway the cold stormy weather caused the crops to decrease wofully.   Northern provinces which had formerly been able to export wheat now had to import it.   The revenues fell off 60 to 70 per cent.   In the wake of these disasters came great political disorder.   All sorts of extremes of climate occurred in neighboring regions.   According to Norlind's careful summary the coldest winter ever known in northwestern Europe was 1323-4,—just when the Caspian Sea rose most rapidly and the Big Trees grew fastest.   Horses as well as men were able to cross the Baltic Sea from Germany to Sweden on the ice.   The next three coldest years were 1296, 1306, and then 1408.   According to Pettersson the fourteenth century shows "a record of extreme climatic variations."   The winters were so extraordinarily cold that the Rhine, Danube, Thames, and Po were frozen for weeks and months, a thing that almost never happens now.   The cold winters were followed by violent floods, which are recorded in fifty-five summers in the fourteenth century.   Of course the inundations of the great rivers of Europe six or seven centuries ago must have been more devastating than similar floods in our day when the flow of the rivers is regulated by locks and canals.   Still the floods of the fourteenth century "must have surpassed everything of that kind which has occurred since then.   In 1342 the waters of the Rhine

. . . inundated the city of Mayence and the cathedral 'usque ad cingulum hominis.' The walls of Cologne were flooded so that they could be passed by boats in July." This occurred also in 1374 in mid-February, which is an unusual month for such disasters. "Again in other years the drought was so intense that the same rivers, the Danube, Rhine, and others, nearly dried up, and the Rhine could be forded at Cologne. This happened at least twice in the same century. There is one exceptional summer of such evil record that centuries afterward it was spoken of as 'the old hot summer of 1357.' "

Pettersson also states that on the coasts of the North and Baltic seas not less than nineteen storms "of a destructiveness unparalleled in later times are recorded from the fourteenth century." The coastline of the North Sea was greatly altered by these storms. Thus on January 16, 1300, half of the island of Heligoland and many other islands including Borkum were engulfed by the sea. So great was the destruction of sea-coast villages that this storm is known under the name of "the great man-drowning." Again in 1304, on November 1, the Island of Ruden was torn asunder from Rugen by the force of the waves. Many other similar disasters occurred, almost always in the cold season.

From this assemblage of facts, which might be greatly increased, it appears that the fourteenth century, especially its early part, was marked by notable storminess in both of the belts where storms now increase during times of many sunspots. As to what was happening in the sun at that time our knowledge is extremely scanty. European records of sunspots begin only in 1610, and are accurate only since 1755. In China imperfect records are available almost as far back as the time of Christ. Of course these include only years when the spots were visible to the naked eye. Moreover, since there was no official agency for making observations, it must often have happened that great disturbances passed unrecorded because no one happened to set down the fact in writing. Nevertheless it is interesting to find that Wolf, the chief authority on this subject, considers that so far as can be judged from the Chinese records the years 1370-1385 were noted for sunspot maxima, while an absolute maximum greater than for many centuries apparently took place about 1372. This at least lends probability to the supposition that the whole fourteenth century was a time of unusual solar disturbance. Thus we are led to infer that if solar disturbances should increase still more the earth would again enter a glacial period.

Let us inquire further into the effect of this approach to the conditions of a glacial period in the fourteenth century. Take England for example. According to Thorwald Rogers the severest famine ever experienced in England was that of 1315-1316, and the next worst was in 1321. In fact, from 1308 to 1322 great scarcity of food prevailed most of the time. Other famines of less severity occurred in 1351 and 1369. "The same cause was at work in all these cases," says Rogers, "incessant rain, and cold, stormy summers. It is said that the inclemency of the seasons affected the cattle, and that numbers perished from disease and want." After the bad harvest of 1315 the price of wheat, which was already high, rose rapidly, and in May, 1316, was about five times the average. For a year or more thereafter it remained at three or four times the ordinary level. The severity of the famine may be judged from the fact that previous to the Great War the most notable scarcity of wheat in modern England and the highest relative price was in December, 1800. At that time wheat cost nearly three times the usual amount. During the famine of the early fourteenth century "it is said that people were reduced to subsist upon roots, upon horses and dogs; and stories are told of even more terrible acts by reason of the extreme famine. But we must hesitate before we give credence to the stories found in chroniclers, picked up as they were, no doubt, from rumors current in the country, and amplified before they reached the monastery in which they were recorded." Neverthe-

less there is strong evidence that many persons must have died,
for the price of labor suffered a permanent rise of at least 10 per
cent. There simply were not people enough left among the
peasants to do the work demanded by the more prosperous classes
who had not suffered so much.

After the famine came drought. The year 1325 appears to
have been peculiarly dry, and 1331, 1344, 1362, 1374, and 1377
were also dry. In general these conditions do little harm in England. They are of interest chiefly as showing how excessive rain
and drought are apt to succeed one another.

Some conception of the harm done by famine may be obtained
from the following figures. They show how anæmia and tuberculosis increased among the children of Germany during the Great
War on account of insufficient nourishment.

Children entering school	1913	1916	1917
Anæmic	22.48%	22.90%	28.50%
Tubercular	1.07%	2.10%	2.35%
Candidates for confirmation			
Anæmic	21.74%	30.99%	31.20%
Tubercular	1.51%	4.16%	4.90%

This is a terrible record. Among the children twelve to fourteen
years of age an inadequate supply of food caused an increase of
nearly half in anæmia. Still more sinister are the figures for
tuberculosis—three times as much under conditions of malnutrition as under those of a normal food supply. Can anyone doubt
that under the far less carefully regulated conditions of the fourteenth century there was a still greater increase in sickness during
two such years as 1315 and 1316 when a large part of the people
of England were short of food most of the time? In India during
the famines which arise from droughts one of the consequences
that is most dreaded is the infectious disease known as famine
fever, or relapsing fever. In fact, it follows famine almost everywhere.

In the midst of the death and disaster which the climate inflicted directly upon Europe in the fourteenth century there
arrived a still grimmer calamity. We have no positive evidence
that the Black Death or Great Plague, as it was called, had any
direct connection with climate, but there is a strong presumption
to that effect. According to Thorwald Rogers the Black Death
began its virulent course in China about 1333 A. D. "It is said
that it was accompanied at its outbreak by various terrestrial
and atmospheric phenomena of a novel and most destructive
character, phenomena similar to those which characterized the
first appearance of the Asiatic cholera, of the Influenza, and even
in more remote times of the Athenian Plague. It is a singular
fact that all epidemics of an unusually destructive character have
had their homes in the farthest East, and have traveled slowly
from those regions toward Europe. It appears, too, that the
disease exhausted itself in the place of its origin at about the same
time in which it made its appearance in Europe. The storm burst
on the Island of Cyprus at the end of the year 1347, and was
accompanied, we are told, by remarkable physical phenomena, as
convulsions of the earth, and a total change in the atmosphere.
Many persons affected died instantly. The Black Death seemed,
not only to the frightened imagination of the people, but even to
the more sober observation of the few men of science of the time
to move forward with measured steps from the desolated East,
under the form of a dark and fetid mist. The Black Death
appeared at Avignon in January, 1348, visited Florence by the
middle of April, and had thoroughly penetrated France and Germany by August. It entered Poland in 1349, reached Sweden in
the winter of that year, and Norway by infection from England
at about the same time. It spread even to Iceland and Greenland,
with which latter country communication had for centuries been
familiarly kept up. It is said that among the physical changes
which took place, consequent upon the convulsions of the earth's
surface, vast icebergs formed on the northeastern coast of the

American continent, and effectually severed all communication between the Old World and that portion of the New which had hitherto been visited." (Rogers, "History of Agriculture and Prices in England," vol. 1, pages 292 ff.)

In China it is said that the plague destroyed 13,000,000 people. It probably destroyed as many more in other parts of Asia. Fifteen years after its inception, that is, in August, 1348, it reached England at the opposite end of the great land mass of the eastern hemisphere. There and in France and Italy it appears to have slain a third of the population. Its ravages were worst among the common people, but even the king's daughter, Joan, died of it. The way in which it swept people away may be judged from the fact that the bishop's registers of the diocese of Norwich show that in many parishes three or even four vicars were installed within eighteen months. Not till 1368 did the plague finally disappear from England.

I have dwelt on the Black Death because of the way in which the accounts of this disaster combine three great types of phenomena. One type pertains to climate, one to earthquakes and volcanoes, and one to disease. That they were connected in the way supposed by the people of the fourteenth century is not to be supposed. Nevertheless, it seems clear that all three rose to a maximum in the first half of that century. I shall not attempt to show how volcanoes and earthquakes were concerned with the others, although I believe that probably they owe their origin to the same causes as the climatic phenomena. As to disease and the weather the connection is clearer. It will be remembered that the plague first came into prominence in China in 1333. This was in the decade succeeding the coldest known winter in northwestern Europe, one of the driest seasons in England, the fastest growth of the Big Trees in California, and the most rapid rise and highest level of the Caspian Sea. These manifestations of climatic instability were accompanied by excessive storms and floods in China. In countries like China the plague seems always to exist in a mild, endemic form. It apparently rises to virulence when the vitality of a large section of the community falls to a low ebb. In this respect it resembles famine fever, whose dreaded consequences were well exemplified in Ireland during the potato famine about 1845. The same is true of cholera and influenza, and of tuberculosis, as we have seen from the German statistics. In China nothing weakens the people like great floods, which drown the rice-fields and bring famine. Hence it is highly prob- able that the sequence in the first half of the fourteenth century was something like this: great solar activity, climatic extremes, floods in China, failure of the rice crop, famine, pestilence, and death. Thus climatic extremes may have been the cause not only of 25,000,000 deaths in Asia, but of another 25,000,000 which are reported to have occurred in Europe at that ill-fated time.

The importance of such climatic vicissitudes can be seen even in our own time. Although now the extremes are not equal to those of the fourteenth century and still less to those of earlier histor- ical times and of the prehistoric and glacial periods, they cause terrible devastation. Even in our own country large areas in western Kansas, New Mexico, and other dry regions have been settled, abandoned because of drought, resettled, and in some cases even abandoned again and then settled for the third time. Many a farmer has had to pack up all his goods and trek across the country in search of a new home. In India the British gov- ernment has spent hundreds of millions in famine relief and in building railroads to bring food and canals to bring water in the hope of reducing the deaths due to failure of the crops when the monsoon rains are deficient. Yet hundreds of thousands of people still die of starvation or of diseases induced by scarcity of food. In China, too, both droughts and floods still bring disaster as they have done for centuries. Even as I write I have before me a news clipping saying that a million people are even now, in May, 1918, in danger of starvation. Even in so progressive a country as Australia the effect of variations in rainfall is terrible.

My colleague, Professor H. E. Gregory, thus sums up the situation there:

"Ten of the twelve droughts recorded for Australia since 1880 affected chiefly the inland areas, where the rainfall is normally below 25 inches; but the great drought of 1902-1903, which marked the culmination of five unfavorable years, affected the entire continent. In one year 15,000,000 sheep and 1,500,000 cattle perished, and the whole drought period saw the death of 60,000,000 sheep and 4,000,000 cattle from starvation and thirst. Mining operations were checked for lack of water. The wheat production fell in one year from 38,000,000 bushels to 12,000,000 bushels, and flour, as well as other foodstuffs, was imported. Many people left the country, the excess of departures over arrivals for the period 1901-1905 being 16,800. The birth rate decreased; the deathrate increased so that the increase in population dropped to 1.38 per cent, the lowest in the history of the country. During this period the rate of increase for South Australia was only 0.27 per cent and for Victoria 0.18."

Inconsistent as it may seem, the kind of climate which brings such disasters to some parts of the world is also the kind which elsewhere most stimulates mental evolution. Variability is the keynote of the whole matter. Suppose that the conditions which appear to be connected with great solar activity should become much intensified. A glacial epoch would be at hand. Events like those which occurred from 1300 to 1400 A. D. in Greenland, Scandinavia, Great Britain, central Europe, the Caspian region, China, and California would recur with greatly increased intensity. It must be carefully noted, however, that bitter cold, great aridity, severe storms, floods, and the like would apparently not prevail steadily, nor everywhere. On the contrary, part of the time in high latitudes and all of the time in low latitudes conditions might be no more severe than those prevailing at present where civilization is highest. The mildest years of the Glacial Period may have been about like our severer years, such as 1917 and the early part of 1918, when many weather records were broken in the United States. Solar activity, however, characteristically varies in cycles. When the sun is unusually active the cycles become shorter and the contrast between maximum and minimum increases enormously. In the fourteenth century this tendency was strongly apparent, and during the Glacial Period, and especially during its closing epoch, this must have been still more true.

Consider the effect which such extreme and frequent fluctuations would have when they first began to prevail in various parts of the Old World, the only place where man appears certainly to have lived at that time. In northern Europe the terrible storms, floods, cold waves, and droughts must have destroyed both animals and plants. Thus the inhabitants were largely deprived not only of the game on which they chiefly subsisted, but of the nuts, berries, and roots which eked out their scanty diet. At the same time the great extremes must have been mentally benumbing. In addition to the famines which must frequently have affected the primitive human inhabitants, diseases like the Black Death probably wiped out others. The few who remained doubtless subsisted miserably for a while and then migrated southward.

In central Europe one of the most marked effects of the early stages of a glacial climate was probably aridity. This is what happens there today on a mild scale when sunspots are numerous. It happened on a much greater scale in the past, as we know from abundant deposits of the yellow, wind-borne dust known as loess, which is found in the valleys of the Rhine, Danube, and other rivers of central Europe. Similarly in North America the relatively poor crops of the central portions of the United States at times of many sunspots have their parallel in the glacial deposits of loess in the valleys of the Mississippi, Missouri, and Ohio. Such aridity was probably not nearly so bad for early man as the incessant storminess and cold farther north. Nevertheless both conditions must have checked progress and wiped out large parts of the population, which at best was very scanty according to modern standards. Hence it is not surprising to find signs of distinct retrogression among the people of Europe at the height of the last Glacial Epoch. The Neanderthal race persisted, indeed, for its bones are found in caves with those of beasts of the far north, such as the reindeer and Arctic lemming, but the adverse climate denied it the privilege of inheriting Europe.

The weakened Neanderthal people were replaced by the Cro-Magnon race which had weathered the last Glacial Epoch in a climate less severe and far more stimulating than that of central Europe. Twenty or twenty-five thousand years ago, when the height of this epoch was past, this artistic race with its highly developed brains invaded Europe, apparently from the south. Possibly they had evolved in the Mediterranean regions, or more probably they had migrated into the northern confines of Africa from an Asiatic center farther east. There they probably lived not far from the ancestors of the dark, long-headed Mediterranean race which today dominates southern Europe, and of the brown-haired, hazel-eyed, broad-faced Alpine race whose home is in the mountainous center of Europe. These other races also appear to have followed the lines marked out by climate. The Mediterranean people quite surely came from Asia by way of North Africa, while the Alpine race, coming later after the climate had ameliorated, seems to have followed a more northern route. Finally, perhaps six or seven thousand years ago, the fair-haired, long-headed Nordics from whom are descended the bulk of the English, Scandinavians, and Germans, reached western Europe by a still more northern route which caused them finally to pour out of northern Europe southward in the great barbarian invasions of historic times.

At the height of the last Glacial Epoch the ancestors of many races including the Cro-Magnons, the Mediterranean race, the Alpine race, and the Nordics all appear to have lived in what we have called the southern storm belt. There is reason to believe that the ancestors of the Semites, of the Indo-Europeans who dominated India, and of the Chinese and Japanese also dwelt in this same general region. Thus although the matter is of course uncertain, it seems probable that the world's most advanced races all evolved under essentially the same climatic conditions. The southern storm belt, in some part of which man apparently took the last great steps in mental evolution, comprises all, the lands around the Mediterranean, the largest area of such lands being in North Africa. It also includes the lands to the eastward from Asia Minor to southern Turkestan, Persia, Afghanistan, Baluchistan, and northern India.

It is interesting to find that the climate of this region during the Glacial Period was apparently much like that which we have found to be most favorable to man's mental and physical activity. In what follows it must be remembered that these conclusions as to the climate and home of early man are only in a small degree the work of the present author, and that they were framed before any extensive studies had been made upon the exact nature of the climate most stimulating to human activity. Hence their agreement with the conclusions of earlier pages is made more striking. Today the average January temperature of the regions where the most intellectual races of mankind are supposed to have developed ranges from 40°F to 60°. The July temperature averages from 75° to 85°. At the height of the last Glacial Epoch the mean temperature of the earth as a whole is estimated by various authors to have been 5° to 20°F colder than at present. These estimates are based on the height of the snowline as marked by evidences of glaciation. Most authorities, especially those who have worked more recently, are inclined to say 8° to 12° rather than higher. Suppose we say 10°. Then the range of mean temperature in the northern part of the area would have been from about 30° in January to 65° in July, and in the southern part from about 45° to 75°. This is essentially the same as prevails today in the area from southern France northward to southern

Scandinavia, including England on the west and Austria proper on the east. In our own country similar temperatures prevail only on the Atlantic Coast in a small region centering around New York, and in a larger area on the Pacific Coast of Oregon and Washington. Elsewhere either one season or the other is too cold or too warm. In Asia only the central part of the main island of Japan falls within these limits. The southern hemisphere contains almost no regions of this kind. A small area in New Zealand where the two islands approach each other conforms to our limits of temperature, while Patagonia in latitude 45° approaches them closely without actually reaching them. It must be clearly understood that our figures are elastic. In the first place we do not know exactly where man's mind developed most rapidly; in the second place, we do not know at exactly what time this most rapid development took place; and in the third place, we do not know exactly what conditions of temperature prevailed at any particular place at any particular time. Thus with three unknown variables it is obvious that the best we can do is to make a rough approximation. This much is clear, however, the conditions of temperature in the general region where man developed most rapidly were approximately the same as in the regions where today he is most advanced. By far the largest of the favorable areas is in northwestern Europe, the next largest is in the eastern and western parts of the United States, the next in Japan, the next probably in New Zealand and Australia, and probably the smallest in South America. Africa appears to contain no such area. This result agrees with that which has been set forth in "Civilization and Climate" on quite different grounds.

When we have stated the temperature under which man evolved most rapidly we have by no means fully described the climate. We must know the conditions of storminess. At times of increased solar activity it will be remembered that there is also an increase both in the number and intensity of storms. This applies to both storm belts. In the northern belt it leads to three conditions which promote glaciation. First, the precipitation of snow during the winter becomes more abundant; second, the lower temperature at all times of the year lengthens the season when snow falls and also prevents the snow from melting in the summer; and third, the greater cloudiness also prevents the snow from melting. Thus the area where snow lies throughout the year gradually increases. After such an area is once established it becomes a region of high atmospheric pressure. It then resembles Greenland and Antarctica. In those great regions of ice-sheets the general movement of the air is downward in the centers and outward on the borders. Some of the world's most violent winds blow out from the great ice-caps. Since the air in the centers of such regions descends from far aloft, it is cold and thus preserves the ice and snow. Only rarely do storms penetrate far into the high pressure areas. They skirt the edges, however, in large numbers, and their violence increases in proportion to the size and intensity of the high pressure area caused by the ice-sheet.

During the Glacial Period ice covered all of Scandinavia, and much of Great Britain, northern Germany, and the Baltic region. The Alps and to a less degree the Pyrenees were the seat of large, permanent masses of ice which spread out far below the base of the mountains. In winter a continuous cover of snow must have connected these various ice-sheets. Thus all Europe north of the Alps and the Pyrenees was probably a high pressure area for at least six months of each year. Asia north of the central mountains was also a high pressure area. Under such circumstances practically all the storms must have been forced to follow a route along the Mediterranean and across Syria, Mesopotamia, and Persia to northern India. Moreover, even in summer many storms must have been forced to follow this course. From all this it appears that when man was making his most rapid mental evolution he lived in a climate where severe storms were of great frequency. Remember that at that time the direct rays of the sun were probably even warmer than now. Thus when there were

no storms the sun quickly heated the land wherever there was no
cover of snow. Then a storm came along. It drew in warm air
from the south; the warm air rose in the storm's center; and cold
air from the ice-sheets swept over the country from the north and
northwest. Thus the changes from day to day were apparently
much greater than is now the case in any part of the world. At
present the most frequent changes of weather are experienced by
the northeastern United States and southern Canada. Western
Europe, including northern Italy and Austria proper together
with the Baltic coast of Russia, but not including Spain, comes
next in this matter. Then follows Japan. New Zealand is the
most stormy of the habitable areas of the southern hemisphere,
and follows Japan in this respect. Finally at the bottom of the
list come the parts of South America from latitude 30° to 40°.
The rest of the world is either too cold and stormy to be readily
habitable, or else has relatively few storms and an unstimulating
climate. It is highly significant that except in one respect the
order of the different regions in respect to favorable conditions
of storminess is the same as in respect to favorable conditions
of temperature. The one exception is that while western Europe
appears to have the advantage in temperature, the United States
has the advantage in storminess and thus in variability. Thus it
appears that today the distribution of civilization is almost in
harmony with the degree to which the climate of the various parts
of the world resembles that in which man's mind made its most
rapid evolution. Apparently in early days before man became
greatly different from the animals, his body became adapted to
a temperature averaging about 64°. Then when the time came
for his mental evolution, the activity of his mind made the most
rapid evolution where the temperature was somewhat lower. Also
at that time or earlier both his body and his mind became extremely sensitive to the stimulus of changes of temperature.
Thus it appears that the relation of climate and health to the ebb
and flow of business and to other human activities is merely the

inevitable reflection of the physical circumstances under which mankind evolved.

In a later chapter we shall follow man's evolution through still another stage, and see how changes of climate seem to have swayed Rome this way and that. Here let us return to the fourteenth century in order to point out certain facts which may be a mere coincidence, but which are at least worth considering in the light of our study of evolution.

Today the southern storm belt is best developed in Italy. An increase in the intensity of that belt, such as appears to have characterized the Glacial Period, would make itself felt first apparently in that country. Thus at a time like the fourteenth century when great storminess prevailed in northwestern Europe, we should expect that Italy would be stormier than now. The stormy period began with a sudden increase of storminess at the very beginning of the century. This culminated about 1325, but judging by the Big Trees of California the climate did not return to a condition resembling that of today until after 1460.* (See Figure 24.) Thus the fourteenth century and to a less extent the fifteenth up to 1460 form a period which would be expected to be mentally stimulating in Italy by reason of the comparative storminess and variability. Many of the best authorities hold that during the fourteenth century the mental activity of Italy was higher than at any time since the days of Rome. The Renaissance, to be sure, did not come till the next century, but its indispensable precursor, the Revival of Learning, came in the fourteenth. During the Renaissance the arts of sculpture and painting rose to their highest levels in Leonardo da Vinci and Michael

* The justification for using the trees of California as a measure of the climate in Italy will be given later. The student should understand that the statement here made is based upon the *dotted* line given in Figure 72, pp. 209 and 231, in "The Climatic Factor." Studies made since that book was written, especially the study of Owens Lake have shown that the dotted line is probably more correct than the other. They have also shown that during recent decades the curve of storminess appears to be rising.

Angelo. Yet these great masters could never have achieved such fame had not such men as Giovanni, Andrea Pisano, Cimabue, and Giotto done a wonderful constructive work in developing the technique of art during the preceding century. These men were the original pioneers who did most of the inventive work, while Leonardo and Michael Angelo were the reapers. The great men of the Renaissance would never have been crowned with such a halo of glory if the preceding century had not been one of the greatest creative periods in the whole history of art. In mediæval Italy, as in ancient Greece, Egypt, Rome, Syria, and Yucatan, the most striking productions of art and architecture usually represented the flowering of forces which had been in action for some time.

In literature, on the other hand, there is no need of so long a period to develop a high technique. In a great many countries the greatest literary masterpieces belong to a period somewhat preceding the artistic masterpieces. Italian literature of the fourteenth century holds its own without a rival. From 1300 to 1310 Dante was writing his Divine Comedy. A little later Petrarch (1304-1374) was laying the foundations of the great Revival of Learning which flowered not only in the Renaissance, but in the Reformation. At the same time (1313-1375) Boccaccio, whose true greatness is often veiled by the coarseness of some of his work, was building the reputation which places him third among Italian men of letters, unless Ariosto (1474-1533) has juster claim to that place. Doubtless Dante, Petrarch, and Boccaccio would have been great no matter where they lived. Yet may not the stimulating climate of the fourteenth century have had something to do with the energy, originality, and perseverance with which they worked? They, too, like the business men of America, came of a race which is extremely sensitive to climatic variations, and which bears in its blood the inheritance of a stock whose chief development, both physical and mental, has taken place under the influence of climatic crises.

CHAPTER IX

THE ORIGIN OF NEW TYPES AMONG ANIMALS

IN following the steps of the evolution of man and of animals we have seen the conditions under which the most rapid changes occur. We have also seen why it is that during periods of great climatic stress many old forms disappear. But why is it that at the end of such a period we find not only that the old forms have gone, but that their places are amply filled by new forms? Indeed we may almost say that at times of evolutionary crises the development of new types is even more marked than the disappearance of the old. The problem of how these new forms originate has a direct bearing upon man's life today, for the laws that apply to species of plants and animals throughout geological history appear also to apply to races of men today and to human ideas and institutions. Let us begin by considering what modern biology has to say on this subject in respect to animals. Then we shall be ready to apply our results to man in the next chapter.

Charles Darwin filled the world with the idea that natural selection is of the utmost importance in evolution. His work and that of hundreds of his successors have shown that among all the factors that cause selection climate is far the most important, since climate largely controls the food supply and migrations. Darwin believed that very slight differences were enough to give natural selection a free hand. The work of later biologists has shown more and more clearly that this is rarely or never the case. New species do not seem to arise through the cumulative effect

of little differences. The tusk of the elephant, for example, probably did not reach its present size through innumerable tiny incre-
ments. More probably there occurred many larger mutations
whereby the tusks of a certain group of elephants were elongated
to such an extent that the group had an advantage over its short-
tusked comrades.

What causes such mutations? This is today the great question
of biology. Several causes are probably at work. Hybridization
is almost certainly an important factor. Two allied forms are
brought into contact, just as various races of men are brought
together in cities or in new countries. The two forms interbreed;
there arises a hybrid form which is subject to wide variations;
and occasionally some unknown cause leads to extreme types.
These extreme types are genuine mutants, and give rise to new
species. When we have said that hybridization thus leads to new
species, we have not yet explained the matter. In the first place,
why do the two forms, hitherto separate, come together? Generally because of migrations. But among animals migrations are
almost invariably due to the search for food and water, or the
desire to escape enemies. The food and water depend almost
wholly on climate, while the number of enemies depends upon the
food supply of some other kind of plant or animal and thus again
upon climate, although less directly. Putting this aside, however,
and confining ourselves to what happens after the hybrid race is
formed, have we any evidence as to why the extreme mutants
arise?

In attempting to explain why mutants arise, it must be remembered that a mutant is different from a monstrosity which does
not reproduce itself. In order to have any great biological
significance a mutant must be reasonably perfect so that it can
reproduce its kind, and its peculiarities must be capable of being
passed on by heredity. Moreover, the mutation must occur in
enough individuals so that there is a reasonable chance that
animals with the same mutation will mate and thus perpetuate

the new form. Such mutations seem thus far to have been produced artificially by only two methods. One is by exposing the immature ovules or germ cells to some artificial stimulus. The stimulus may be produced through the injection of a weak chemical solution into the ovary at an early stage of development. In this way MacDougal appears to have obtained a genuine new species of primrose. Other possible stimuli are mechanical shocks, electricity, and light of different colors, but none of these seems to have led to the production of really new forms. The other method of causing mutations is by keeping the developing germ cells under extreme conditions of temperature or humidity during certain critical periods. In the case of plants it is probable that this has occurred again and again although it is not easy to point to specific cases. In the case of animals, with which we are now chiefly concerned, it has occurred in a number of well-authenticated instances, some of which we shall now describe.

One of the best-known instances of changes in animals through the effect of climatic extremes is the butterfly. Standfuss, Fischer, Merrifield, and others have experimented along this line. To take the work of only one of these students, Standfuss raised about 42,000 pupæ belonging to about sixty species. His method was to expose the eggs of the butterflies to various temperatures for longer or shorter periods. By exposure to both cold and heat he found that the coloring and other conditions of the butterflies are altered. For instance, a butterfly called *Vanessa levana* has two distinct generations each year. The summer form of the creature lives during the warm part of the summer, while in the fall there appears a distinctly different type. By subjecting the eggs which would naturally give rise to the summer generation to cold, the fall generation can be secured, or the reverse can be done by warming the eggs of the fall generation. When the eggs of another form called *Vanessa urtica* are subjected to low temperature they hatch as the variety *polaris* which lives in Lapland. When the same eggs are subjected to great heat they hatch into the variety *ichnuse* which lives in Corsica and Sardinia. In another experiment Standfuss subjected the nymphæ, or newly hatched young, of fifty species to temperatures ranging from —4°F upward. The method was to expose the nymphæ to the low temperature twice per day for a period of from two to four hours. This was done for five or six days. Betweenwhiles the nymphæ were kept at a temperature-of over 40°F. The change from warm to cold and back again was always gradual, lasting about half an hour. When the nymphæ of these various species developed into butterflies it was found that from 2 per cent to 15 per cent were variants from the ordinary types. Some of these variants were so extreme that they might be classed as mutants. The degree of variability was in proportion to the lowness of the temperature. No mutants were observed when the temperature was reduced to 32°, even though this continued twelve hours, but when it was lowered to 23° unusual forms began to appear. When the same experiments were tried with high temperatures running up to 108° and even 113°, the same variability appeared. In some cases the form of the mutants was the same as in the cold experiments, but generally there was a difference. Some of the unusual forms are found in nature, and may be regarded as ancestral forms. This is especially true of the ones due to heat. This is natural, since temperatures above 100° may occur on hot banks where the eggs are exposed to the sun, while extremely low temperatures are almost unknown at times when the nymphæ are developing. In general, both extremes of temperature retard the development of the insects, and the slower development is accompanied by other changes. When the aberrant insects were bred under normal conditions there was a very slight inheritance of their abnormality, but not enough to be of great significance.

For our present purpose the importance of these butterfly experiments lies in the fact that they show how brief extremes of either heat or cold may alter the form of a species. It will be remembered that in a former chapter we saw that such extremes appear to have been the most notable feature of the climate of the Glacial Period. In earlier times during the Permian glaciation they appear to have given rise to the habit of metamorphosis which the nymphæ of the butterflies illustrate. Moreover, such extremes, though less severe than in the Glacial Period, are one of the most marked characteristics of the climate of the United States. Cold waves alternating with hot waves occur in this country not only in winter but in summer when the eggs of creatures like the butterfly are hatching.

Another set of experiments on insects has been conducted by Tower, chiefly in Tucson, Arizona, at the Desert Laboratory of the Carnegie Institution of Washington. To that dry region he brought beetles from Mexico, Illinois, and other less arid regions. In this way he obtained many mutants, some of which bred true, and thus perpetuated their variations. In many cases the new environment selected certain types for preservation and destroyed others, so that the inherent character of the insects was changed. These changes were evident not only in the color and pattern of the insects but in other respects also. For instance, one type of beetle was brought from Chicago to the Desert Laboratory at Tucson. During the first winter many insects died because they were not able to stand the drying effect of the arid climate. Those that survived were bred in Tucson for some generations and then a part were taken back to Chicago. There they proved quite unable to stand the cold winters because they could not give up their moisture fast enough. In Arizona they had been forced to hold much moisture, but in Chicago this caused them to freeze so that all perished. In still other cases Tower's beetles showed marked mutations which were passed on to later generations. In all cases he found that whatever changes take place occur quickly. A given species is subjected to climatic extremes to which it is not accustomed. In the next generation mutants arise; these start new lines; those that are not adapted to the new conditions die off, while those that are adapted persist and give rise to new varieties. Here among the beetles we have the same sort of changes as among the butterflies, but with greater success in producing new and permanent varieties.

Let us take now some other insects where the exact mechanism of changes has been followed. The drosophila is a little fruit fly about an eighth of an inch long. Everyone has seen it hovering in swarms over decaying fruit. This little creature has been the subject of some of the most careful biological studies ever made. They have been carried on by Morgan with the help of his students. For many generations the flies have been raised and their pedigrees have been kept as carefully as those of race horses. In one of the experiments on these flies Miss Hoge selected those that had an unusual number of bristles on the sex-comb, which is part of the leg. Normally the male, which alone has the comb, has ten bristles in each comb. Miss Hoge selected those having eleven or more in order to see whether she could gradually obtain a strain having more than the normal number. During the fifth generation of these many-bristled flies there suddenly appeared various duplications of the legs that bore the combs. What caused this mutation no one knows, and all attempts to produce it in other animals have been in vain.

When the abnormal flies were bred, their mutation was inherited. It did not always take the same form, but there was some kind of a doubling of the limbs. When the flies lived at ordinary temperatures the abnormality was slight and did not accord with the Mendelian laws of inheritance which determine the proportion in which the qualities of the parents will reappear in the offspring. For example, to take a very simple case, if white peas are pollenated from the flowers of red peas, a quarter of the next generation will be white, a quarter red, and the remaining half will be pink, showing the result of mixture. In the case before us the matter is merely more complex, but the probable occurrence of a given quality can be worked out in exact mathematical proportions. In cold weather, however, the abnormalities increased, and came much nearer to following the Mendelian laws. Therefore some experiments were tried similar to those already described in respect to butterflies. The eggs were placed in a temperature of about 50°F instead of about 70° which was the usual condition in the experimental rooms. The results of the best experiment are shown in the following table:

Age of Eggs or Larvæ when Placed in the Lower Temperature	Number of Eggs that Hatched	Number that were Abnormal	Per Cent that were Abnormal
Age less than 1 day	12	12	100.0
Age 1-2 days	506	341	67.4
Age 2-3 days	290	148	51.0
Age 3-4 days	417	98	23.5
Age 5-6 days	752	79	10.5
Age 6-10 days	2169	207	9.5
Control, not cooled	1711	174	10.1

The important part of this table is the right-hand column. It shows that when the eggs were cooled at a very young stage all of those that hatched were abnormal. If there was some delay in cooling the eggs, the proportion of abnormality decreased until an average of about 10 per cent was reached. In other words, if the eggs were not cooled till after the fourth day there was no more effect than when they were not cooled at all. Consider what this means. Suppose that for some unexplained reason this mutant happened to arise in nature. If the flies were living in a climate where the temperature rarely fell to 50° during their breeding period the mutation would doubtless soon die out. If the climate should change, however, so that cool waves came frequently during the summer and lasted three or four days, the mutant might thrive so that before long it would become as abundant as the old species. Thus a new species or even a new genus with an extra pair of legs might conceivably arise. This would be the more likely to happen because Miss Hoge's experiments show that when the eggs are cooled the number that hatches is less than at higher temperatures. Thus the cool spells would diminish the normal forms and relatively increase the abnormal. All this is highly important, for we are working out certain far-reaching biological principles which apply to man as well as to the lower insects.

In connection with Miss Hoge's experiments Plough, another of Morgan's students, has carried on a still more conclusive series. Using the same fruit-fly, drosophila, he has tested what is known as "crossing-over." Microscopic study of the nuclei of the reproductive cells shows that the factors which make up the inheritance of any organism are carried by the minute threads known as chromosomes. Ordinarily the corresponding chromosomes from the male and female nuclei fuse into one and then split longitudinally in such a way that exactly half of each goes to each of the cells of the new organism whose development is beginning. Sometimes, however, the chromosomes do not unite in this simple way, but wind about one another, or "cross over." Hence when the splitting begins, the parts of the nucleus that go to the two daughter cells are not exactly alike. This leads to a new combination of characteristics in the offspring, so that decidedly new types are formed.

In his experiments Plough found that the amount of crossing-over varies according to the temperature. This is illustrated in Figure 25. The high parts of the curve represent the normal conditions where the offspring resemble the parents according to the Mendelian laws. The low parts mean that the percentage of abnormal or new forms increases. The little hooks at the ends of the curve are of little importance since they are based on relatively few data, and might disappear if further experiments were tried. At temperatures above and below those indicated in the curve the flies perish. The meaning of the curve is evident. When the mother flies are kept at low temperatures of 45° to 55°F during the critical period of the development of the eggs there is a high percentage of crossing-over. This reaches a minimum at about 71°, remains low till about 80°, and then increases rapidly at higher temperatures. An exposure of about two days is necessary in order to produce the new forms. This exposure is effective only when the eggs are in their earliest stages.

Plough's curve is significant in many ways. It is essentially the same as that which Ewing has worked out for similar changes

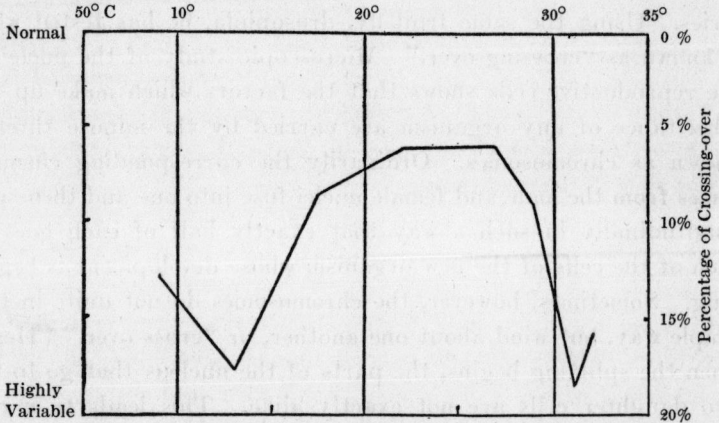

FIGURE 25. The Relation of Temperature to Variability in Drosophila. Adapted from Plough

in the insects known as aphids. At a temperature of 65°F this creature produces the maximum number of wingless, non-reproductive forms, while at lower and higher temperatures the number of winged forms with fully developed sex characteristics increases. Another similar curve has been found by Howell for the contraction of the muscles of a frog's leg, the contraction being strongest at about 80°F. In "Civilization and Climate" I have given a series of similar curves which include (1) plants with a maximum growth at about 85°, (2) infusoria which reproduce most rapidly at about 83°, (3) crayfish which are most active at 74°, (4) factory operatives who do the most work when the temperature for day and night averages about 60° with a noon temperature of 65° to 70°, and (5) the work of students with a maximum when the temperature averages about 40°. We have seen in previous pages that a similar curve can be drawn for health with a maximum at an average temperature of 64°F. Thus it appears that for each species there is a certain temperature at which the various functions take place most nearly in the normal fashion. Above or below that temperature there are departures from the normal, and among insects these departures take the form of new varieties or mutants. Likewise, as appears from Tower's work and from our study of the human deathrate, there is an optimum humidity, above or below which there may be similar changes although this is not so well demonstrated.

Let us now turn from insects to some of the higher animals and see what effect changes of environment have upon their offspring. Kammerer has caused what seem to be hereditary changes by subjecting the nurse-toad (Alytes obstetricans) to a high temperature. This animal is a small toadlike amphibian about two inches long, with a gray color, plump form and warty skin. It is remarkable as the only European batrachian in which the male helps in rearing the offspring. Hence the name. The eggs are larger than those of related animals. They are also fewer and have more yolk. At the time of spawning they are stuck together in two strings which the male twists around his legs. He then returns to his usual haunts among stones and sticks. The nurse-toad is thoroughly terrestrial, but prefers moist places, and feeds at night. On very dry nights it may enter the water in order to keep the eggs sufficiently moist. Three weeks after the eggs have been laid the male regularly enters the water and stays there until all the eggs are hatched and the young tadpoles are swimming freely about.

Kammerer kept the toads at a temperature of 77° to 86°F, a temperature which is rare in the cool, shady places frequented by the animals in central Europe. This led them to seek the water, and there the egg-laying and fertilization took place. The gelatinous envelopes of the eggs which usually remain unswollen and sticky on the land, swelled up and would not adhere to the male's legs. Hence the young developed freely in the water without the paternal care. After this had happened during several of the breeding periods, of which two, three or four occur each summer, the toads acquired the habit of going to the water, and the eggs became more numerous and smaller.

More important than this, however, is the fact that, according to Kammerer, the offspring produced in this way showed a change of habits like that of their parents. At the time for reproduction they sought the water, even when kept at the normal temperature, and laid their eggs there. Moreover, in the fourth generation there appeared on the forefinger of the male a swollen pad which was absent in the race that Kammerer began experimenting with, but which seems to have belonged to ancestral types. Thus a change in climatic conditions seems to have caused a permanent mutation. The mutation, to be sure, like some of those of the butterflies, seems to have been back toward an ancestral form. This, however, by no means indicates that mutations may not take place in the opposite direction. Such seems to have been the case with Hoge's drosophila where the change if carried far enough might lead to a wholly new type of fly with an additional pair of legs.

By exposing the larvæ of the nurse-toad to cold conditions, Kammerer produced results of quite a different kind. He prolonged the larval condition even to the time of sexual maturity. When the offspring of such forms were placed under normal conditions of temperature the abnormal duration of immaturity was found to be inherited. Here, as in the other cases, the inherited effects appear to be produced very early in the life of the organism. The heat to which the toads were subjected apparently influenced the eggs while they were still in the mother's body, and the cold of the other experiment was effective at an almost equally early period. In this respect the toads resemble all the insects for which exact data are available.

· Thus far we have been dealing with changes produced in the offspring of cold-blooded animals. Let us now take up some experiments with warm-blooded creatures whose response is presumably much the same as that of man.

During the years 1906 to 1911 Sumner carried on a series of experiments to test the effect of heat and cold upon white mice. He divided his 2,300 animals into two groups which were kept in separate rooms from the beginning of November to the end of March. One room resembled an ordinary unheated attic. Its mean temperature was about 39.5°F and the mean relative humidity approximately 75 per cent. The other room was heated, and had a mean temperature of 72.5°F and a relative humidity of approximately 30 per cent. The rooms varied a good deal, however, especially the cool room which was subject to essentially the same fluctuations as the outside air. During the remaining seven months both sets of mice were transferred to a common room which averaged a little cooler than the warm room, although it became decidedly warmer in midsummer.

On four occasions a second generation was raised from mice that had been subjected to either the warm or cold rooms. The total number of such mice for which measurements are available is 879. It was impossible to raise a third generation, for the mice were attacked by some disease or weakness which prevented reproduction. This happened to both the warm-room and cold-room animals. It apparently had nothing to do with the temperature. The warm-room animals suffered more than the others, however, which suggests that their relation to temperature may be like that of man.

The mice which lived in the warm and cold rooms respectively from their very birth showed distinct and systematic variations when measured with great accuracy at various ages. The cold-room animals seemed to depart most widely from the ancestral type. The most notable differences were that when the length of the tail and foot were compared with the length of the body, the warm-room mice had relatively longer tails and feet. This accords with the conditions among many tropical animals when compared with related species in the north. Perhaps the large feet of Negroes are due to similar conditions. Lengthening of the ear appeared in many of the warm-room animals, but was by no means so distinct as the lengthening of the tail and foot. In general the length of the body was greater in the warm room than in the cold, but this was not constant. Other characteristics, such as weight and hairiness, seemed to have no direct relation to temperature. Thus it appears that while the low temperature produced modifications in the relative length of different parts of the body, it did not produce what may be called adaptive modifications. It is true that in general the rodents of warm countries appear to have greater length of tail and foot than those of cold countries, but there is no evidence that this is of any particular value in the struggle for existence. Apparently mutations may occur in any direction without respect to the causative agent. It may happen that they are useful, as would be the case if the hair were thicker in the coats of the cold-room mice. Under such circumstances the mutation would be of value, and would presumably be preserved.

When the mice that had been reared in the warm and cold rooms were bred separately in the common room, their offspring displayed the same characteristics as their modified parents. This happened even when a period of five months had elapsed since the parents were removed from the cold and warm rooms and placed in the common room. Therefore it seems to represent a real inheritance. Moreover, the variations in the second generation were more constant than in the first, so that the relative weight and the length of the ear seemed to vary as constantly and regularly as did the relative length of the tail and foot. This appears in the following table based on 752 mice. The figures show the average amount by which the warm-room mice exceeded the cold-room mice when comparisons were made between animals having the same length of body.

EXCESS OF WARM-ROOM MICE OVER COLD-ROOM MICE WHEN ANIMALS WITH THE SAME LENGTH OF BODY ARE COMPARED

	Weight	Length of Tail	Length of Foot	Length of Ear
Males	0.367 grams	1.345 mm.	0.120 mm.	0.122 mm.
Females	0.324 grams	1.269 mm.	0.223 mm.	0.199 mm.

Every one of these numbers is positive. Therefore it seems hard to avoid the conclusion that the parent mice were themselves modified directly by the climatic conditions, and that they passed these modifications on to their descendants. This does not mean necessarily that there is any such thing as the inheritance of acquired characteristics. It seems rather to mean that during the very early life of an animal its germ plasm or reproductive tissue is subject to changes in response to external environment. This is suggested by the fact that when Sumner exposed adult mice to low temperatures neither they nor their offspring were affected. On the other hand, a small number of mice were born of parents that had been kept in the cold room during the first two weeks of their lives, but were then transferred to the warm room. The offspring of these mice showed the characteristic cold-room variations. Thus it looks as if the first two weeks were the critical time. This is especially interesting in view of the fact that during early life, as Sumner conclusively proves, the blood temperature of the white mouse, as of all young mammals, is not constant. It varies in response to the external air. In the adult mouse, however, the variations in temperature are very slight, and can be detected with certainty only when the animal is subjected to very sudden and marked changes of temperature. Thus it appears that when the animal is young and its body temperature can be reduced to a low level, the germ plasm is influenced.

This conclusion is of the utmost significance. It agrees with all that we have seen as to variations in butterflies, beetles, fruit flies, aphids, and toads. It shows especial agreement with the highly exact work done by Morgan's pupils on the drosophila fly. Of course the body of evidence thus far available is slight, but it all points in one direction. Apparently the tissues of animals are especially sensitive to extremes of heat or cold during a limited stage in their development. Among insects the most sensitive period seems to be as soon as the eggs begin the process of growth within the body of the mother. Since insects are cold-blooded, the mother's body necessarily shares the changes of temperature occurring in the outside air. Among warm-blooded animals, if the white mouse may serve as a type, the most sensitive period appears to be immediately after birth. While the young are within the mother's body they probably are not influenced by changes in the outside temperature. At birth, however, they are still extremely immature, and their germ plasm is apparently still susceptible of changes. In other words, while inheritance from its parents gives to the young animal most of its characteristics, the conditions of the air immediately after its birth apparently have a certain modifying effect. The new characteristics thus acquired appear to be measurable and to be capable of transmission to offspring. This fact perhaps explains why glacial periods have been times of such rapid evolution. Not only have the sudden extremes of heat and cold then caused the rapid extinction of old species, but the same climatic extremes may have caused rapid and pronounced mutations so that new species and genera were produced in great numbers.

If these conclusions are true, the animals of extremely hot or cold regions ought to show large numbers of new or unusual characteristics. A. H. Clark has investigated this question in respect to the crinoids, near relatives of the starfishes. He finds that the optimum temperature of the crinoids is not far from 60°. Those living in water near this temperature conform quite closely to the standard type of their class. In unusually warm or cold water, on the contrary, aberrant types are numerous. This looks as if the warm or cold conditions caused variations, while the optimum allows the standard type to reproduce itself unchanged. That this is really the case is further suggested by various other cases cited by Clark. For example, the asymmetrical narwhal is exclusively arctic, while another group of equally aberrant whales lives within the tropics. The anthropoid apes, which are pronouncedly left- or right-handed, live in very warm regions; the hornbill *Rhinoplax*, with an uneven tail, a solid casque, a naked patch on the back of the head, and other peculiarities, is found in warm Malayan regions, while the crossbills with the tips of the mandibles crossed and a corresponding distortion of the bones of the head are all subarctic or cold temperate forms. So, too, Clark points out that the owls with one ear greatly larger than the other all appear to inhabit cold regions. Among the fishes the very asymmetrical *Anableps* lives in the warm tropical littoral, and the asymmetrical forms of "Amphioxus" (using the term in its broadest sense) occur in warm regions; while the flatfishes are chiefly developed either in warm tropical waters or in those that are cold.

Since the great majority of animals are symmetrical, any departure from symmetry attracts attention and makes this quality an easy one to study. Lack of symmetry may or may not be important in the life history of the animal, but it is at least an indication that the creature has suffered some mutation. The chances are large that other mutations also accompany the changes in symmetry. Among the crinoids Clark's work seems to demonstrate that this is the case. Hence the relative abundance of asymmetrical or aberrant forms in temperatures which depart far from the optimum seems to suggest that mutations are actually due to extremes of temperature. If this is so, it may have a most important bearing upon the powers and capacities of mankind.

CHAPTER X

THE ORIGIN OF NEW TYPES AMONG MEN

HAVING inquired into the causes of variations among animals, we are ready to ask why they occur among men. Why did so many races of men arise during the Glacial Period? Why were there so many great men in ancient Greece? Why so many in Italy during the fourteenth century, and in England since the days of Shakespeare and Newton? In a gang of boys why is there generally a leader who starts things? In his little way such a boy is a Napoleon or an Alexander. He is one of the variants, or perhaps even one of the mutants, whose biological importance we have been discussing in the preceding chapter.

Does the world need mutants? In the Harvard Library the catalogue contains seven and one half drawers, or about 4,700 cards, under the name of William Shakespeare. The two names before and after that of the great poet are Shakery and Shakhmatov, each with only one card. Why such a discrepancy? Why should Abraham Lincoln have 498 cards, while Barnabas Lincoln has only one, and Benjamin Lincoln three? The same catalogue contains 157 cards under the name of that strange mixture of good and bad called Macchiavelli, and 38 under the sentimental brute named Nero. Still more remarkable is the fact that there are seven cards under Jukes, a name that stands for the lowest depths of crime, vice, and degradation. Why should this be when millions of most estimable citizens find no place either in the catalogue or in history?

The answer is that estimable citizens are usually much like other people, while Shakespeare, Lincoln, Macchiavelli, Nero, and the Jukes family were very different. Variability is what attracts attention. It is the variant, the man with new ideas, new methods, and new impulses who makes the great success in business. It is the variant, with new ideas, who commits the crimes that curdle the blood. If an individual departs far from the average on the bad side of the ledger we try to suppress him during life, and hold him up as a terrible example after death. If he departs far on the good side, we laugh at him, oppose him, misunderstand him, praise him, or neglect him as the case may be, while he lives, but after he is dead we write books about him and give his name to our streets, our clubs, and our children.

It is almost impossible to overestimate the importance of variability. Every gardener knows that if plants always bred true we should never have such things as the double rose, the seedless orange, and the sweet corn. We should have to be content with the single wild rose, the sour wild orange, and the small and tasteless wild corn. Among animals this same variability has given us the stocky percheron, the slender race horse, and the shaggy pony, all from the same species. Among men we have not only white and black, Jew and Gentile, Teuton and Slav, but "high-brows" and "low-brows," and dainty society belles and coarse-featured factory girls. Such variability is a great advantage. It is indeed regrettable that every high type must have its corresponding low type, but society can restrain the activities of the low far more easily than it can dispense with the guidance and inspiration of the high. Blot out a thousand names from religion and philosophy, another thousand from politics, and equal numbers from art, literature, and science. These 5,000 amount to about one in 300,000 compared with the people now living, or perhaps one in ten million or more among the people who have lived since the days of the Hebrew patriarchs. But take away the contribution of this ten-millionth of the human race, and where would civilization be today?

Since the men who cause most of the world's progress—and also its worst misery—are all extreme types, it becomes highly important to discover the reasons for such variations. Doubtless there are many reasons, but only two seem as yet to be well enough understood to warrant attention in this book. The first is mixture of races or types, a process whose effect few students would question. The other is climatic extremes like those discussed in the last chapter. Their effect is so little understood that we must consider some of the evidence in detail.

To begin with the mixture of types, in an ordinary peasant village of almost any long-settled country, especially in regions that are backward, one family is almost like another. For centuries few brides have been brought from other villages, and few men have come from outside. All the families are therefore related and have virtually the same inheritance. Hence new types rarely arise through the union of parents with divergent qualities. If by any chance such a type does arise, it is frowned upon and discouraged. Only minds of more than usual originality can appreciate the new ideas evolved by similar minds that depart from the standard type.

Among the upper classes and among people who travel, diverse types intermarry much more than among conservative peasants. In cities this tendency is accentuated by the fact that the unusual minds of the villages are apt to drift cityward, where they mate with others of their kind. Thus, for good or for ill, city children vary more than country children. This is one reason why Cattell's study of men of science shows an increasing tendency for the proportion of eminent men born in cities and their suburbs to increase faster than the general population of such places. New countries are like cities. As the "moody" or "trifling" country boy goes to the city and is recognized as a genius, so the Pilgrims, Puritans, Huguenots, and others came to America

because their "queerness" made them a misfit at home. It made
them great, however, in the world's history. Such immigrants,
unfortunately, are scanty now, but when a Russian Nihilist
marries a Spanish artist in the environment of Chicago, the children are likely to be unusual. Thus new countries even more than
old cities are apt to produce mutants. It is not by accident that
Radosavljevich finds that the study of thousands of American
and European school children shows that while the *average* conditions of height, weight, head-form, hair, lung capacity, dynamic
power, activity of the senses, and so forth, "are very much alike
for both American and European pupils, . . . the Americans
vary more than their European brothers and sisters at all the
school ages." Such variability promises men of genius, but it
also promises an equal number of exceptionally low and dangerous
types.

Mixture of races is clearly not the only cause of the variability
that insures progress. The Jews furnish strong evidence of this,
for though they are one of the purest races they are also one of
the most variable. It is highly probable that they owe this characteristic in part to some one or more factors which as yet are
completely beyond our ken. Nevertheless, a study of the Jews
suggests that the climatic conditions which seem to cause variations in butterflies, beetles, fruit flies, aphids, nurse-toads, and
mice may also cause similar variations in man. This is of such
great importance in guiding man's future development that we
shall consider it fully. We shall confine ourselves largely to the
Jews because they are the only race for which sufficiently full
data seem to be available. There is, however, every reason to
suppose that the lessons to be learned from the Jews apply to
all races.

In studying the Jews we must satisfy ourselves as to three
points. First, is there good evidence that the Jewish race is
highly variable? Second, how far is the Jewish race a pure

stock? And third, is there any reason to think that the Jews really change in response to their physical environment?

As to the variability we may quote Radosavljevich in regard to his study of European and American school children: "Hebrew children, both in America and abroad, show the greatest variation; then come the Anglo-Saxon, then the Latin. The least variation is shown by Slav pupils." Another evidence of the extreme variability of the Jews is our own observation. Is there any race among which we have known a greater contrast between the ones whom we admire and those whom we would gladly do without? Turning to the world at large we see strong evidence of the variable quality of the race in the number of men of genius whom it has produced. Moses, David, Isaiah, Peter, Paul, and Jesus, these are a few of the great names of the past. The two Mendelssohns, Neander, Heine, Brandes, the Herschels, the Rothschilds, and Disraeli show in how many lines modern Jews have risen far above the average level. Compare this race with the Negroes. Both have endured most bitter persecution, but the Jew has always bobbed up, as one may say, while the Negro has stayed down. Look through any scientific bibliography, or any list of business leaders in a city like New York, and see how thickly the Jewish names are sprinkled. Make what allowance you will for opportunities and environment. Perhaps southern slavery was worse than the repression and *pogroms* of the Russian Pale. In New York, however, it is hard to see wherein the Jews whose parents were slain and tortured in the Russian massacres have any greater advantage than the Negroes whose grandparents were whipped in Louisiana. Yet see how the Negroes drop out of the upper grades in the elementary schools, become scarce in the high schools, and disappear from the colleges. See how the Jews, on the contrary, elbow the Gentiles out of Columbia, New York University, and other higher institutions. Scores of those same Jews will later sit in high seats as business men, professors, diplomats, and philanthropists. To be sure there are about ten times as many Jews as Negroes in New York, but in the higher walks of life there must be a hundred Jews for one Negro.

The difference between the Hebrew and the colored races is far greater than the amount by which the *average* Jew excels the *average* Negro. Few scientists would dare maintain that the Jews as a whole average twice as capable as the Negroes. Yet today and throughout most of history Jews have been tenfold, perhaps a hundred-fold, more influential than colored men. Since in places like New York the social and physical environment can play only the smallest part in this contrast between the races, it seems as if the difference must be due to the fact that the Hebrew race is highly variable, while the Negro race goes to the opposite extreme and displays great uniformity.

The variability of the Hebrew race seems to manifest itself not only in the number of unusually gifted men, but in the degree to which the race as a whole appears to adapt itself to new environments. In order to understand this matter let us try to gain a clear idea of the physical characteristics of the Jews. It is well recognized that there are two main branches. The Ashkenazim center chiefly in Poland and spread out to the neighboring parts of Russia, Germany, and Austria, and even to Roumania and the Caucasus. They form nearly nine tenths of the race. The other branch is the Shephardim who center in Spain and Portugal, but have spread to other Mediterranean countries as well as to Holland and England. Among the Ashkenazim blond or red hair, and gray or blue eyes are much more common than among their Mediterranean brothers. Speaking roughly about 20 per cent belong to this type. The beard of the Ashkenazim is apt to be shorter than that of the Shephardim, the body stouter, and the general aspect less melancholy. An even more widespread quality is that the heads of the northern Jews, that is, of the Ashkenazim, are broader and have higher cheek-bones than those of the southern Shephardim. So great is the difference that the Jews of the Caucasus are uncommonly broad-headed, while those of North

Africa are markedly long-headed. In addition to the general
difference between the two branches of the race, there are still
more significant differences between the various parts of the
Ashkenazim. A comparison of the Jewish and non-Jewish parts
of the population in different sections of Germany, Poland,
Austria, Russia, Roumania, and Bulgaria shows that both the
stature and the shape of the head vary among the Jews almost
exactly as among the Gentiles. On the other hand, the degree of
blondness by no means varies in harmony with that of the surrounding non-Jewish population. Thus it appears that the Jewish
race is so variable that its different portions present distinct
racial characteristics.

This brings up the extremely difficult question of racial purity.
There are evidently three main physical traits in which the
Jews vary from place to place. These are, first, stature, with
which may be associated weight; second, complexion; and third,
the form of the head. Are the variations in these due to intermarriage with the surrounding Gentile population? The only
other possible causes seem to be economic conditions and climate.
Let us begin by seeing what relation complexion has to each of
these three, that is, to racial mixture, economic conditions, and
climate. Whatever may have been the case in later times, it is
almost certain that in Biblical days the Hebrews intermarried
with various other races who may have introduced a blond strain.
One of these was the Amorites, who are supposed to have been an
Aryan people. Esau was "red," and David was "ruddy." Later
the Jews intermarried somewhat with other races in the early days
of the Christian era, and also received some converts who were
presumably more or less blond. Thus from remote times there
has been a blond strain among the Jews. Among the Shephardim
of the Mediterranean regions this strain has largely disappeared.
Possibly this is due to intermarriage with the dark Mediterranean
races, but there is no direct evidence of this. The same darkening
of the race has taken place among the Greeks, Romans, and

perhaps the Spaniards. In classical times the proportion of fair-haired, blue-eyed persons among the Greeks and Romans was quite surely much larger than at present. Witness the painted statues in the museum on the Acropolis at Athens. This type doubtless disappeared in part because the victorious Greeks and Romans intermarried with the dark slaves whom they brought from the provinces. In addition to this, however, it appears that in countries as hot and sunny as the lands around the Mediterranean Sea a fair skin is a disadvantage. The blond type is there more prone to disease than the dark type. Hence it gradually disappears. Economic conditions may possibly favor people of one complexion more than those of another, but this is very doubtful. The disappearance of the blond type, however, seems to have been hastened by the climatic changes which we have discussed, for those changes apparently decreased the cloudiness and storminess which are favorable to people with fair skins. Hence even if the Mediterranean Jews have not inter-married with their neighbors, we should expect them to have become darker during the past two thousand years.

Farther north the case is different. In his monograph on the Jews, Fishberg gives tables showing that on an average about 20 or possibly 30 per cent of the Jews in central and eastern Europe are more or less blond. It is hard to see how economic conditions could have much to do with this, but it accords with what we should expect on the basis of the climate. The fair complexions derived from the early Amorites would persist in the more northern climate while they would die out farther south. Of course the degree of blondness would vary from region to region in accord with the character of the original settlers. But how do we know that the blondness comes from remote ancestors and not from intermarriage with the surrounding Gentiles during recent centuries? Fishberg makes this clear. The blondest Jewish population is by no means found in the regions where the surrounding population is fairest. If the complexion of the Jews depended upon intermarriage with their neighbors, the greatest percentage of blond Jews ought to be found in such places as northern Germany where the Germans are fair, while the percentage should be much smaller in places like Galicia where the non-Jewish population is dark. Yet such is by no means the case. In fact, the reverse is more nearly true. I emphasize this point because the complexion is one of the characteristics which most clearly indicates racial mixture. Everyone knows how a strain of white blood shows itself in a Negro, or a strain of Italian blood in an Anglo-Saxon family. If the complexion does not indicate intermarriage between the Jews and their neighbors, it is hard to believe that much mixture of the races has taken place.

The question of stature, unlike that of complexion, will not help us much in determining whether the variability of the Jews is due to intermarriage or to environment. The Mediterranean Jews are shorter than those of central Europe, but this may be due equally well to climate, to intermarriage, or to economic conditions. In central and eastern Europe the Jews are systematically a little shorter than their Gentile neighbors. This may arise either from some racial inheritance dating to remote times or from economic conditions. Poverty, indoor occupations such as tailoring, and life in villages instead of on farms are quite enough to account for the relative shortness of the Jews. But how about the fact that the Jews vary in height almost exactly as do their Gentile neighbors? Where the Gentiles are tall, as Fishberg's tables show, the Jews are also tall, although not quite equal to the others. This looks like an effect of economic conditions in some cases, but not in all. Although the most poverty-stricken regions such as Galicia show the shortest stature for both Jews and Gentiles, the taller statures do not show so obvious a relation to economic conditions.

When we consider the form of the head, we find ourselves confronted by a most puzzling problem. So far as we are aware the shape of people's heads cannot be influenced by their food, their

occupation, or their social and economic condition. Nor can we
see how climatic selection could weed out one type of head as it
weeds out one type of complexion. In fact, the shape of the head
has been supposed to be one of the most stable racial characteristics and to be one of the most invariable features of man's
physical inheritance. Yet the heads of the Jews appear to vary
in harmony with those of the people who live around them. Look
at this little table adapted from Fishberg. It shows the width
of the head in percentages of the length, that is, the cephalic
index. The first column shows the index for Jews and the second
for the non-Jews who live in the same region. A high index, it
will be remembered, means a broad head.

	Cephalic Index of Jews	Cephalic Index of other Races	Difference
Caucasus	87.5	87.4	0.1
Galicia	83.6	84.4	0.6
Baden	83.5	84.1	0.6
Little Russia	82.9	83.2	0.3
Turin, Italy	82.4	84.9	2.5
Lithuania	81.7	80.6	1.1
Russian Poland	81.9	80.9	1.0
White Russia	80.9	82.5	1.6

A few scattered facts from Holland, where the cephalic index
of the country as a whole is not far from 80, indicate that the
Jews also have a lower index than any given in the table. In
North Africa, where the people are very long-headed with an
index not far from 76, only four measurements of Jews are available, but they average 75.8. When it is remembered that according to Ripley the cephalic index of the races of Europe varies
from 73 to 87, it will be seen that the differences indicated in the
third column of the table are slight. Fishberg, following the
ordinary canons of anthropology, attempts to explain this as
the result of intermarriage. He thinks that there must have been
so many illicit unions of Hebrew women with Gentile men that

the head-form of the two parts of the population has everywhere become the same. This can scarcely be the case. In the first place, it is inherently improbable. Jewish men have doubtless had many children by Gentile women, but they are not reckoned as Jews. Jewish girls, on the other hand, are more carefully guarded than Gentile girls, they are married young, and they are strongly imbued with racial prejudices. In the second place, as we have already seen, Fishberg has himself shown that the complexion of the Jewish population gives no hint of much racial mixture in recent times. It is scarcely possible that the form of the heads of a race should change through intermarriage, while their complexion remains unaltered. Hence, in spite of Fishberg's aspersions upon the women of his own race, there seems reason to believe that the Jews are racially comparatively pure, and that the peculiar facts in regard to the shape of their heads are susceptible of some other explanation.

This brings us to our third question. Is there any reason to think that the Jews really change in response to their physical environment? About a decade ago Boas measured some 30,000 immigrants and their children in New York City. These measurements apparently show that the stature and form of the head among children born to immigrants in this country differ systematically from those of their parents. This conclusion was received with great scepticism. I confess that on reading Boas' preliminary report I shared this feeling. Lately, however, I have read his final report where the full figures are given, and have considered it in the light of the biological experiments described in the preceding chapter. This, together with the facts already outlined as to the Jews in Europe, has led me to revise my opinion. Although Boas' work has been severely and even bitterly criticised I cannot see that the criticism does more than show that in minor details the work might be improved, and that he has sometimes used such phrases as "exceedingly long" when he ought to have said "longer than usual." As he himself says, the investigation was made hastily, and the results are so important that they cannot be accepted as final until a great deal more work has been done. Nevertheless, it seems to me that in the face of all the facts we can scarcely avoid the conclusion that a change of environment may cause an alteration in man's physical form and presumably in his mental reactions. If this is true, we must at once recognize that one of the most pressing scientific problems of the next few decades is the discovery of just how these changes act when people of various races migrate from one environment to another.

The results obtained by Boas are briefly as follows. In 1908, under the direction of the United States Immigration Commission, Boas measured approximately 30,000 immigrants and children of immigrants. His object was to see whether there is any measurable physical difference between immigrants and their children, or between children of the same parents born in this country and abroad. One of the races included in the study was the Scotch, but they showed no appreciable effects, probably because the change in their environment was much less than in the case of the other immigrants. Another race was the East European Hebrews, including those from Poland and the neighboring regions in Russia, Germany, Austria, and Roumania. These showed the maximum effect, and were in all points influenced as we should expect from the facts already before us. Another group was the Bohemians, Slovaks, Hungarians, and Poles from the same general region as the Hebrews. They showed the same changes as their Jewish countrymen. As all of these non-Jewish types react similarly, and as it is not easy to separate them, they may be grouped together. Two other groups consisted respectively of Sicilians and of Italians from the part of Italy south of Rome. These two groups showed distinct changes, especially the Sicilians, but the changes were not of the same type as those of the Jews and the Bohemian group.

Before we describe the changes a few general facts should be before us. In the first place, Boas found no evidence of any distinct physical change in adult immigrants. In the second place, he found that when very young children come to this country they suffer slight changes of the same kind as those occurring in children born here, but not of great significance. Thirdly, children born in this country show distinct and systematic differences from their brothers and sisters born abroad. These differences increase in proportion to the length of time since the mother came to the United States, or at least they are greater in the children born after the mothers have been here ten years than when the mothers have been here a shorter time. Finally, the break between the foreign-born and the American-born is sharp, and is far more pronounced than the difference between the children born earlier and later in this country.

Now as to the nature of the changes. One of the first subjects of inquiry is complexion. This was examined with care, but no consistent changes were observed. Apparently the complexions of children born of foreign parents in this country are identical with what they would be if the children were born abroad. This agrees with what we have seen as to the Jews in Europe. It is quite possible that life for generation after generation in some parts of America might weed out the blond children, while life in other parts might weed out the darkest type. Thus there might arise a change such as that which seems to have differentiated the Mediterranean Jews of the Shephardim type from the Central European Jews of the Ashkenazim type. Such a change, however, is quite different from the sudden changes with which we are now dealing.

The next point to claim attention is stature. From the age of five years at which the measurements begin, the stature among the American-born children of East European Jews and of the non-Jewish group from the same region is greater than the stature of similar children born in the old country. Among the Italians, on the contrary, the reverse is the case. The Sicilian children

born in this country are distinctly shorter than their brothers
and sisters born in Sicily. Among the immigrants from the
southern mainland of Italy, who are mostly Neapolitans, the
same tendency is observable, but to a less degree. The question
arises whether these changes can be due to economic conditions.
If the stature increased in all cases, we might feel quite sure that
the greater opportunities, higher wages, and more varied food
of America were the cause. If all the American-born children
showed a decrease in stature we might attribute it to the congestion of life in a big city. Among the Jews the change in the
mode of life on coming to America is less than among any of the
other races. They were town-dwellers and sedentary workers in
the Old World, and so they are in the New. It is doubtful
whether they change their food any more than do the others, if
as much. Therefore the group that suffers the smallest change
in general habits shows the greatest change in stature. This is
surprising, but perhaps it is merely an evidence of the great
plasticity of the Hebrews as a race. If economic conditions are
the cause of the increased stature of the non-Jewish Bohemian
group we must suppose that better food offsets the disadvantage
of city life compared with country life, and thus leads to greater
stature. Among the Sicilians, on the contrary, we must suppose
that the confined city life of New York and possibly the absence
of the fresh fruit and vegetables to which they were accustomed
in Sicily have a depressing effect upon stature. The other
Italians are influenced a little in the same way. On the whole
we may conclude that the changes in stature may perhaps be due
to economic conditions, although there is nothing to prove that
this is the case. The state of affairs in this respect is almost
identical with that which we have described in relation to stature
among the Jews in Europe. An economic explanation may be
possible, but it is not convincing.

Turning now to the form of the head we find that the Jews
show the greatest change. The heads of the children born in this

country are longer and narrower than those of similar children born abroad. This causes the cephalic index to be lower by about three points. The difference is not great, but it is remarkably systematic so that its reality can scarcely be doubted. Among the Bohemians and other non-Jewish peoples from east central Europe both the length and the width of the head decrease, but as the width decreases more than the length, the heads become a little narrower. Hence the cephalic index drops a little, but not so much as in the case of the Jews. Here we have essential unity between the Jews and the people who live around them. If we suppose that the environment causes the changes in head-form we at once find the explanation of the fact that in Europe the cephalic index of the Jews everywhere approaches so closely to that of the other races in the same region. Turning now to the Italians we find that among them the form of the head changes, but not in the same fashion as among the more northern people. In both Italian groups the length of the head decreases and the width increases, so that the cephalic index, contrary to that of the Jews, shows an increase.

In estimating the importance of the work of Boas, it is highly significant that the most systematic difference between children born abroad and in New York is in the shape of the head. Stature may be influenced by economic conditions, but in the head we have an organ whose form apparently has nothing to do with such conditions. The objector may say that there are other possible causes of changes in the head-form. Boas has carefully investigated this. For instance, he considers the kind of pillows on which children lie, and the practice of swaddling infants which prevails largely in Europe but is soon given up on coming to this country. There seems no reason, however, to think that the changes in the shape of the children's heads are due to any such mechanical causes. Another possible objection is that it is unreasonable that the same environment should act in one way on the Italians and in another on the people from farther

north. The answer lies in one of Æsop's fables. Was it the fox
or some other animal that refused to have anything to do with
an inconsistent creature like man who blows on his fingers to
warm them and on his soup to cool it? We all know that coffee
that is painfully hot to one throat may be highly refreshing to
another. And does not alcohol make some people affectionate and
others pugnacious? The south Italians, it must be remembered,
and especially the Sicilians, represent the extreme Mediterranean
type of man; while the Jews and the Bohemian group represent
quite different racial types. Moreover, the physical environment
of Italy with its long monotonous dry summers is very different
from that of east central Europe with its long monotonous cold
winters. Both, again, are in strong contrast to New York with
its cold variable winters and its warm variable summers.

The fact that no changes could be detected in the Scotch children strengthens the force of Boas' argument. When the Scotch
come to the United States the change both in physical environment and in mode of life is much less than for the other races.
Yet even among the Scotch the new environment may cause
changes of many kinds that were not measured by Boas. There
may be pronounced changes in mental reactions which cannot be
detected by the calipers. It is indeed most significant that the
greatest evidence of physiological changes arising from a new
habitat should be in the head. We have already seen that the
most noteworthy fact in all man's later evolution is the rapidity
of mental development. The brain appears to be the most plastic
part of the human organism. We have also seen that at the
present time the effect of environment and of health upon mental
processes seems to be even more important than their effect on
the so-called lower functions such as nutrition. If a change of
environment can alter the form of the head, it seems only reasonable to agree with Boas in the conclusion that it is still more
likely to alter the mental processes.

Finally, let me hark back once more to the surprising agreement between the results of Fishberg in his study of European Jews and of Boas in his study of immigrants.   I emphasize the importance of this because the strength of any conclusion is much more than doubled when it is based upon two independent lines of evidence.   Moreover, although Fishberg and Boas assisted one another, Boas, whose work was done later, does not appear to have recognized the remarkable way in which his results are supported by those of Fishberg.   This arises partly from the fact that Boas, in accordance with long habit, is prone to attribute as much as possible to purely economic causes and to events which happen in accordance with man's own artificial surroundings, while Fishberg, in accordance with the well-established usage of ethnology and anthropology, is inclined to attribute as much as possible to racial mixture.

Since racial mixture obviously has nothing to do with Boas' results, and since it probably has only the slightest influence upon the facts described by Fishberg, we seem forced to conclude that the differences between American-born and foreign-born children of immigrants are due to environment.   The question then is, What particular features of the environment are responsible?   Boas, as I have said, seems inclined to attribute the changes to the urban environment.   He shows that Ammon in Baden and Livi in Italy have found evidence that on the whole the people of the cities have slightly longer heads than those of the country districts around them.   These authors, however, believe that this is merely because the cities that they investigated lie in regions where the average length of the people's heads is less than in the more remote districts whence many of the people of the city were originally drawn.   Hence the presence of people from a distance increases the average length of the city heads.   Boas accepts this idea, but tries also to show that in Italy this factor is not enough to account for the observed differences.   His argument is interesting, but unlike his study of immigrants in New York, it is based largely on assumptions, and hence is not conclusive.

Several facts seem to oppose the idea that the change from country to city is the cause of the changes in head-form. In the first place, the Jews, in whom the head assumes the most distinctly new shape, are the very immigrants whose former life is most like that of their new homes. The South Italian who has lived, or at least worked all day, under his own vines and then is suddenly dropped into a New York tenement and a New York factory suffers a tenfold greater economic and industrial change than that experienced by the Jewish tailor or shopkeeper who has always lived in a stuffy room in the midst of a closely packed village. In the second place, the change to city life offers no explanation of the peculiar conditions in Europe where the form of the Jewish heads agrees so closely with that of the non-Jewish. Yet this fact can scarcely be separated from the phenomena in New York. Therefore it seems necessary to fall back on some other explanation.

The explanation which seems to me most reasonable is that the changes in head-form are due to the conditions of the air, including not only what we commonly call climate, but also the indoor air and ventilation. I am well aware that already the reader has said to himself that I am doing exactly what I have accused Boas and Fishberg of doing. I am letting myself be influenced by a mode of thought which has become habitual. I grant this freely. No man, no matter how unbiassed he may attempt to be, can dissociate himself from the ideas which have been in his mind for years. I can only say that from 1910 when I first heard of Boas' results until early in 1918 I refused to let my climatic predilections persuade me. Then, for quite a different purpose, I assembled the biological facts presented in the last chapter. They seemed to indicate conclusively that extremes of heat, cold, and dryness may cause distinct and far-reaching changes in animals of many types. Therefore I was forced to believe that in man the same thing may happen.

The changes in head-form and probably in the stature of the

Jews appear to be closely analogous to those in the length of body, tail, foot, and ear in white mice. They also appear to be analogous to the changes in flies and other insects. We have already seen that the changes in the bodily form of the Jews from place to place in Europe can scarcely be due to racial mixture, economic conditions, or climatic selection. Neither can the changes in the bodily form of the children of immigrants in New York be due to these causes. So far as I can see the one factor that does differ from place to place in such a way as to produce the observed results is the variability of the climate. This factor, as we have seen, is extremely susceptible to variations not only from place to place, but from year to year, and month to month. While the mean temperature of a given month varies only a few degrees from year to year, one month may have four or five times as many cold waves and hot waves as another. The most marked climatic difference between eastern and western Europe is the greater monotony of the cold winter weather in the east. Similarly the chief difference between Italy and Poland, for example, is the monotony of the long Sicilian summer compared with the relative variability of the same season farther north. Finally the outstanding contrast between the eastern United States and Europe is the much greater variability of the weather here than there.

From these facts it appears that when Jews or Gentiles from eastern Europe come to New York they suffer one kind of climatic change. When South Italians come they suffer another kind, but in both cases the change is pronounced. When Scotch or English come to New York, on the contrary, they certainly experience a climatic change, but it is by no means so pronounced as that to which the people from less stormy climates are subjected. Hence the failure of Boas to find any measurable changes in Scotch children is what we should expect.

Turning now to the effects of climatic variations upon racial characteristics, we have seen that even the slightest change of

temperature from one day to another has a truly extraordinary
effect upon the deathrate. No other known factor appears to be
anything like so important. Moreover, the effect is plainly
visible not only in summer when people live with open windows and
breathe the outside air, but also in winter when the houses are
closed. Still more remarkable is the fact that the changes in
the outside temperature produce the strongest kind of effect upon
sick people, even though such individuals are protected from the
outside air in winter far more carefully than are persons in ordinary health. If changes in temperature, either through their
direct effect or through some indirect means which we do not yet
understand, can swing the deathrate back and forth so remarkably, it seems reasonable to assume that they must have a pronounced effect upon creatures so highly sensitive as newborn
infants. This effect would be accentuated by the fact that the
immigrants from eastern and southern Europe have had the habit
of swaddling their infants, but give this up when they come to
America. Thus the children not only are born in a climate far
more variable than that whence their parents have come, but are
more completely exposed to its variations. Even if they do not
greatly feel the direct differences of temperature, they feel the
varying conditions of humidity and perhaps of electricity which
accompany each change of temperature.

The conclusion that variations of temperature, either directly
or indirectly, produce corresponding alterations in bodily form
and presumably in mental activity is fraught with the gravest
consequences. It may mean that the climatic conditions during
the first few months of a child's life have much to do with its
ultimate development both in mind and body. What conditions
are best no one can say as yet, but on general principles it would
seem as if exposure to fairly low temperatures was probably better
than to high, since low temperature is apparently favorable to
mental activity. The conclusion that variations of temperature
cause alterations in body and mind may also mean that the present

world-migrations are giving rise to revolutionary racial changes. Immigrants who come from the Old World to New York may experience one kind of change, those who go to southern California another, and those to Alabama a third. Moreover, people from one part of Europe are presumably influenced differently from those from another. Which changes are good and which are bad no one can tell. If our conclusions are correct, the whole human race is in a state of flux, and the future may see profound readjustments in harmony with the new environments. Remember that two forces may be producing these changes. One is the sudden mutations which apparently arise when people migrate to new countries, or perhaps when children at the critical age are exposed to climatic extremes. The other is the selective effect of the entire environment which in the course of generations will weed out some types and give others a free opportunity. The mutations and still more the selection may prove to be largely within our control. Whether this is so or not, the world has before it no more pressing task than to discover how and why the environment influences heredity.

Before we leave this chapter a word of warning is necessary. I am afraid that the people who magnify environment at the expense of heredity will quote me in a sense that I have never meant. I believe that in the long run environment—and by that I mean physical environment—is the greatest of all factors in evolution. From this point of view heredity is merely the sum of all past environments, and training depends entirely upon the powers and faculties developed as the result of past heredity and past environment. But notice that I have said "*all* past environment." Part of that past environment is very far back. It includes the early geological times when animals first emerged from the water to the dry land, the times when certain feeble animals acquired the power to warm their own bodies, the hundreds of thousands of years of the last Glacial Period when man's mind was evolving most rapidly, and the thousands of years since the present races took their place upon the stage of history.   During these past ages, and even in the period since the present lines of racial cleavage appeared, man has passed through a great many changes as important as those to which he is now subjecting him-self.   The effect of these has become part of his inheritance.   It cannot be eradicated.   Grant if you will that the artificial con-ditions to which man now subjects himself are causing his evolu-tion to proceed much faster than ever before.   Yet the case of any two races is like that of two buds.   Here is the bud of a pear and yonder that of an apple.   You may hasten or retard their development.   You may mutilate them or protect them from wind, storm, and insect.   You may enrich the trees or tear off their branches.   You may do a thousand things which will cause the buds to result either in wee, knotty, shrivelled nubbins, or in great, luscious, juicy fruits, but after all is said and done, one is a pear and one is an apple.

So it is with races.   Environment has made them, but it cannot unmake them.   For good or ill, each race has acquired certain characteristics.   These may be modified, just as the pear and the apple may be modified, by long and careful selection or by sudden accident, but they can never be wholly destroyed.   In this sense those who talk about the immutability of races are correct.   The whale immutably breathes air, and can never evolve into a fish again.   Even when a creature is said to revert to an ancestral type, it really goes back no more than a step or two on a road where it has taken thousands of steps.   The Chinese, the Negroes, the Anglo-Saxons, the Jews, and the Italians cannot be made alike either by the influence of physical environment or by educa-tion and training.   This we must recognize.   Mankind is bound to change in the future, but it would be the height of folly for a nation on this account to incorporate into itself elements whose mental and moral aptitudes it does not now approve.

CHAPTER XI

THE EXAMPLE OF ROME

IN almost every phase of man's life today we see that the air which he breathes and in which he moves is one of the chief factors. Whether we turn to Civil Service Examinations, the use of liquor, business fluctuations, immigration, or crops, climatic conditions are in one way or another a variable factor upon which variations in the others depend. In almost every phase of man's earlier evolution the same appears to have been true, no matter whether we turn to the emergence of life from the water, to the change from the cold-blooded to the warm-blooded condition, to the evolution of mind, or to the mutations which gave rise to new forms of life. Between the geological past and the present lies the historic past. Does it, too, show this same dependence upon climatic variations?

For several reasons Rome will be the best text for this historical discussion. In the first place, we have heard a thousand times that as a guide to modern conduct the example of Rome is perhaps the most significant in all history. In the next place, in previous writings upon Rome, I have emphasized the economic effects of the climatic changes which she has suffered. Here I wish also to emphasize the new point of view which comes to light with our study of health. Finally, we have already discussed mediæval Italy, and have seen how in North Italy at least there was apparently a remarkable response to the climatic crisis of the fourteenth century.

What do we know as to the climate of Rome for the past two thousand years or more? This is not the place to discuss the evidence of climatic changes. In the publications listed in the Appendix, I have gone into the matter in great detail. Here it is enough to say that after a decade of vigorous discussion the geographers of America, and to a considerable degree those of other countries also, seem to have come to the conclusion that climatic pulsations of considerable amplitude have occurred during historic times. As Colton puts it: "The summation of all these different lines (of evidence) makes the *theory* of climatic pulsations become the *doctrine* of climatic pulsations." Moreover, Antevs has carried out a most careful study of all that has ever been written on "The Annual Rings of Tree Growth and Their Meaning as Climatic Indicators." He believes that the present author has underestimated the magnitude of the climatic pulsations indicated by the trees of California.

The best available measure of the climate of the past is the growth of the Big Trees of California as determined by the width of the annual rings of hundreds of stumps. The curve thus obtained is shown in Figure 24. Where it is high the climate was relatively moist and rainy, and storms were abundant so that the stimulating qualities were at a maximum. Where it is low the reverse conditions prevailed. Since the southern half of California and the southern half of Italy lie in essentially the same kind of climate, the pulsations of the two places appear to be practically the same. That this is so appears from the rainfall of March to July, the critical months for agriculture and tree growth. Let us compare the rainfall at San Diego and San Francisco since 1851 with the growth of one hundred and twelve sequoia trees in the Sierra Nevada Mountains and with the rainfall in Italy. We will arrange the years of each record in order according to the amount of rain in California, and then divide them into the four groups indicated below. For the trees, however, we will use first the three-year period beginning with a certain condition of rainfall (E), and second the growth in the third year of each three-year period (F). This is because the huge sequoia trees

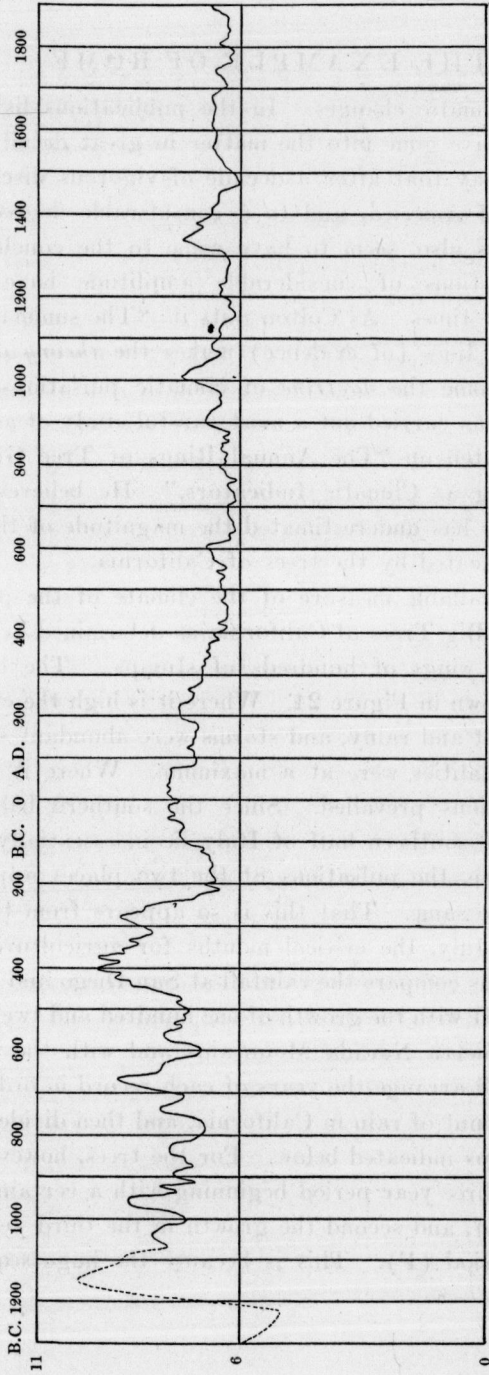

FIGURE 24. Climatic Pulsations of Historic Times

do not feel the full effect of a given rainfall for two or three years. Jerusalem is added for comparison.

Groups of Years

I.   7 years with heaviest rainfall in California. Average 6.5 inches and over at San Francisco and San Diego combined.
II. 18 years with heavy rainfall in California. (3.9 to 6.4 inches.)
III. 17 years with light rainfall in California. (2.7 to 3.8 inches.)
IV. 13 years with least rainfall in California (less than 2.7 inches).

| | Average Rainfall | | | | Average Growth of Trees | |
| | A | B | C | D | E | F |
	San Francisco and San Diego	Rome	Naples	Jerusalem	3 Years	Third Year
I.	8.3	10.7	11.5	7.0	3.02	3.07
II.	4.5	10.6	11.0	6.3	3.00	3.04
III.	3.4	9.8	9.2	5.6	2.98	2.99
IV.	1.9	9.6	8.6	5.2	2.92	2.84

Without exception all the columns from B to F vary in harmony with A. At Rome the agreement with California is less marked than at Naples, while at Naples, when reckoned in percentages, it is less noticeable than at Jerusalem. At Palermo in Sicily, however, the agreement is probably at least as marked as at Jerusalem, as appears from the following table for the twenty-six years for which records at Palermo are available at the time of writing.

(1) 10 years averaging 5.8 inches in California average 8.3 at Palermo
(2)   8 years averaging 3.6 inches in California average 7.6 at Palermo
(3)   8 years averaging 2.4 inches in California average 6.2 at Palermo

From these facts it seems quite clear that the curve of tree growth in California can safely be used as an approximate measure of the storminess in the southern half of Italy. Turning now to Figure 24 we see that from about 450 to 250 B. C., California, and presumably Italy, was blessed with much more rainfall than at present. During those two centuries the Big Trees grew perhaps 30 per cent faster than during the last hundred years. The difference in rainfall, however, and still more in the variability of the temperature was probably much greater. While we cannot speak positively, it seems probable that in those days the variability at Rome may have been twice as great as at present, and the stimulating quality of the air correspondingly important. Today Rome lies near the border between the highly stimulating climate of northern Italy and the relatively enervating climate of the extreme south. From 450 to 250 B. C. the climate was probably decidedly more stimulating than in any part of Italy today. In fact, it is open to question whether there is today in any part of the world a climate better than that which Rome then enjoyed. July and August were doubtless too hot, for they now average 77° and 76°F respectively, and were then probably only three or four degrees cooler. Yet the summers were not so hot as those of Philadelphia, and were probably blessed more frequently with cool waves. The winters were much better than those of Philadelphia, for they must have had greater variability, while the temperature from December to January did not fall so low, and probably averaged a little above 40°F.

In such a climate, provided the people had a good racial inheritance to begin with, we should expect a most healthy, vigorous, and strong-willed population. Among them there would presumably prevail conditions such as those which accompany our periods of prosperity. If anything, however, we should expect greater powers of self-control because the average health ought to have been better than with us. Not that the deathrate was anywhere so low as with us, for there was no real medical science, but when people were well they presumably had that superabounding health which makes them work with a will, and enables them to resist temptation. What do we actually find? For fear that I may overstate the case, let me quote various passages from Ferrero's account of this period. The Romans were then so unlike the people of more enervating climates—this is my phrase, not Ferrero's (he does not mention climate)—that even the patricians, the most wealthy part of the population, "were peasants like their fellows, and not above handling the pick and the plough." Similar conditions, so far as we can gather, prevailed among the neighboring tribes. "The cause of [Rome's] success lay in the vigorous discipline of her constitution, which was strong enough to control that spirit of self-indulgence which is the most powerful solvent of national life. It was this that maintained a pure and simple morality among her rich and powerful class, which would have been the first to succumb to the vanity and vice that too frequently attend on the pride of conquest. The Romans were a primitive people without the defects peculiar to a primitive people." Theirs was "a stern and difficult discipline of the spirit." They accustomed their boys "to reverence and purity, to labor and sobriety, to the careful observance of laws and customs and of a narrow but tenacious patriotism." They taught the girls to "be gentle, obedient and chaste, attentive only to housework and children." Everyone knows how democratic was the form of government among the early Romans. Officials were judged by their deeds, and the slightest dereliction from duty was severely punished. No officials were paid, but it was deemed sufficient honor to be allowed to serve the State. Ancient Rome was in many ways remarkably like the early Puritan colonies in New England.

Between 450 and 250 B. C. the Romans extended their power over most of the peninsula of Italy. This brought them great wealth. "But this increase of wealth did not at first tend to weaken the ancient traditions nor was it immediately followed either by a change in manners or by a political revolution. The thrift and simplicity of the old times were still the proudest virtues of every noble family. . . . If by the end of the third century B. C. Rome had become paramount in Italy, it was because the most admired virtues of every class of her State were those that are distinctive of a well-disciplined rural community.

The Roman was sober and self-restrained in all his habits and simple in all his ideas and customs. He had a deep and loving knowledge of the small world in which he lived, and a quiet and imperturbable intensity of purpose. He was honest, loyal, persevering, and displayed that curious absence of excitability so characteristic of a man who has no vices, who does not waste his strength in self-indulgence, and has but a limited stock of knowledge."

The basis of this sturdy, simple life of the early Romans was intensive agriculture. We are told that in the days of the Roman Republic seven jugera, or about four and a half acres of land, sufficed to support an average family. Agriculture was so intensive that farms of this small size, supplemented presumably by pasture land, supported a contented and self-respecting population. As Simkhovitch puts it: "The farming of the Romans on seven-jugera farms was like the farming of the Chinese and Japanese, very intensive, their small grain fields being planted in rows, hoed, and weeded and carefully manured with excrements and ashes and dung. The experience of China and Japan has shown that on very small land-plots such intensive agriculture can maintain itself indefinitely without any recourse to scientific repletion of the soil by mineral fertilizers."

So much for the period from 450 to 250 B. C. That period ended in a great decline in rainfall and storminess, as appears in Figure 24. Up to 250 B. C. the climate still appears to have been highly favorable. Then by 220 or 210 it had apparently fallen to about the present level. For a hundred years nearly the same conditions prevailed, and not for a century and a half did the climate return to a condition as favorable as in 240 B. C. Even then it by no means rivalled the two preceding centuries. Theoretically such a change of climate should produce at least three kinds of results. First, we should look for a decline in health, energy, and moral fiber. Second, economic difficulties would be almost certain to arise. Third, political conditions could scarcely fail to be affected.

As a matter of fact, we find exactly what would be expected. In order to preserve the chronological sequence I shall not attempt to keep the three types of results separate. To quote Ferrero once more: "Towards the middle of the third century [that is at the very time when the climate was changing most rapidly], through the increase of wealth and the continuance of victory, this spirit of discipline and rural simplicity began to show symptoms of decline. . . . Social simplicity began to be impaired and domestic discipline to loosen its bonds. The family council was more rarely summoned; sons, thanks to the proceeds of campaigning, became more independent of their fathers, women less submissive to husbands or guardians; the nobility neglected its duties toward the middle class. . . . The new spirit was fatal to the old friendly coöperation between class and class. A selfish and grasping nobility that looked to Carthage for its model inevitably provoked popular opposition."

In these quotations Ferrero follows the usual method of attributing the decay of Rome to luxury. I do not question that this played an important part, but is it not also probable that the decline in vigor due to the changing climate had much to do with the matter? It is significant that the change in the Roman spirit is closely analogous to the difference in spirit today between a country like Scotland or Denmark where the climate is highly stimulating and one like Spain or Mexico which fails to give people the vitality so essential to high ideals.

In political, as in moral and social life, we find a change in Rome at the end of the third century B. C. "In the Gallic War (225-222), for the first but not the last time in Roman history, the people, not the nobles, were the aggressors. It was the democracy that cast its eyes upon the great plain that stretches at the foot of the Alpine barrier—a plain rich in fresh and fertile soil, covered with immense oak forests and huge tracts of marsh and lake-

land, dotted with Celtic villages, watered by hurrying streams.
. . . No noble of great lineage, but the head of the popular party,
gave his name to the first great road, the *via Flaminia*, that joined
Rome to the Valley of the Po. . . . The old aristocratic, agricultural and military society was nearing the limit of its greatness.
If it was to play a further part in history it must be through a
transformation of its character and institutions."

The eagerness of the common people for a war against the Gauls
in the plain of the Po sounds as if poverty and distress might
have been prevalent. With a decline of rainfall such as is indicated in Figure 24, how could it be otherwise? It is extremely
difficult, however, to distinguish between the effects of different
causes. In 218 B. C. the Second Punic War introduced seventeen
years of bitter fighting. How far this war was due to the economic
and political stress arising from the diminished rainfall in both
Italy and Carthage we cannot tell. It is equally difficult to determine whether it was the war or the climate which about 200 B. C.
"hastened the advent of the commercial era in a society which
had hitherto been military and agricultural." Certain it is that
Italy now needed food, and had to import it from abroad. The
year 196 saw the first public distribution of grain in Rome. Such
conditions were one great reason for the development of commerce.
It is also certain that in spite of this demand for food, farming
became less profitable. Especially in southern Italy, where the
effect of a climatic change would be greatest, land fell to a low
value. Speculation became rife, the peasants fell into debt, their
lands were bought by capitalists or large proprietors, and the
cultivation of wheat gave place in large measure to the raising of
sheep and goats. Many country people flocked to the cities, huge
wooden tenements were erected, and bakeshops were established
to furnish bread to the many unmarried tradesmen and laborers
who could not get it at home. So great was the influx of country
people to the cities that in 187 and 177 B. C. the Latin towns
lodged complaints with the Senate. At first an apparent era of

prosperity prevailed because of the expansion of commerce and
the great booty obtained by Rome from her conquests of Carthage, Spain, Macedonia, and other regions. "The passion for
enjoyment, so long restrained, burst out in all the primitive and
animal indulgences; in gluttony and sensuality, in the craving for
violent excitement, and in that gross form of ostentation and
display which marks the first blundering efforts of the country-
man grown rich. . . . It is true that those plebeians who
remained in the country still lived a sober and honorable family
life, after the manner of their fathers, respecting with equal
simplicity the nobility and the law; but those who had settled
at Rome in order to devote themselves to commerce or shopkeep-
ing or contracting [which was a most lucrative occupation] . . .
acquired all the vices that corrupt . . . a rich commercial city."
Both in city and country "the deadening spirit of caste exclu-
siveness, the regard for family and friends and dependents, the
calls of ambition or avarice, superseded the old-fashioned
promptings of duty; while attempts to hasten the transformation
of the old agricultural society became more pronounced and
determined."

In political life the tendencies were the same as in social life.
"There grew up, even among the aristocracy, a generation of
arrogant and ambitious politicians, who transformed the reasoned
and moderate Liberalism of Scipio and his followers into a revolutionary movement at variance with all the ancient principles
of social discipline, and destined to set public and private life at
the mercy of passion and self-seeking. . . . Nowhere was the new
school of policy seen to less advantage than in the sphere of
foreign policy. . . . To despise all foreigners, to be always in
the right, to make the end justify the means; these were the principles of the new diplomacy, which with a perfidy that grew with
each success, reduced the allied States of Rhodes, Pergamus,
and Egypt to a position of ignominious dependence, and, alike
in the independent republics of Greece and the great monarchies

of Asia, fomented discord and espionage, sedition and civil war.
. . . In its dealings with barbarians it acknowledged no code of
honor; they might be attacked and exterminated without cause
or excuse or declaration of war."

This disgraceful state of affairs lasted through the second
century. "At the first symptoms of its decadence," in the third
century, "the Roman public had burst out in a passion of pride
and savagery which swept Carthage and Corinth clean from their
foundations." Then followed other wars which were less successful, as might be expected from so decadent a people. The
Spanish War from 153 to 133 B. C. was "a costly inglorious cam-
paign which lasted twenty years and almost reduced Rome to
bankruptcy." When the great Slave Revolt took place in Sicily
from 139 to 132 the government had real difficulty in suppressing
it. In this revolt, as in many other occurrences, we see signs that
the trouble lay chiefly in the southern part of the country. The
healthy growth of the Roman Empire came to an end during this
sad century. Expansion, to be sure, still took place, for other
countries were suffering even more than Rome, but it was at best
a sickly growth.

What caused this second century to be so disastrous? Is such
disaster the inevitable accompaniment of growth? Must there
be decline to balance progress? Perhaps, but the study of evolution as it is seen in geology emphatically insists that such a
decline always has a physical cause. Was the decline due to the
wealth and luxury that came from foreign conquest? Or was it
due to the importation of slaves who caused deterioration in the
racial stock of Rome? Doubtless both these causes are highly
important. Their importance is much lessened, however, by the
fact that a similar decay took place in Greece, Egypt, Carthage,
Syria, and many other countries. So far as wealth and slavery
were concerned many of those countries were the opposite of Rome.
They were plundered and not plunderers: they lost slaves instead

of gaining them. Yet the general course of events was the same. Hence it would seem that we must look farther.

Many historians have thought that agricultural decline was one of the chief elements in the fall of Rome. Such a decline unquestionably occurred. Some authors ascribe it to competition with other countries, such as Sicily and Spain. That seems unreasonable, however, for the Italian soil is as fruitful as that of the other countries. Moreover, the farmer who lives nearest the market has a great advantage, especially where transportation is as primitive as it was in the Mediterranean region two thousand years ago. Others, like Liebig, who was a student of history as well as of chemistry, hold that the depletion of the soil by constant cropping was the main factor. Recently Simkhovitch has ably revived this idea. It seems untenable, however, as I have shown elsewhere. This is chiefly because this theory clashes with the long survival of China and Japan. It also clashes with the sudden decline of Roman agriculture at the same time when agriculture collapsed in many neighboring countries. It is scarcely possible that the soil of all these countries was in the same stage of exhaustion at one particular time. Moreover, the theory of chemical exhaustion of the soil does not explain the revival during the days of the Roman Empire. Finally, there is no need of such a theory, for everything which may be attributed to the exhaustion of the soil may also be ascribed to a change of climate. There is good evidence of sudden changes of climate, but no evidence of sudden crises in the composition of the soil. Moreover, climatic changes explain much of the loss of physical and moral strength among the Romans, a loss which is not easily explained in any other way.

It must be remembered that the climatic change which overwhelmed Rome at the end of the third century before Christ may have affected the character of the Roman people in at least three chief ways. First, economic distress may have had a powerful moral and mental effect. A poverty-stricken man finds it much harder to be honest than does one who has all that he wants.

Second, new diseases such as malaria may have been introduced. And third, there may have been a general weakening of health and thus of moral fiber such as seems today on a small scale to result sometimes from our climatic fluctuations from year to year.

In considering both the economic and moral effects of climatic changes, it must be remembered that the *change* is what counts. A chronic invalid thinks nothing of taking to her bed; it is no great change. A man who has never been sick, on the other hand, has a perfect horror of being sick. He actually feels ashamed if he is obliged to go to bed. So too, a carpenter with $1,500 a year feels prosperous, whereas a banker who has had $50,000 a year feels himself in dire poverty if his income is reduced to $5,000. The banker can in time accommodate himself to his diminished income, but meanwhile he may be sorely tempted to recoup his fortunes by dishonesty. Suppose that his income falls to $4,000, then $3,000, and finally only $2,000. He will still have more than the carpenter, but when he sees his boy at work instead of in college, his daughter learning stenography instead of dancing, and his wife riding in a street car instead of an automobile, he feels defeated, bitter, disgraced. So in Italy, her climate and resources in the second century before Christ may have been as good as today or even better. Yet the change and the lack of adjustment to it may have produced most deplorable consequences.

We have already spoken of the evidence of agricultural decline in Italy. Not only is there direct proof of this, but such events as the Slave Revolt in Sicily probably sprang from it. Even in good years during the second century B. C. Rome was never entirely immune from partial famines. Little by little the troubles of the farmers became the greatest political problem. Finally in 133 B. C. Tiberius Gracchus tried to remedy them by a series of laws for the redistribution of the land. He paid with his life for his attempts to change the old order. Ten years later his younger and greater brother, Caius, took up the problem once more, but without permanent success. Yet at that very time relief was in sight. Pliny states that in 121 B. C. Rome became aware through the cheapness of wine that a change had taken place in the methods of agriculture. Vines and olives, so it appears from Cato and others, had been substituted for grain in many places at the beginning of the century, that is, immediately after the climate became driest. Now, nearly a century later, there is evidence of an agricultural change. Perhaps this was due to improved methods, but much more probably the new methods were due to the improvement in rainfall. Figure 24 shows that about 120 B. C. a slight amelioration of the climate began to make itself felt. A decade later, in 111, Spurius Thorius succeeded in enacting a land law which is supposed to have been much better than those proposed by the Gracchi. Thus he receives credit for the solution of the great problem which had been vexing Rome for a century. But does he deserve the credit? Agricultural disturbances certainly declined and the price of land rose rapidly after the law was enacted, but look at Figure 24 and see how the rainfall and hence the crops improved at just this time. Nature often does the work which man thinks he has done.

At the end of the second century before Christ, Rome was in the state of a sick man who is just beginning to be convalescent. As he grumbles, so she grumbled. "There were interminable discussions on the diseases from which Rome was suffering," says Ferrero. One of these diseases was a deluge of crime. "Murder, poisoning, theft, assassination, even family tragedies, became alarmingly frequent. A large category of crimes committed by women and young persons went entirely unpunished, being still outside the cognizance of the law, and no longer dealt with by the family. Even recognized offences, when committed by Roman citizens often evaded a penalty." Another disease was anæmia. "No one tried the remedy of action. Men frittered away their energies in a morbid inertia, pouring vain encomiums upon a golden past, and childishly appealing for the intervention of some heaven-sent deliverer." The Romans did not recognize that their grumblings, their crimes, and their inertia were products of physiological disease any more than we have recognized that crime and hard times are similar products. Yet it is difficult to avoid the conclusion that such was the case.

One specific disease as to which we have detailed information is malaria. Anyone who has lived in a malarial country knows its ravages. The form which prevails in countries like Italy rarely kills people. Most persons who have it keep about their daily work except when actually having a chill. But watch the work of such people. See how feebly they act, how irritable they are, how careless, and how ready to leave a task half finished. Note, too, how soon such conduct becomes habitual with people who suffer frequently from malaria. In our own day malaria is still the great scourge of Rome. A few years ago it was worse, for the value of careful drainage and of the extinction of mosquitoes was not then understood. In the days of the Roman Empire malaria was apparently a far greater handicap, for then the use of quinine was not known. In the Rome of the second century B. C. more than half the people probably had the disease, or at least had had it during childhood in so severe a form as to cause a permanent enlargement of the spleen. At any rate medical examinations carried on by Ross show that today this is actually the case in similarly affected parts of Greece.

So important is this matter that W. H. S. Jones has written a little book on "Malaria: a factor in the decline of Greece and Rome." He finds that previous to the second century before Christ malaria was merely epidemic in Rome. It occurred sporadically as it occurs in some of our American cities, but its ravages were unimportant. Then, in the second century, as appears from the work of Latin medical writers and others, it seems to have become endemic. It was always present and every child was expected to have it just as children in America are expected to have the measles. Ross and Jones believe that such prevalence of malaria would go far toward giving the Roman people the listless, complaining, inert character and also the cruelty and licentiousness which became so common in those times. We may perhaps question whether malaria alone would do this, yet having seen the potent effect of climate upon business in America today, we may at least query whether the general ill health combined with the economic effects of poor crops may not afford a sufficient explanation of the low estate of Rome in the second century B. C.

The most significant feature of the whole question is the *coincidence* of a great many symptoms, all of which are what would be expected as results of a deteriorating climate. Here seems to be the sequence of events. First, a climate with less rainfall and less variability than formerly, but with more liability to the occasional severe showers which are characteristic of regions of light rainfall. Next, poorer crops, the abandonment of many fields, the substitution of olives, vineyards, sheep and goats for grain and vegetables. This would lead to the pasturing of the sheep and goats on thousands of hillsides. The already sparse cover of grass would be still further diminished, as would the young trees and bushes which were already suffering from lack of rain and which are greedily eaten, especially by goats. The animals' feet would break up the soil, and the heavy, but infrequent showers of spring and fall would carry it away. Thus, not only would the slopes be denuded and many fields spoiled, but large deposits of silt would be laid down in the valleys and lowlands. Over these the streams would wander in many channels. Moreover, the streams would become intermittent because of the prolongation of the summer dry season, and undrained swamps and pools would abound. These would form ideal places for the mosquitoes that carry malaria, and the dryness of the summer would insure a continual supply of the insects. Thus malaria would abound, and with it would come a large amount of apathy, indolence, and vice.

Pursuing another line of thought we find that poor crops would lead to debts, to usury on the part of heartless creditors, and to complaints against taxation. This would also lead to the concentration of wealth and land in a few hands, to emphasis upon class distinctions because of the growing gulf between rich and poor, and to migration from country to city. Thus would arise the ills which result from congestion, overcrowding, and lack of family life. Along still another line of thought we find that the change of climate which apparently took place in Rome at the end of the third century would diminish people's energy, increase the death-rate, and render people much more liable to the many little ailments to which mankind is heir. Such ill health would weaken a people's judgment and will power. The Romans would tend to acquire more of the qualities that we associate with tropical countries and to lose those that we associate with cool and variable countries such as Scotland, Norway, and Canada. Finally, another line of thought leads us to conclude that the climatic conditions of the second century would make the anæmic, malarial Romans less warlike, less honorable in their foreign relations, and less able to conquer, protect, and wisely govern the peoples with whom they came in contact.

Rome's later history is no less consistent with our climatic theory than is the earlier. Ferrero's picture of the mixture of the old forces of decay and the new forces of revival about 100 B. C. is most suggestive. The great proletarian uprising, or Social War, was approaching, the disorder of the past century was gathering itself together for a final attack on the established order, and "the day of reckoning was felt at last to be at hand. Yet it would be a mistake to imagine that decadence and ruin filled the whole picture. Even amid the chaos of society and politics there were promising symptoms of intellectual advance." Reformers like the Gracchi, strong, if misguided, spirits like Marius and Sulla, and great men like Julius Cæsar were beginning to arise. Roman law was taking shape, handsome houses of imported marble were beginning to be erected in the metropolis, sculptors and painters were developing their art, and the literature of the Augustan Age had its first forerunners. We have already seen signs of an agricul-

tural revival. A little later, almost on the morrow of the sangui-
nary struggle of the Social War, B. C. 90 to 89, there was "a
marked increase in the general luxury and comfort." By the
time when Varro wrote his *De Re Rustica* in 37 B. C. some of his
characters could say that Italy was the best-cultivated land in
the world, and had become almost entirely one vast garden.
Another states more modestly that Italy was better cultivated in
his time than in preceding centuries. Many other indications
point to a return of prosperity and also of vigor. The period
from 75 B. C. onward was marked by a high degree of luxury and
affluence. Though vice and sensuality abounded, they did not
play such a part as in earlier times. In their place came more
desire for the graces of life, for art and literature, for serious
studies in science such as the work of Varro just mentioned and
the more poetic Georgics of Virgil. This was the time of Cicero
and of the men who made the succeeding Augustan Age the most
famous epoch in Roman history.

Turn again to Figure 24 and see how the climate improved
from the end of the second century B. C. to the middle of the first.
Then it remained favorable for seventy years after the birth of
Christ. This period corresponds closely with what is often called
the greatest age of Rome. It was an age when the Roman arms
were once more invincible, and the city by the Tiber was the mis-
tress of the world. It was an age when the ideas of the earlier
Roman Republic flowered and bore fruit in the great system of
Roman law which still so largely guides modern jurisprudence.
Yet this was not really Rome's greatest period. It was a vast
improvement over the second century B. C., but it lacked the
idealism and the high moral purpose of the earlier, simpler days.
It was like the health which a man enjoys after a deadly illness—
something to be devoutly thankful for, something that may enable
him to achieve the master stroke of his life, and yet not equal to
the young vigor with which he laid the foundations of his career.

After the time of Augustus the character of the Roman Empire did not change greatly at first. As the "Encyclopedia Brittanica" puts it, even Nero's wild excesses (54-68 A. D.) "scarcely affected the prosperity of the empire at large; the provinces were well governed, and the war with Parthia led to a compromise which secured peace for half a century." At the end of this time, that is, after 80 A. D., there occurred a decline in rainfall, but the conditions were by no means so bad as during the second century B. C. As might be expected under such circumstances, the Emperor Nerva (96-98 A. D.) and his successors began a series of attempts to take care of the food supply both of Italy and the Empire. These attempts included vast irrigation works in North Africa and Syria. In Italy capital was advanced at moderate interest to landowners, and the profits were devoted to the maintenance and education of poor children. Time-expired soldiers received grants of land, a proceeding which helped to give Italy a well-to-do class of cultivators. "Although the system was not successful in lower Italy, where economic decline could not be arrested, there can be no doubt that central and northern Italy, where the vine and olive were largely cultivated, and manufacturing industries sprang up, enjoyed a considerable measure of prosperity." "Yet even under Trajan, Hadrian, and the Antonines (98-180) we notice a failure of strength in the empire as a whole. . . . The ceaseless labors of Hadrian were directed mainly to the careful husbanding of such strength as still remained, or to attempts at reviving it by sheer force of imperial authority. Among the symptoms of incipient decline were the growing depopulation, especially of the central parts of the empire, the constant financial difficulties, the deterioration in character of the local governments in the provincial communities, and the increasing reluctance exhibited by all classes to undertake the now onerous burden of municipal office." Here we see repeated the conditions of the second century B. C., although not on so serious a scale, as befits the somewhat more favorable climate. During the reign of the odious Emperor Commodus (180-193)

famine and pestilence brought Rome to a low ebb. The reign of
Severus (193-211) saw an improvement in the government and
in general prosperity corresponding not only to the relatively
strong character of that ruler, but to the comparatively favorable conditions of climate.

Soon after 200 A. D. there began in full force the long period
which Gibbon describes in the "Decline and Fall of the Roman
Empire." War, plague, famine, misgovernment, and barbarian
invasions vied with vice, crime, and incompetency to drag the
world lower and lower. In Italy, as well as in other lands,
depopulation progressed apace, infanticide became widespread,
great areas of formerly fertile land were left desolate by proprietors who fled to avoid the exactions of the taxgatherer. How
could they pay the old taxes when decade after decade saw their
crops declining? The prosperity of the towns decreased with
that of the country districts. All over the Roman Empire there
were repeated riots and insurrections among the poverty-stricken
inhabitants. Political disorder due to starvation and misery
extended from Gaul on the one side to populous cities like Antioch
on the other, and Italy had its share. Civil war and the rule
of tyrants like Maxentius and Maximus added to the confusion.
Men's energy and power of self-control, as well as their crops,
were suffering at the behest of the inexorably changing climate.
Worst of all, the barbarians were constantly swooping down first
on one part of the empire and then on another. They, as well
as the Romans, were in distress because of lack of rain and hence
poor crops and scanty pasture for their flocks and herds. Or
if they themselves did not thus suffer, they were driven out of
their homes by other tribes who years before had migrated because
of drought. For generation after generation such unfortunate
tribes moved restlessly this way and that, seeking homes and
peaceful prosperity, but finding only war and slaughter, drought
and poverty. When the barbarians came down upon them from
the more vigorous north, what could the enervated Romans do

to repel them? Ill health, anæmia, vice, misgovernment, were scarcely the means of repelling fierce invaders. So Rome fell, and her fall was followed by that period of unfavorable climate which is known as the Dark Ages.

From first to last the general outlines of the history of Rome conform to what would be expected on the supposition that climate is one of the chief determiners of the strength and habits of a nation. We have seen that this is so in our own country today, and that it has been the case all through the course of geological evolution. Now we see that when Rome and southern Italy had a highly stimulating climate there arose the stern, yet admirable Roman Republic. There right was might, and conscience played as large a part as in almost any civilization that the world has ever known. Next came a sudden change of climate, and the Italy of the second century B. C. showed itself base, weak, and wicked where its ancestors had been noble, strong, and pure. Again, the climate improved in the first century before Christ, and once more Rome rose, although not to her former level. A century of greatness and a century or two of slow decline agreed once more with the climatic conditions. Then once more a long and painful downward sweep of civilization occurred hand in hand with a prolonged downward sweep of climate. The Dark Ages were the period of least storminess, and presumably of least climatic stimulus and poorest health at any time for at least three thousand years. Since those days there have been two great periods of recovery. Both appear in general to have agreed with climatic pulsations.

Today in spite of the vicissitudes of climate Italy still holds her place among the Great Powers. Is this inconsistent with our theory? It would be, were it not that there are two Italies. The Italy of ancient times was the country from Rome southward. Again and again we have seen that it was southern Italy whose disorders chiefly brought calamity. Today's Italy is the country from Rome northward. Every student of Italian affairs knows that there is a marked difference between north and south. If the south were by itself, it probably would have not a whit more influence than Spain, and perhaps less. Thus, even at present, Italy illustrates the fact that man's actions and capacities depend largely upon the health and energy, and thus upon the strength and stimulus which he derives from his climate.

CHAPTER XII

THE PROBLEM OF TURKEY

TURNING from our survey of the past, let us apply to modern problems the lessons learned from a study of man's relation to his physical environment. In the Great War we recognize Germany and Turkey as the two main types that we were opposing. Austria and Bulgaria are intermediate between the others, and therefore need not claim our attention. Both Turkey and Germany furnish striking examples of the results which arise when physical evolution proceeds to its logical ends without being duly guided and moulded by the spiritual factor of altruism. Germany illustrates what happens under the most favorable physical environment; Turkey what happens in a much less favorable, but not the worst environment.

Let us begin with Turkey. If I were to choose a text for this chapter, it would be from Eliot's "Turkey in Europe," that best of books on the Turk: "The crimes with which the Turks are frequently reproached, such as treachery, fratricide, and wholesale cruelty, are characteristic not of them, but of the lands which they invaded." We all know those crimes. Our hearts have bled for the hundreds of thousands of massacred Armenians, and for the Syrians suffering torture and starvation. Our purses have been opened that we may bind up a few of the wounds that the Turk, backed by the German, has inflicted on his miserable Christian fellow subjects, or perhaps I should say slaves. With these dire facts in mind it is hard to judge fairly. Yet if we do not judge fairly we run the risk of falling into the very errors for which we fought the old régime in Germany. So let us patiently try to understand why "treachery, fratricide, and wholesale cruelty are *characteristic*" of the lands that the Turks invaded.

Let me begin by telling a few stories of things that I have heard or seen in Turkey. Before the war I was talking with a certain Herr Winter, an engineer in charge of the extensive irrigation works which now bring water from Lake Bey Shehir to the dry plain of Konia in the center of Asia Minor. As we talked, an assistant engineer entered the room, and was introduced as a Greek. Soon came another, a Bulgarian; then a third, a Belgian. When a fourth was introduced as an Italian, Herr Winter laughed, and said: "This is not all. I could introduce you to an Armenian engineer and to those of still other races. This irrigation company is German; but I'm the only German here, and I'm an Austrian. Our laborers are just as mixed—Turks, Armenians, some Kurds, a few Greeks, and I don't know what else. Of course we don't understand each other. We don't try to."

In saying that they did not understand one another Herr Winter referred to language. His words have a deeper significance, for in Turkey one race rarely or never understands another's purposes. They do not wish to understand. Hence comes vast misery. It arises I believe from lack of mental activity. Hence differences in religion, or in speech, dress, and manners, form insurmountable obstacles. We shall come back to this, but first let us look further into Turkish character.

From Lake Bey Shehir, thirty miles long, a clear river flows southeastward to a smaller lake, Kara Viren. At most times this second sheet has no visible outlet, for the water escapes underground through several exits whose location is evident from swirling eddies. During flood seasons, however, a little water overflows and passes down a mountain valley to the Konia plain. For a thousand years the Turks and their predecessors have longed to prevent the loss of water through the underground outlets and to carry the whole supply to the thirsty plain. They have dumped rocks into the swirls, and at low water have tried to place covers of beams and felt over the holes in the limestone where the water escapes. They have also tried to deepen the channel at the outlet. Their greatest effort, however, was a vain attempt to build a practically horizontal canal for a dozen miles around the smaller lake from inlet to outlet. The idea was excellent. The only trouble was that they went to work with characteristic lack of foresight, and apparently made little effort to secure a proper slope. Now with greater foresight the Germans have given their canal the right slope and are watering the plain.

Of a piece with this bit of Turkish lack of foresight was the remark of a Turkish peasant. One of the engineers was telling him what a fine thing it would be when his land was finally irrigated; "When we turn the water into the canals, your crop of grain will average five times as large as now." At first the peasant did not seem impressed. Then an idea struck him: "Allah be praised! Do you know what I'll do? I'll sell all but one fifth of my land, and work only one fifth as much as now!"

Equally stupid is the Turkish attitude toward massacres. Why does the Turk massacre the Christian? Is it because he is by nature more cruel than other people? More likely it is sheer stupidity. The Turk reasons thus: "Look at these Christians. They occupy good land; they prosper; they lend money to Turks and make the good Moslem pay interest; they 'eat' better than we do. Let us tax them and make them disgorge the wealth which by right belongs to the Children of the Prophet." So the screws are turned and the Christians are pinched. Naturally the Christians protest and squirm. "Aha," says the Turk, "you are against the government, are you? We'll settle that. The Kurds shall kill and plunder you, and we will share the plunder and enjoy your lands." The stupid Turk does not realize that he is killing the goose that lays the golden eggs.

I happened to visit Adana just after the massacres of 1909 in which fifteen or twenty thousand Armenians were killed. That case illustrates the extraordinary stupidity and also the lack

of reasoned self-control which are among the most prominent
Turkish characteristics. The first massacre was stirred up by
reactionary Mullahs, or Moslem priests, whose object was to
discredit the constitutional party and restore the old régime. As
soon as news of the atrocities reached Constantinople, the Young
Turk Committee, which then seemed still to be actuated by high
ideals, ordered troops from Salonika to proceed to Adana and
restore order. The Salonika troops had been the chief agent in
forcing Abdul Hamid to grant a constitution. They were supposed to be especially imbued with principles of fraternity and
progress. What happened? The troops reached Mersina, and
were entrained for the short ride to Adana. As they disembarked
from the train, long-robed Mullahs with white or green turbans
went among them: "Thank God you have come. Ever since the
massacre we have been in terror of our lives. These Christian
dogs—may Allah curse them—are sly and cunning. Look out or
they will shoot you in the back. Thank God you are here, and
our wives and daughters are at last safe." Thus they talked,
lying, and the poor simple peasant soldiers believed them. In the
middle of the afternoon a soldier was shot in the back. Later it
was proved that the shot must have come from a Turkish house,
and moreover the Armenians had all been disarmed. But the plans
of the Mullahs worked well. "To your arms," they cried, for
they were still whispering lies among the soldiers. "Kill the
Christians or they will kill you." In a moment the unstable,
unthinking Turkish soldiers were out of hand. Their officers,
so they claim, could not restrain them, and perhaps did not want
to. At any rate the troops that had arrived to save in the morning went out to massacre in the afternoon. And their massacre
was worse than its predecessor.

The Young Turk Committee tried to save its face in the sight
of Europe. It executed about six Turks—I think that was the
number—for killing fifteen or twenty thousand Armenians, and
perhaps two Armenians in penance for the score or two of Moslems

who had been killed by a few armed Christians. As I went into the interior from Adana, the news was just spreading. We heard a city Turk relate it to some countrymen. "What," said the countrymen, "hang a Turk for killing a Christian! Impossible!" That was no pose on their part. It was actually beyond the limits of their thought that a Moslem should be punished for killing a Christian in the same way that a Christian would be punished for killing a Moslem.

As I went farther into the interior, to the most Turkish portion of the country, I inquired repeatedly as to the effect of the new régime.

"What do you think of the new constitution?" I would ask.

"Constitution?" they would answer, "What does that mean?"

"Oh, I mean this new liberty, this new government. What difference does it make in your village?"

"Ah, yes, now we understand. This liberty? What do we know about it? They tell us we have it, and all will now be right. Perhaps it will. God grant it. But we see no difference. Oh, yes, the officials do not take quite so many bribes as formerly, but that won't last. They are afraid now, but you wait. They want money as much as ever. They seem to want more soldiers than ever, and they take our sons to die in Yemen. We don't mind being soldiers, but Yemen! Allah be merciful! Men die like flies there."

Then they went on to talk about the new government. "Did we vote for a man to go to parliament? We don't know what you mean. Oh, the big meeting in Stamboul? Did we send a man? Oh, no, we heard that they sent one from the city, but we had nothing to do with it. Why do you ask all these questions? How can we tell about liberty? We don't know what it means. We don't know anything. You are from the city, you have read books. *You* ought to tell *us*, and not ask us to tell you. What do we know except that we are poor and God is great. God grant that we get enough to pay the taxes and live this dry year."

Another example of the workings of the Turkish mind is seen in the relation of the government to the nomadic Kurds of the mountains and the wandering Arabs of the desert. Take the case of Dersim, a rugged tract of high mountains between the two branches of the upper Euphrates. The Kurdish inhabitants raise some grain, but depend in large measure on flocks. In 1907-1908 the crops were bad and the sheep did not do so well as usual, for grass was scarce. The Kurds needed supplies from without. In the old days they would merely have robbed the neighboring villages. I myself have been in a village on the Dersim border when the Kurds drove off the flocks, killed a shepherd, and had a fight with the villagers. In 1908, however, having recently been chastised by the government, they purchased grain, and made up a great caravan to bring it home. Instead of helping them in this peaceful and righteous course and thus paving the way for permanent good relations, the stupid officials said: "Aha, now is our chance. We can strike a blow at the Kurds without injuring ourselves."

So the caravan was seized. Naturally the Kurds flared up, and began to rob and plunder on all sides. The authorities sent a large body of troops, 20,000 it is said, who hung around the borders of the mountains, not daring to penetrate the fastnesses. Half a million dollars was spent. The only result was to embitter and impoverish the Kurds, and encourage them to engage in further raids. A few years later those same Kurds were turned loose to kill the Christians, and blot the page of history with the last—let us hope—of the fiendish massacres which have been one of the chief entries on the debit side not only of the Turks and Kurds but of the land in which they dwell.

We might go on to tell a hundred tales of the way in which Turks mistreat Arabs, Arabs plunder Syrians from whom they might otherwise buy bread, while Syrians use every petty contrivance to get the better of one another or of the government. But is there no race in the whole Turkish Empire that lives up to some higher standards? The Greeks of the coast and the Armenians of the interior succeed better than the Moslems, but even they succeed very poorly according to the standards of the world's advanced nations. Their Christianity helps them. Moreover, I am inclined to think that they inherit greater mental powers than do the Turks, who come of a long line of nomadic ancestors. Even so, however, they suffer from a sort of inertia which prevents them from sticking long to a new attempt. Moreover, they are not notable for self-control. More than one thoughtful Armenian has said to me: "It is useless for us to talk about self-government. No half dozen of us can agree. We all want to run things our own way, and no one is willing to submit to the majority. If we governed ourselves we would not be much better off than under the Turks, except when the Turks start massacres." The Greeks are similar. Is there not a saying "Five Greeks, five generals"? Athens swarms with half-educated men whose one thought in life is to talk and argue, and ultimately to obtain office.

It is easier to describe the weaknesses of the Turkish Empire than to agree upon their causes. These begin with misgovernment, lack of education, and the absence of high religious ideals. Important as these are, however, I pass them by. Again let me insist that I by no means underrate these things. Good government, sound education, and high ideals are absolutely essential. The question is merely whether they are fruits or roots. Are the people of the Turkish Empire inert, weak-willed, self-indulgent, cruel, and stupid because of their government, education, and religion? Or are they misgoverned, ignorant, and superstitious because of their own lack of energy and will-power? The case of the Turkish Empire today apparently resembles that of Rome in the second century except that it is far worse.

The climatic conditions which seem to lie at the bottom of much of the trouble in Turkey produce profound economic results. For example, we have spoken of the Kurds of Dersim, and of the government's interference with their attempts to procure food in a dry year. The trouble in that instance was primarily lack of rain, and hence poor crops. Some of the coastal regions of Turkey get a fairly abundant rainfall and are correspondingly prosperous. Nowhere, however, except in a small area on the Black Sea coast does much rain fall during the summer. In most parts of the country no rain worth mentioning falls from the end of May to the first of October. Often May and October have little rain, while in bad years April and November may both be dry. In mountainous regions like Dersim, which are at best scarcely able to support their population, dry years bring great distress. In the case under discussion the Turkish officials were extremely foolish. They said that the Kurds were a bad lot and needed a lesson. They failed to realize that the trouble with the Kurds is not innate depravity, but the hunger of the moment and the despair arising from century after century of unsuccessful struggles against nature. Half a million dollars spent in furnishing labor on public works instead of in paying for a military expedition would have enabled those particular Kurds to buy five times the food they needed, and would have kept them perfectly quiet. The fundamental mistake is in assuming that the Kurds are by nature robbers, a dangerous element to be sternly repressed. The remedy lies in so adjusting matters that the evils of their physical environment shall be neutralized.

The Arabs are other members of the Turkish Empire who are victims of similar circumstances. Before the Great War accustomed men's ears to tales of distress and cruelty, I could have harrowed your souls by telling how the people of the borders of the Arabian Desert starved in the early seventies, a period of unusual drought, while the Arabs plundered them unmercifully. The Arabs pressed in from the desert by thousands. They were hungry; their sheep and camels were weak and thin; the young animals including the babies were dying for lack of milk; and food of all kinds failed for the adults. Therefore the Arabs scourged the starving villages, stripping men and women of every rag, and leaving them weak and wounded to find the way home for miles in the blazing sun. We grow eloquent over the infernal wickedness of the Arabs, and the criminal weakness of the Turkish government in permitting such devastation. But why should we blame the Turk and the Arab? They are acting absolutely in accordance with the stage of evolution which they have reached and with the physical environment in which they are placed. If we would do anything, we must show the Arab how to find food where there is no food, and the Turk how to be so wise and energetic that he will forestall the hunger and violence of the Arabs. If the new government which must be established in Turkey can find a way of helping the Arabs in times of drought, it can preserve its borderlands from desolation. Raids will never cease so long as the Arabs are hungry and have the desert as a refuge.

Here is another example of the economic handicaps which keep the people of the Turkish Empire so backward. Everyone familiar with Constantinople wonders at the desolate character of the surrounding country. On the Asiatic side, to be sure, villages are fairly numerous in spite of the relatively high mountains. On the European side the beautiful plateau stretching northward to the Black Sea and westward a hundred miles to Adrianople, is well-nigh uninhabited. It lies only a few hundred feet high; the soil is deep; the slopes are gentle; and everything appears propitious for agriculture. Yet one may walk for miles and see nothing but flocks of sheep, and at long intervals a little village in a secluded valley. To test the common opinion I made inquiries of three friends who have lived in Constantinople. All are far better informed than the average traveler, and one is among the chief authorities on the country. My inquiries took the form of this question, "Why is the country around Constantinople so sparsely settled?"

The first reply was: "Lack of energy on the part of the Turks. They might have some fine gardens there; they have them in some places around the city—splendid ones—and if the Turks were an energetic people they would turn the whole region into fine farms."

The second reply emphasized another point: "It is because the Turks don't know how to do things wisely. They keep sheep up there on the plateau. You can see them any day close to the city, eating away, and cleaning up the grass so that the ground is smooth as a floor. The Turks ought to give that up and take to farming."

The third answer carried the matter still farther: "The trouble is that it is not safe outside the city. [All this, of course, was before the war.] It is dangerous to go out alone there on the hills; all over the plateau the shepherds are unfriendly. Soldiers from the city go out there and insult or rob respectable citizens. So people do not live there. The government is to blame."

All these answers are true, but not the whole truth. Lack of energy, lack of knowledge, and lack of good government all seem to be largely the result of unfavorable physical environment acting either through economic conditions or through health. Consider the economic side of the matter. The plateau west of the Bosphorus does not blossom with gardens partly because it is too dry. In the spring it is beautifully green, and in exceptional years it remains verdant well toward autumn. Usually, however, it dries up at the beginning of summer. Even early crops such as winter wheat and barley often fail. The gardens to which two of my friends referred are all artificially irrigated, or else lie in valley bottoms enjoying natural, that is, underground irrigation. Under present conditions water for irrigation cannot be brought to the plateau, which therefore is left to semi-nomadic shepherds. Across the Bosphorus where the mountains are higher, the rainfall is greater and there is more chance for irrigation. Hence the more abundant villages.

On the European side the sparsity of population due to the dryness allows the plateau to become the haunt of miscreants from the great city. If agriculture were profitable thousands of poor people would gladly take up farms; villages would spring up; and in a few years comparative safety would prevail.

That the absence of cultivation is not due wholly to lack of energy or to bad government appears from the fact that in the fall of 1909, when the deposition of Abdul Hamid had assured safety in the minds of many, a considerable area of the plateau near the city was planted with grain. The results are said to have been disappointing. The crop was by no means such as to tempt further expansion of agriculture. Yet the season of 1909-1910 was not one of the worst, although not one of the best. The rainfall of Constantinople varies from eleven to forty-four inches. Sometimes it continues all summer, but not often. Usually the effective rains end about the first of June and begin again in September. Occasionally the rainfall almost ceases as early as April and does not begin again until October. In such years agriculture without irrigation is impossible. Dr. Washburn, who for many years was president of Robert College on the Bosphorus, states that he has known the water supply of the College to fail completely because of the delay of the rains until the end of October. That year, as at other times, the little *chiftliks*, or villages, on the plateau suffered severely because their wells dried up. They were forced to bring water from long distances, and their cattle suffered greatly. An occasional group of years of this kind is enough to keep all people except shepherds away from the plateau.

The effect of such conditions upon the people of Turkey is illustrated by another incident. As I drove one day over the plain of Axylon, northeast of Konia, the parched brown land gradually became transformed into a carpet of short thick grass, beautifully green. Yet not a trace of village or field was visible, nothing but the tents or little mud huts of nomads. Hitherto my Greek driver had not been sparing of opprobrious epithets when he spoke of the local inhabitants. Now he broke out into renewed and more vehement exclamations at the laziness, ignorance, and incompetence of the "poor swine" who inhabited the plain. "Look at this fine plain," he exclaimed. "See how green it is. Look at that brook. If only some Greeks were here, or even some Muhajir Turks, they would make a perfect garden of this. But these vile Turks! What do they know! They are animals without a speck of sense in their noddles."

The Greek's remarks throw an interesting sidelight on racial psychology. He had no theory as to the incompetence of the Turks as a race. Muhajir Turks are those who have come from Roumania, Bulgaria, or other European regions because of the change from Moslem to Christian rule since 1876. Racially they are among the purest of the Turks. Yet they are generally accounted among the most active and progressive farmers in the empire. The reason appears to be largely that they have lived for some generations in an environment more stimulating than that of most parts of Asiatic Turkey.

Another interesting feature of the Greek's remarks is that his mental attitude illustrates that of almost the whole world. He judged by outward appearances, and utterly failed to hit the mark. How far he was from the truth appeared when the Kurdish chief with whom we spent the night showed me his garden. "It's hard work," said the Kurd, "to make a garden here. You see what a good little brook we have. We ought to have good gardens. A few years ago I tried to make one over there where you see those dead saplings. It was all right the first year, but the second season the ground became hard, and most things would not grow. Now I am trying here where the soil is more sandy. This is the third year. Some plants do pretty well, but I don't know why so many trees die."

I saw another new garden where likewise the trees had mostly died after a year's growth while many of the vegetables seemed stunted. The reason was plain. We were in the bed of an ancient salt lake. The soil was strongly impregnated with salt, and the brooks were slightly saline. Irrigation concentrated the salt, as it always does, and after a few years the ground was fit only for tough grasses. We saw traces of earlier gardens all of which had met the same fate. Nature had been too much for the Kurds just as it had been for the Arabs in the desert and the Turks and others around Constantinople.

Down in Beersheba, the most southerly town of Palestine, I saw a young Syrian official defeated by nature in the same way. He and two partners had attempted to raise grain on a large scale. Seeing many square miles of good land lying unused, they leased from the government a large tract at a rental of about $2,000 per year. In 1908 they planted several acres and reaped an excellent crop. The next year they increased the area, hiring many laborers, and investing all the money that they could lay hands on. The spring of 1909 was unpropitious with no rain from February till the end of April. At the end of April, when the fields should have been at their best, those at Beersheba looked almost as if they had never been planted. There was no crop to reap, and camels were turned in to browse on the scanty stalks of grainless wheat and barley. Each man lost $1,500 or more, which is as much as $10,000 would be for an American official.

The untilled plateau of Constantinople, the stunted Kurdish gardens, and the withered grain at Beersheba represent the constant experience of the Turkish Empire. Men fail to improve their condition because natural obstacles are insurmountable. In view of the repeated failures of the past the number of attempts at improvements is highly commendable. It shows that in spite of much inertia and stupidity many of the people of the Turkish Empire are blessed with quick, active minds and a good deal of persistence. But no one can be blamed if nature refuses to coöperate with him. In ancient days, when the climate of the Turkish Empire was favorable, the ancestors of some of the present inhabitants were the leaders of civilization. Today their descendants are crushed and discouraged by the insurmountable obstacles of nature. No wonder their spirit is broken, their children ignorant, their religion corrupt, and their government diabolical.

In the preceding paragraph I have twice used the word "insurmountable" with a definite purpose. Are the natural obstacles so insurmountable? It all depends on who is to surmount them. Have you never seen a toddling infant stumble and fall over a threshold? Have you seen a sick man clutch at his heart and sway breathless at the top of three or four easy steps? Think what ill health does to business in New York. Consider the effect of an adverse climate upon Rome. Remember that delicate climatic adjustments have been one of the chief strands in the long cord of evolution. Then ask what the climate of Turkey does to its inhabitants. It is not a disagreeable climate. In fact, it is in many ways delightful. Rarely have I found nature more charming than on a spring day when the purple Judas trees along the Bosphorus— all probably cut for firewood by now—were in full bloom, and the day was ushered in by a full chorus of nightingales. Equally beautiful were some of the bracing autumn days when the first showers fell on the mountains of the interior, and our horses' hoofs struck fragrance from the dry leaves of the hardy little sage bushes. Four years of residence in the interior, extensive later travels, and constant intercourse with relatives in Constantinople and with friends all over the country have given me abundant opportunities to sum up the net effects. Long before I had any climatic theories I remember how we used to talk of the jaded feeling which seemed to pervade all the foreigners at the end of the long monotonous summers. Day after day was exactly the same. How we longed for the first break in the fall—the day when the clouds that had gradually been gathering should drop the first rain, wash the dusty air, and bring a *change*. I lived there just after leaving college; I never had a sick day and scarcely a cold; during the vacations of Euphrates College where I taught at Harput I travelled and lived out of doors most of the time; and at other times I always had plenty of exercise and spent much of my spare time on horseback or geologizing. A healthier, saner life would be hard to imagine, for we were so remote that there was no chance for the social engagements that interfere so much with healthful hours of sleep. Yet I know that I sometimes had a jaded feeling which I almost never feel now although I am sixteen years older and work harder and sleep less.

My experience is like that of many others. I recall a letter from a friend who had lived in Constantinople for some years. In other letters he had spoken of the beauty of many a day on the banks of the famous Bosphorus. He had also mentioned the depressing effect of a month or so of steady cloud and gloom during the winter, for the winters as well as the summers are relatively monotonous. Now he was writing from Copenhagen. This is essentially what he said: "You don't know how good it is to get here. This air is like wine. I don't know when I have felt so energetic. I just want to skip about and do everything." That is it. The Turkish climate may be most pleasant; it is never very bad. Yet it lacks stimulus. I have watched people who live there. I have seen how on their return to New England they are at first very sensitive to our extremes of heat and cold; how they declaim against it and want to get back to Turkey. Later I have heard them speak of how much better they feel here than there, and of how much more they can accomplish. Again I have compared the American colleges in Turkey with similar institutions at home—the faculties, I mean, not the students. It would be hard to find a finer set of men, physically, mentally, and morally. They go out to Turkey imbued with the highest ideals and filled with the greatest zeal. What happens? At the end of twenty years their ideals are still as high as ever, and their zeal as great. Yet they are not working as their college classmates at home are working. They have slackened their pace little by little. They do not attempt to keep so many irons hot; they are much more likely to stop for afternoon tea; they have more largely given up their ambition to do something original, and are content with the faithful accomplishment of life's daily routine. This is no discredit to them. It is merely a wise and often unconscious adjustment to the new environment. I remember one who wished that he could work with the untiring energy displayed by his wife and by others who had just come from America. Two years later he said, "My wife, unfortunately, has learned that in this climate she cannot work so steadily as at home."

I might go on to cite hundreds of such cases. One has only to study the climographs of an earlier chapter and the facts as to health in New York to see that this response to the environment of Turkey is exactly what would be expected. If people with the finest inheritance, the best training, and the highest ideals thus find themselves obliged to reduce their lives to a lower *tempo* in Turkey than in more favored lands, what can we expect of the natives? Malaria is rife among them, many are underfed, and those who have plenty of food often do not have the ambition and energy to learn proper ways of cooking it and of varying it. Any number of small ailments prevail constantly, and do their share toward keeping a large part of the people in a state of more or less anæmia. Not that they are visibly sick, or that they would acknowledge that they were less strong than the strongest. But have you not noticed that just when people are most in danger of breaking down they are loudest in their assertions that they are all right? Have you not also noticed that when you are "under the weather" you are apt to neglect all sorts of little things? In Turkey people are under the weather for generation after generation; this difficulty is aggravated by economic distress; it is intensified by the mixture of many races who fail to understand each other partly because their lack of health and energy predispose them to be self-centered and conservative.

So Turkey, like all the other countries with which we have dealt, seems to have a civilization corresponding to her physical environment. This does not mean that she is forever doomed to misgovernment, race hatred, and massacre. It does mean, however, that there is little hope of any favorable development from within. The stronger nations must give Turkey a good government. They must keep the peace between the different races, and, so far as may be, break down their prejudices.

Another pressing need is a thorough revision of the economic system. This matter is so important that even at the risk of digression I shall discuss it somewhat fully. One possible method of revision is through some sort of insurance against years of scarcity. In good years the Turkish Empire is most fruitful. A Joseph is needed to store up food so that the good years may feed the bad. The new government which will be inaugurated after the war might well compel the peasants to deposit a share of their grain in public warehouses after good harvests. Part of this might be in the nature of an advance on taxes, so that when the lean years come, the taxes could be remitted. The rest might well be in the nature of insurance. Since the chances of crop failure are high, the premiums would have to be high. Suppose that the crop fails absolutely once in ten years. An average payment of three bushels per year for nine years would perhaps be enough to cover operating expenses and to allow the payment of twenty-five bushels to the beneficiary when his crop failed. In actual practice allowance would of course be made for partial as well as complete failures.

Consider how such a system would not only help the farmer, but would steady the general market. Suppose there is a good year with exuberant crops. In such years prices ordinarily drop to a low level; transportation facilities, especially in a backward country like Turkey, are overburdened; and a good deal of grain is wasted. Even if it does not spoil, it is consumed more rapidly than is advisable and some is fed needlessly to animals. Thus at the end of an unusually favorable year the farmer is no better off than at the end of a moderate year. Things would be quite different, however, if great insurance warehouses were located in every district. As soon as the crop was harvested and the fall work was over, the farmer would take much of his surplus to the warehouse. He would not need to pay any commission to a middleman, nor to pay expensive transportation charges. With his own beasts he could easily travel fifty miles if necessary. So much grain would go to the warehouses that the price would not fall so low as is now the case at such times. The next year the crop might be moderate. Little would be deposited in the warehouses and little taken away. Then would come a poor year. Some people would draw on the warehouses for their own consumption and others in order to sell. Prices would not go up much, for the presence of a large stock in the warehouses would hold them down. If a series of good years filled the warehouses to overflowing, it would be easy to sell to foreign markets. If a series of bad years depleted the stock, the government could buy from abroad.

Such a plan of state insurance is not easy to inaugurate. It would require much time for its full development. It would necessarily have to go hand in hand with the building of roads and railroads. The people, too, would need to be educated up to it. Yet there is nothing insuperably difficult about it. Once its benefits were understood, it would find rapid favor among a simple people like those of Turkey. The prime necessity would be confidence in the government. If the people once became convinced that the administration was absolutely impartial and was in the interests of the general public and not of the rulers, success would be assured. England in many of her colonies has gained that kind of confidence. The Turks themselves could never gain it. Perhaps the day may come when they will change so much that they can administer such an enterprise, but it is far distant. In all such backward countries as Turkey, it seems probable that the races from the more stimulating climates will have to be the administrators for an indefinite period.

The situation in respect to health is as hopeful—and as difficult—as in respect to economics. Within a generation we have discovered the causes of malaria and the measures to prevent it. We have also found that hitherto unrecognized disorders such as pellagra and the hookworm disease are responsible for no end of ignorance and inefficiency. All of these diseases seem to be closely dependent upon climate. Further investigation will doubtless disclose many other ailments whose effects are so mild that we have not hitherto called them diseases. Yet their combined effects may account for a large part of the contrast in health and energy in different parts of the world. When they are eradicated we perhaps should not expect the people of unfavorable climates to work as steadily and energetically as those of the best parts of the world. Yet we may reasonably expect that much of the seeming stupidity, and much of the indifference, vice, and crime will disappear. The medical rebirth of countries like Turkey is as important as their political and economic rebirth. The first great step toward medical rebirth is an exhaustive study of the causes of the present inertia. It is good to think that science, through the study of biology and evolution, offers such hope for the regeneration of backward nations.

CHAPTER XIII

GERMANY AND HER NEIGHBORS

THE principles developed in this volume have a direct application to the Great War. The pages of history show that in the long run the outcome of wars is in accord with the health and energy of the people. Of course there are many exceptions. The distance from home makes a great difference. A strong people fighting at long range may occasionally be unable to defeat a weaker nation which has the advantage of being close to the battle-ground. So, too, a great leader may be of more avail than the activity of his opponents. Again, a people in distress through hunger may overwhelm others of greater energy by the sheer impetuosity of their frenzied outburst. Yet ultimately health and energy, and therefore climate, appear to be the deciding factors. Racial character is unquestionably most important in this respect as in others, but in spite of our prepossessions to the contrary, it is becoming evident that much of what we call racial character is really the effect of physical environment acting upon generation after generation.

Glance at the course of history for a moment. Egypt spread her dominion far to the south and into the confines of Arabia at a time when her people appear to have been blessed with health and energy because of the variable climate which then prevailed. So, too, with Babylonia and Assyria. In the wars between these two we cannot tell what part was played by differences in health, but both of them conquered the surrounding countries at times when they were probably stimulated by a bracing climate. In Palestine we see this same phenomenon. That country apparently

rose to temporary greatness a little after 1000 B. C. not merely
because David was a great leader, but because his followers were
energetic. A much clearer case is that of Greece. She appears
to have been victorious over the "barbarians" across the seas so
long as her climate retained the extremely stimulating quality
which it possessed until the time of Alexander. It must have
been an immense advantage to Alexander that his army was
invigorated by long years—yes, by generations of life in one of
the best environments that the world has ever known. So, too,
Rome overthrew Carthage at a time when the climate of North
Africa had become decidedly unfavorable, while that of Italy had
deteriorated far less. Again, in the Middle Ages Italy was dominant during periods when the climate—or perhaps it would be
better to say, the weather—was highly variable, while her power
was usurped by more northern nations when they in turn were
favored with the atmospheric conditions that stimulate activity.
In our own day every explorer knows that in unfavorable environments the endurance of men from better climates is much greater
than that of the natives.

In spite of these considerations it is hard to persuade one's self
that climate and health are really so important. Other factors,
such as the character of the commanders, the strategic advantages
of topography, and the availability of supplies certainly dominate
the details of most combats. The part played by health and
energy can be fairly estimated only from a comprehensive view
of decades or centuries. As I have shown in "Civilization and
Climate," wherever and whenever the climate is stimulating, civilization seems to rise to a high level. The character of the civilization of course varies according to the race and training of the
people. Yet no matter what the race, it seems under such circumstances to acquire the power to originate new ideas, to stick to
them until they are carried out, and to impress its rule and its
civilization upon the less favored people with whom it comes in
contact. One may of course say that it is the higher civilization,

the better training, the better government, or the stronger racial fiber which causes the more advanced race to conquer and dominate, but that begs the question. It seems to be a rule in history that the following conditions generally go together: a stimulating climate, health, energy of body and mind, originality and persistence, high civilization, conquest and dominance of weaker races, and spread of the type of civilization which has grown up where the climate is stimulating. The civilization and energy of the people cannot be the causes of the climate. On the other hand, there is abundant evidence that the climate has a great deal to do with the energy of a nation and with its capacity for progress and conquest. Hence in the broad view much of what is ascribed to the race, training, and civilization of a nation is really due to health and climate.

This brings us to the question of where Germany stands in reference to climate. We may say at once that the German climate is much superior to that of her enemies who live east and south of her. This is illustrated in Figures 26 A-B, two maps of energy and civilization respectively, which I have described elsewhere. Even in a country like Germany there is, as we have seen, much anæmia and many other types of ill health, but not nearly so much as in most other countries. When Austria first clashed with Serbia, the Serbians gave a good account of themselves even though they were fighting with a power far larger than their own. They had a fighting chance, as we may say, because they were contending with a country whose average energy is not much greater than their own. When Germany took charge of operations the case was altered, and Serbia quickly succumbed. Of course the size of Germany, her education, her science, her racial habit of obedience, all played a part in this. At present, however, we are merely showing that in her relation with the other belligerents Germany's energy has been in accord with what would be expected on the basis of her climate. Perhaps if the Balkan States had had as stimulating a climate as that of Germany for

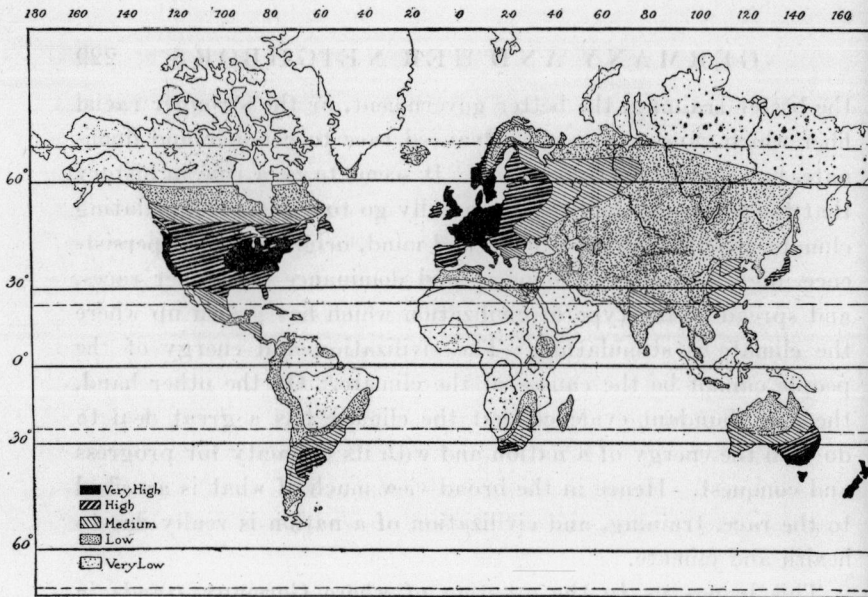

FIGURE 26 A.　The Distribution of Civilization

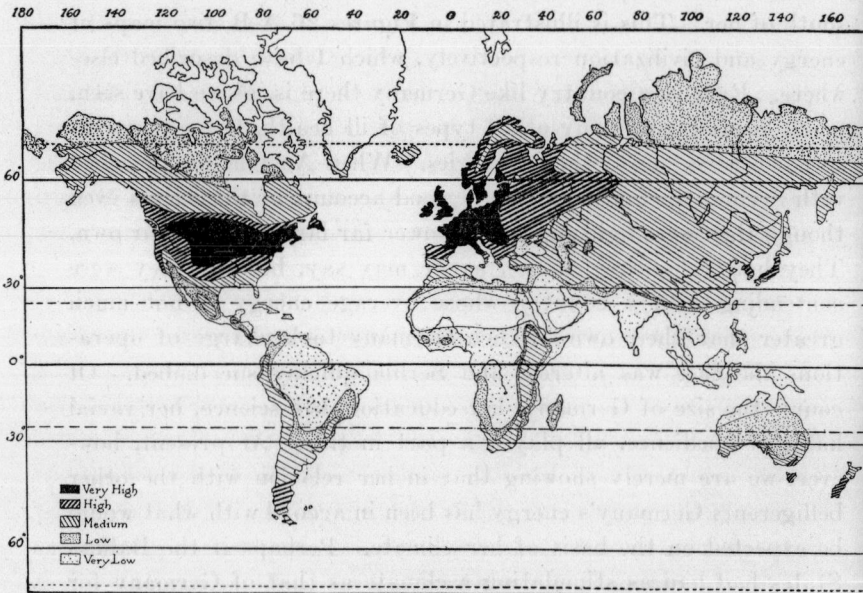

FIGURE 26 B.　The Distribution of Human Energy on the Basis of Climate

a few hundred years, they might have had the strength and self-control to sink their racial differences and unite into a nation as competent as Germany.

Perhaps the reader will say: "Why choose Serbia? Why not talk about Belgium? Germany hit her as hard as she hit Serbia." True, but the contrast between Belgium and Serbia is one of the best illustrations of the point we are making. Belgium suffered because she was small. How much has she cost Germany, however, compared with what Serbia has cost? At the end, after four years of fighting, a Belgian army still held an important part of the battle-front. How Germany would have rejoiced to substitute Serbians for Belgians along that front! She would have broken through in a week behind the British and would have seized the channel ports.

Take another of Germany's eastern antagonists, Roumania. Here, too, we have a country whose climate, like that of Serbia, is not bad, but is merely by no means so stimulating as that of Germany and Belgium. What happened? Roumania went into the war for motives far lower than those which actuated the Belgians. She looked out mainly for her own selfish interests, and she reaped a bitter harvest. Belgium reaped an even more bitter harvest, but she has a twofold satisfaction. She knows that she fought only in self-defense. She also knows that having begun to fight she never lost her grip, while Roumania, being once defeated, ceased to be a factor of any importance.

When we come to Russia we find a country larger than Germany, and from that point of view able to fight on equal terms. In other respects, however, the fight was very unequal. Russia is a northern country and has none of the disadvantages of the torrid zone. Yet her climate is a terrible handicap. I know that in this chapter I shall seem to some readers to go beyond the limits of reason in the importance which I ascribe to climate, but remember what it does in New York. Remember that a change of only one degree in the mean temperature has an easily measurable effect

upon the deathrate and hence upon human energy. Remember
that the brain is the most sensitive of man's organs and that
climatic changes were apparently the greatest external factor in
controlling its development. Remember, too, that among all the
faculties of the human mind none is so sensitive to external circumstances as is the power of invention. Do we not all know
that an interruption bothers us far more when we are trying to
solve some difficult problem than when we are merely doing a bit
of routine figuring? Is it not notorious that people who are
gifted with the creative impulse, whether in art, music, literature,
or science, are more sensitive than any others to conditions of
health? In rare cases like Darwin, and Stevenson in his later life,
a man succeeds in doing a great work in spite of ill health. Ask
an ordinary scientist, however, as to the effect of a headache when
he is trying to write the report of some complex investigation.
Many a time I have heard my colleagues say that on days when
they feel right they can do five times as much as when something
is wrong with their health. Often such a man throws away what he
has written at such a time, and rewrites when he feels more "fit."

This may seem like a digression from Russia, but it is not.
Having lived for over a year among the Russians, and having
learned to admire both the common people and their great men,
I would be the last to underrate them. Yet many of my Russian
friends have made a remark which my own observation fully bears
out: "We Russians are not like you Anglo-Saxons. We are more
sensitive to external impressions. We lack your power of concentration. That is our greatest trouble. We become filled with
high ideals, or with great plans for remodelling the world. We
begin on them with great enthusiasm, but we do not stick to them.
Fits of depression come over us, and when we are close to a great
achievement we often give up in despair."

Presumably this is in part, at least, a *Slavic* characteristic.
Yet after observing the effect of the weather in New York and
in many other regions, I cannot but think that climate and health

have much to do with it. The Russian climate, as we have seen, varies extremely from season to season. The long cold winters are deadening. The air becomes cold and stays cold. There are indeed changes of temperature, but the *variety* of weather during the winter is not nearly so great as in a place like New York. Thus health is impaired more than in the northeastern United States. The spring and fall, however, are admirable. In summer, on the other hand, although large parts of the country are so far north that they do not become very hot, the monotony of the climate or some other cause raises the deathrate enormously. Whatever may be the reason, the deathrate of Russia in July, according to official figures for a long series of years, is 45 per cent greater than in May and 55 per cent greater than in October. Such extreme and sudden fluctuations in health must have a corresponding mental effect. Moreover, where the health of the community varies so greatly from season to season it also varies much from year to year. Thus in the Russian people we should look for fluctuations between optimism and pessimism similar to those which our own business men experience, but on a much greater scale. That is what we actually find. We see it in daily intercourse with the Russians. It pervades their literature. A good example is Tolstoy's novel, "Resurrection." During his youth the hero is filled with high ambitions. Then he succumbs to sensualism, but is overwhelmed with remorse. Finally he decides on a course of expiation, but carries it out in an inconclusive, half-hearted manner that is most irritating. Finally when the hero leaves the girl whom he has wronged and lets her continue on her way to Siberia, the reader closes the book with the same pitiful and disappointed feeling that we all have when we think of the events in Russia during the second half of the Great War. The Russian revolution after the Japanese War was quite in accord with Russian character—a revolution that promised much but accomplished little. And the Great War furnishes an example of the same proneness to begin a task with great enthusiasm and fail when it is half done. When such a nation is pitted against a nation like the Germans, with steady purposes to which they hang like death, the result is certain. Steady energy always vanquishes a fitful energy which may fail at the critical moment.

There is still another way in which Russia is at a terrible disadvantage compared with Germany. Over 85 per cent of the Russians are either peasants or depend on agriculture in some other way. For six months the rigorous winter shuts them up in their houses. There is almost nothing to do except cut and haul the necessary firewood and take care of the animals. So the peasants sit in the close, stuffy houses day after day and do nothing except talk and dream. Such a life of idleness leads many to sensuality which permanently weakens their powers of real achievement. With many others there is a strong tendency to make great plans during the long, idle winter. But when the spring comes the routine farm work takes every hour of the day, and people who have been idle all winter are not in fit condition to carry out new plans or achieve great improvements. Thus the severe cold of the winter tends to foster in the Russians a tendency toward speculative idealism which bears fruit in words but not in deeds.

On the Italian battle-front the Germans found a more persistent foe than the Russians. In Figure 26 we see that about half of Italy has a climate of the kind marked "very high," while only a small fraction of Russia has such a climate. This does not mean, however, that the climate of all North Italy is as good as that of Germany. Nevertheless, the frequency of storms and the absence of depressingly low temperatures in winter give northern Italy, to about the latitude of Florence, one of the world's admirable climates in spite of the hot summers. Even there, however, the difference between the deathrate of the worst and the best months is two or three times as great as in Germany. When Austria and Italy were pitted against one another, they seemed almost equally matched, which is about what would be expected on the basis of energy.   When Germany threw herself against the Italians in the fall of 1917 the balance was at once changed.   Whatever may be the reason, German energy is more than a match for that of Italy.

In the Great War two nations, France and England, fought Germany to a standstill.   Another, the United States, falls into the same class.   When the war ended, France, England, the United States, and Germany all emerged with unimpaired prestige, so far as prestige depends upon the energy and determination with which they had fought.   Here again I can only point out that this is what would be expected on the basis of climate and energy.   Let us compare the climates of the chief cities of these four countries. Perhaps it is worth while to remind the reader that these are also the four chief cities of the whole world.   Here are the figures as to the mean temperature from month to month.   The smaller figures preceded by plus or minus signs indicate the amounts by which the various months differ from the same month in London.

MONTHLY MEAN TEMPERATURE

	London	Paris	Berlin	New York
January	$38°F$	$37°-1°$	$31°-7°$	$30°-8°$
February	$40°$	$39°-1°$	$33°-7°$	$31°-9°$
March	$42°$	$43°+1°$	$37°-5°$	$38°-4°$
April	$47°$	$51°+4°$	$46°-1°$	$48°+1°$
May	$53°$	$56°+3°$	$55°+2°$	$59°+6°$
June	$60°$	$62°+2°$	$62°+2°$	$67°+5°$
July	$63°$	$65°+2°$	$65°+2°$	$74°+11°$
August	$62°$	$64°+2°$	$63°+1°$	$72°+10°$
September	$57°$	$59°+2°$	$57°±0°$	$67°+10°$
October	$50°$	$51°+1°$	$48°-2°$	$56°+6°$
November	$43°$	$43°±0°$	$38°-5°$	$44°+1°$
December	$40°$	$37°-3°$	$33°-7°$	$34°-6°$
Difference between				
highest and lowest	$25°$	$28°$	$34°$	$44°$

Among these four it is difficult to decide which is the best. As may be seen from the lowest line they present a series in which the contrast between summer and winter becomes progressively greater. So far as mean temperature is concerned, London appears to be the most favored, although its difference from Paris is negligible. In both places the January average is close to the temperature which is best for mental activity (40°), while the July average almost coincides with the optimum for physical activity (64°). The fact that London is damper than Paris probably makes its climate a little the better of the two, for we have seen that in spite of our prepossessions a damp climate is better than a dry one, provided it is not too hot. Berlin is too cold in winter, but of just the right temperature in summer. New York is not only too cold in winter, but too hot in summer. So far as mean temperature and humidity are concerned, it seems probable that the cities are arranged in order of excellence, London being first and New York last.

It is not enough to look only at temperature and humidity. Changes of temperature are equally important. Viewed from this standpoint the order of the four cities is reversed. New York easily stands at the head, while London is least favored. As yet our investigations have not gone far enough to enable us to balance the advantages of the one against the other. If I were obliged to express an opinion in the light of present knowledge I should have to confess that Berlin may have a very slight advantage over any of the others. At any rate there is no denying the fact that Germany is today blessed with as fine a climate as any in the world. How far this accounts for her tireless energy and her ceaseless preparations I dare not attempt to say. That it is an important factor seems almost certain.

Before we discuss this matter further let us see how many people actually live in highly stimulating climates. Here again, we must proceed with great caution, for we are only on the threshold of this subject. The figures that I shall give are based

on a careful weighing of the facts set forth in this book and in
"Civilization and Climate." They must, however, be regarded as
merely preliminary and as in the nature of suggestive estimates.
Here they are:

POPULATION IN REGIONS WHERE THE CLIMATE IS HIGHLY STIMULATING

Our Allies

England and Scotland .	45,000,000
Canada and Australia .	9,000,000
France . . .	30,000,000
Belgium . . .	7,000,000
Italy	16,000,000
United States . .	50,000,000
Total . . .	157,000,000

Teutonic Allies

Germany . . .	72,000,000
Austria . . .	18,000,000
Total . . .	90,000,000

Neutrals

Denmark . . .	8,000,000
Holland . . .	7,000,000
Norway . . .	2,500,000
Sweden . . .	6,000,000
Switzerland . .	3,500,000
Total . . .	27,000,000

Possibly something should be added to Austria, but if that is
done, allowance must be made for Russia on the other side. Since
Belgium was put out of the running at the beginning of the war
because of her small size, and since the United States did not
really get into the war until the summer of 1918, the war for four
years was waged between about ninety or one hundred million of

the world's most energetic people on each side. A part of the Japanese should perhaps be included among the people living where the climate is exceptionally stimulating, but since they took little part in the war we may omit them.

From what has been said thus far it appears that the advantages of a highly energizing climate were almost equally divided during the first four years of the war. Notice, however, that in the table Germany is credited with over seventy million people, while England has only forty-five million and even the United States only fifty million who live in the best kind of climate. Thus while Russia and the United States, and also India and China, have more people than Germany, *no other nation in the world has so many people who live under a highly stimulating climate.* This, I believe, is one of the most important features of the whole situation. Not only are the Germans comparatively homogeneous in race, not only are they united under a single government, but they are all under the stimulus of one of the best climates in the whole world. To that in part, at least, they owe their constant energy. Like the ancient Romans in a similarly stimulating climate, they are capable of the stern self-discipline which held them together in spite of hunger and sorrow. It is as foolish for us to make light of the German virtues as it would be to condone their sins. In enmity born of war we exulted over the breaking down of moral standards, the increase of autocracy, and then the spread of revolution. Yet, if we are open-minded, we cannot deny that the Germans to a remarkable degree showed their devotion to the state. We fondly hoped for a revolution to help fight our battles; we have taken pleasure in deriding the peasants and professors alike as the stupid dupes of autocracy. That is a mistake on our part. They were doubtless the dupes of their own false system of education, but they were thoroughly convinced that their system was right, that man's first duty is to yield his own will and his own pleasure to the upbuilding of the state. This conception may be right or wrong, but at any rate it is terribly formidable to its enemies. It is a sign of great strength of will, and of a power to endure which is the greatest of assets in a struggle that tests a nation's power to the limits. The German devotion to the national cause is like that which made early Rome so formidable. In a mistaken way it is the spirit that animated our revolutionary ancestors in early New England. Although they were ardent individualists, they were ready to sacrifice everything to what they believed to be the public welfare, and they had the will to stick to that determination.

I am not praising the Germans. I am merely trying to point out what seems to be one of the great causes of their power. So far as they direct their course toward right ends the energy and alertness which seem to result from their environment are highly admirable. So far as they pursue wrong ends those same qualities are the world's greatest danger. Because the Germans are so strong and live in such a wonderfully favorable environment, the Allies should strive the more mightily to help Germany to set her house in order. For the moment this is the chief lesson to be learned from a study of climate and health. The world's most favored regions have been divided into two great camps. Both owe much of their strength to the favorable environment. One camp has stood for a policy which is genuinely great in its emphasis on the duty of the individual to sacrifice himself for the good of the state, but which is despicable in other ways. It stifles the individuality which is the root of all progress; it inculcates scorn of all that is not its own; it leads to brutal cruelty, and to a system of public and private morals that would make the world unlivable. The other camp likewise has its faults, but at least it tries to give all men a chance. It does not hold that its own system is infallible, but it does believe that the world will make progress only if we stimulate all men to their best, and encourage each individual and each race to make its contribution to the general welfare along its own chosen lines.

This completes our survey of the course followed thus far by the ship of human progress. We started when man's ancestors were still spineless creatures living in the vast ocean. We have seen that again and again great crises have depended largely upon climatic conditions. When the primitive animals came out upon the land, when they began to crawl in the mud and thus develop the limbs which finally became hands, and when they at last evolved the power of warming their own bodies, the circumstances which brought about the change appear each time to have been largely climatic. Other factors must unquestionably have played most vital parts, but none stands out more clearly than climate. In later days man's brain, the most sensitive of all his organs, made by far its most rapid evolution under the stress of great climatic extremes. The greater the climatic changes, the more rapidly new types were evolved not only among plants and animals, but in the human species. Whatever may be the inner causes of the rise and extinction of new forms of life, there can be no question that these have occurred most rapidly at times when the climate of the world swung rapidly from one extreme to another.

Side by side with this great fact stands another. Today man's body is more sensitive to the temperature and humidity of the air than to any other feature of his environment. This is proved by our daily experiences of discomfort because the air is too hot, too cold, too dry, too stuffy, or too actively in motion. It is also proved by the measured work of thousands of factory operatives and students, who achieve most under certain narrowly defined limits of temperature and humidity. Further and still more conclusive proof is found in the fact that deaths, which all physicians recognize as by far the most sensitive index to the general health of a community, are least frequent when the conditions of the air approach closely to the optimum for physical activity. Moreover, not man alone, but every plant and animal that has yet been carefully tested possesses the same close adaptation to certain distinct conditions of climate. Such an adaptation among all living creatures appears to be the inevitable result of

millions upon millions of years of evolution.   Unless we assume
that man's evolution has been something entirely apart from that
of the rest of the world, we cannot for a moment expect that he
will be free from this intimate dependence upon the air.   He may
mitigate the effects of conditions which depart from the optimum,
but he cannot alter the fact that he is part and parcel of a world
of life in which the condition of the air has been the determining
factor in the rise and extinction of type after type.

Another step in our study of the relation between man and the
air around him is taken when we study history.   We have seen that
in Rome the ups and downs of the ancient Republic and the later
Empire followed the vicissitudes of climate with extraordinary
fidelity.   Here, indeed, we recognize that we are studying a problem so new that there is much more opportunity for a difference of
opinion than in the general conclusions that climatic changes have
been a main factor in evolution and that all forms of life are now
extremely sensitive to the condition of the air around them.   One
of the most interesting phases of the historical studies of the next
generation is bound to be the conflict of opinion as to the effect of
climatic changes upon history.   Yet already the evidence seems
strong enough at least to warrant the careful attention of seekers
after truth.

In this final summary we are arranging our main points in the
approximate order of their probability.   Many people who will
accept the idea that the history of Greece, Rome, and Babylonia
was greatly influenced by climatic conditions will scornfully reject
the idea that the trend of modern business is subject to any such
control.   Their attitude is not surprising.   The idea that climate
through its effect upon health exerts a controlling effect
upon mental activity, upon drunkenness, upon the ebb and flow of
business and upon the influx of immigrants ought not to be accepted lightly.   On the contrary, it ought to be weighed and tested
from every possible angle.   It cannot be held as proved until it has
been demonstrated in scores of different ways.   Yet here, too, the

evidence is already strong enough to cause us to ponder most thoughtfully. We dare not do otherwise, for if this conclusion is true it will alter our present methods in a hundred different ways. Somehow we must explain the fact that statistics as to the ebb and flow of some of the greatest activities in the United States and Germany appear to show an intimate relation to the ebb and flow of health and of weather.

To some minds it will seem difficult to believe that the strength of Germany on the one hand and of her enemies on the other is due in considerable measure to the stimulus of their climates. Oddly enough, people are willing to believe that tropical countries are backward because of their bad climate, while those same people balk at the idea that the strength of their own countries owes much to the good health and constant vigor which arise from good climates. They seem to think that such a belief overlooks the importance of racial character and of education and religion. That is by no means the case. Racial characteristics, on the one hand, and the many influences which we may call training on the other, determine the direction in which a country's energies shall be expended. Climate, on the contrary, acting not only on the present generation, but on an infinite series of past generations, determines how great those energies shall be. Even here its effects are modified by food, by training, by ideals, and in many other ways. Nevertheless, a broad survey of civilization, both today and in the past, makes it appear that along this line also the effect of climate deserves most careful study. Could Germany, for example, have defied the world four years or even four months if she had been located in equatorial Africa? That is the kind of question that we must answer once and for all. If we decide that the progress of a nation depends largely upon the health and energy of its individuals and thus upon climate, the responsibility of the more favored races is correspondingly increased. If we admit that Germany shares this tremendous energy which arises from a favorable physical environment, it becomes more than ever important that by fair treatment we should win her to a spirit of idealism, a spirit which many of her sons showed most clearly in the generations before the Great War. Bad training, indeed, led her astray, but the power of Germany for good is as great today as ever. On other nations quite as much as upon Germany lies the responsibility for seeing that every strong nation uses its strength for the general good and not for its own selfish advancement.

Finally, we come to the part of this book which is sure to be most fiercely assailed. Today the swing of evolutionary thought is all toward the side of heredity. Therefore scores of biologists will feel that in placing so much emphasis upon the effect of environment I have committed a cardinal sin. They will say with justice that there is far more proof of the importance of heredity in causing stability from generation to generation than of the importance of environment in causing mutations. Undoubtedly the evidence as to the cause of mutations is still slight. That is inevitable when a subject first comes into the realm of scientific investigation. On the basis of such scattered facts as are yet available we have framed the hypothesis that the commonest cause of mutations and thus of the origin of species is germinal changes due to the action of extremes of heat and cold upon the organism in its early stages of growth. If such an hypothesis is accepted, it will doubtless demand a readjustment of many old ideas, but there is nothing about it at all inconsistent with the strongest possible belief in the importance of heredity. The scales have swung too far in one direction because one side has been heavily weighted with some of the most important and interesting facts that have ever been discovered. Now we must find facts of other kinds and throw them into the scales. It happens that the facts set forth in this book fall into the side of the scale marked environment. By and by we shall have more facts. As we dig them out we must carefully inspect them to see whether they belong in one scale or the other. It is easy to mistake the scale in which a given fact should fall, and sometimes we may have done so in this book. Yet even so there remain many facts which indicate that extremes of heat and cold, dryness and moisture, are somehow associated with pronounced changes in the form and function of the organs of the body. That single fact, if it be a fact, is more important than all else that we have here discussed. Part of its importance lies in that it opens up the possibility that some day mankind may learn not only how to select the best variations in a given plant or animal, but how to cause a great number of widely diverse mutations from among which he may select. In all this the human race is merely one among the species of animals. For aught we know, his migrations and the many new and artificial conditions to which he subjects himself may be altering some of his most deep-seated qualities. We spend millions in the attempt to improve plants and animals. Is it not time that we learned how the highest of all animals is being changed and how his future evolution may be directed along the right path?

APPENDIX A

ELIMINATION OF THE SECULAR TREND

THROUGHOUT this book, except where otherwise noted, the secular trend has been eliminated from all diagrams showing the course of events for a series of years. The secular trend is the progressive change arising from causes which act with comparative regularity throughout long periods. Thus the secular trend of the production of pig iron in the United States is upward, for under normal conditions the production increases from year to year. On the other hand, the trend of the deathrate is downward because of the improvement in medical science. Nevertheless, the total number of deaths in a given city may trend upward because of growth in population.

The purpose of eliminating the secular trend is to bring into true proportions the irregular or cyclical variations, which trend first one way and then the other without apparent system. The method of elimination is illustrated in Figure 27. The lower of the three irregular lines represents the variations in bank clearings at New York for a period of over forty years. Note the maxima in 1873 and 1906, for example. Our problem is to determine their relative importance. To do this we divide our forty years into periods of five or ten years or other convenient length, and plot the average clearings for each period. With the points thus obtained as guides we draw a smooth curve such as the solid line in the lower part of Figure 27. This represents the normal course of bank clearings, or the course that clearings would have followed if there had been no disturbing influences such as bad crops, panics, and the like. The steadily increasing upward tendency of the secular trend is obvious.

Having obtained the normal for each year, it is easy to eliminate the secular trend by calling each year's normal 100, and finding the

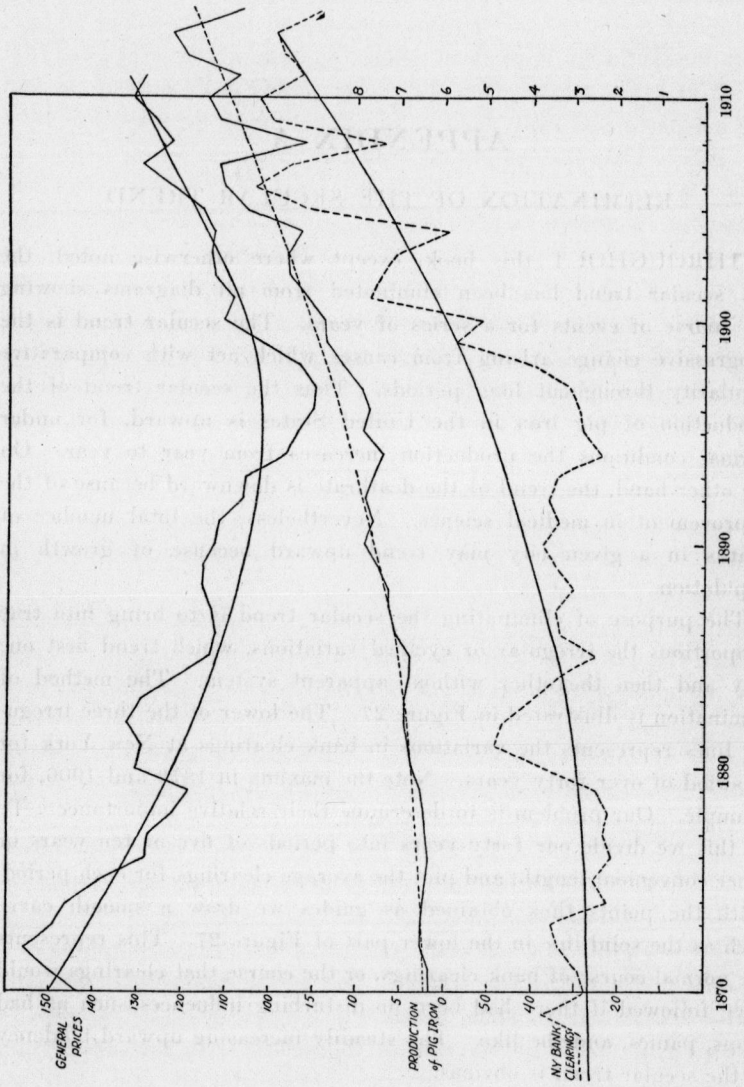

GENERAL PRICES

PRODUCTION of PIG IRON

NY BANK CLEARINGS

150 140 130 120 110 100

15

10

5

0

50

40

20

1870 1880 1890 1900 1910

8 7 6 5 4 3 2 1

FIGURE 27. Elimination of the Secular Trend

percentage by which the actual clearings depart from it. Thus the
bank clearings in 1873 were approximately 30 per cent above normal,
while those of 1906 were about 35 per cent above the normal for that
year. In other words, when the secular trend is eliminated we find
that a departure of about eight million dollars from the normal in 1873
was only a little less important than one of twenty-seven million in
1906. When the percentages for each year have thus been computed,
a curve can be drawn showing the cyclical variations without the secular trend. This is what has been done in this book.

The normal curves showing the secular trend may be convex, straight
or concave. In Figure 27 the line for bank clearings is decidedly concave, and that for pig iron is nearly straight, but both rise rapidly on
the right, since business in the United States increases at a constantly
accelerating pace. The curve for prices, on the other hand, is quite
different from the others. On the left it descends rapidly, for from
1870 to 1890 prices fell because of improvements in manufacturing
processes, transportation facilities, etc. In the nineties, however, the
excessive production of gold began to lead to inflation of prices, so
that the later part of the curve rises.

In plotting the normal curves mathematical accuracy is not possible.
Sudden changes in the direction of the smoothed lines must be avoided,
and too much weight must not be given to temporary fluctuations.
Thus personal judgment must play some part. When the work is
checked by averages, however, this is reduced to small proportions.
Moreover, a considerable deviation from the absolute position of the
true normal does not affect our conclusions. Suppose that the position
of the normal is too low by 5 per cent, which would be a large error.
Three successive years which actually departed from the normal by
30 per cent, 10 per cent, and —10 per cent would appear to depart
by 36.8 per cent, 15.8 per cent, and —5.3 per cent. The difference
between the two extremes, however, that is, the intensity of this particular fluctuation, would be nearly the same, namely 40 per cent in
the first case, and 42.1 per cent in the second. On the other hand,
suppose that the secular trend were not eliminated, and that two
exactly similar series of years occurred thirty years apart so that the
normal in the second case was twice as great as in the first. The

difference between the extremes would appear to be a hundred per cent greater in one case than in the other. Since the changes in the normal during the period from 1870 to 1910 amount to 50 per cent even in the case of general prices and to several hundred per cent in most cases, it is evident that the elimination of the secular trend adds greatly to the accuracy of our judgment as to the importance and character of successive cyclical fluctuations, and that is its sole purpose.

APPENDIX B

CONSTRUCTION OF CLIMOGRAPHS

IN the preparation of the climographs which illustrate this book the first step was to select a series of cities or districts so located as to cover all parts of the area to be investigated. The number of such cities was fourteen in France, fourteen in Italy, fifty-two in the United States, and also Tokio in Japan. Then the deaths at each place during the years 1899 to 1915, or for as much of that period as possible, were tabulated by months for each year. Allowance was made for the fact that some months are shorter than others. This was done by multiplying the figures for short months by $^{31}\!/_{28}$, $^{31}\!/_{29}$, or $^{31}\!/_{30}$ as the case might be. Thus figures were obtained representing the actual monthly *degree* of mortality.

The second step was to find how much this actual mortality differs from the normal mortality for the year in question. The normal may increase because of the natural growth in population. It may also decrease because of improved medical and sanitary efficiency. The method of obtaining the normal is illustrated in Figures 28 and 29, where Chicago serves as an example. In both figures the broken dotted line shows the actual number of deaths from year to year, or from month to month. The straight dotted lines show the normal number, that is, the number that would have occurred had there been no irregularities due to epidemics, weather, and so forth. In most of the cases employed in the preparation of climographs in this book the normal is represented by a straight line. The exact direction of the line is found by dividing the years into an earlier and later half and getting the average for each half. The two averages are plotted in their proper places and then connected by a straight line. In some cases, however, the normal forms a curve instead of a straight line, and must be plotted with more reliance upon the judgment of the investigator as has been explained in Appendix A.

After the normals had been obtained, the third step was to find the percentage by which the actual mortality exceeds or falls short of the normal. For example, in April, 1914, the actual number of deaths in Chicago was 3,298. Since April has only thirty days this number needs to be corrected to 3,408 so as to show how many would have occurred if there had been thirty-one days. The normal mortality for 1914, as shown by the straight line in Figure 29, is 2,998. If we reckon this as 100 per cent, the true mortality was 113.8 per cent.

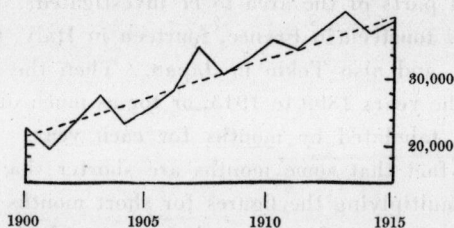

FIGURE 28.   Annual Deaths in Chicago,
1900-1915

When the true mortality for each month at each place had thus been reduced to percentages of the normal the fourth step was to tabulate the percentages according to the temperature and humidity of the months in which they occurred. To take an actual example, among the twenty-eight cities of France and Italy a month having a mean temperature of 19°C and a mean humidity of from 61 per cent to 65 per cent occurred ten times. The places where these conditions occurred are shown in column A of the following table. Column B shows the mortality in percentages, and C the weight to be assigned to each place according to the number of inhabitants. The weighted average of column B, 91.4 per cent, indicates the mean mortality rate in French and Italian cities when the temperature averages 19°C and the humidity 61 per cent to 65 per cent. The average may equally well be expressed as a departure of −8.6 per cent (100 per cent—91.4 per cent) from the normal.

A Place	B Mortality in Percentages	C Weight
France		
Claremont	91.9	9
Paris	95.6	60
Lyons (first year)	85.8	13
Lyons (second year)	82.1	13
Marseilles	97.4	14
Perpignan (first year)	73.1	4
Perpignan (second year)	80.3	4
Perpignan (third year)	103.8	4
Italy		
Milan	90.2	30
Brescia	89.0	11
Average	91.4	

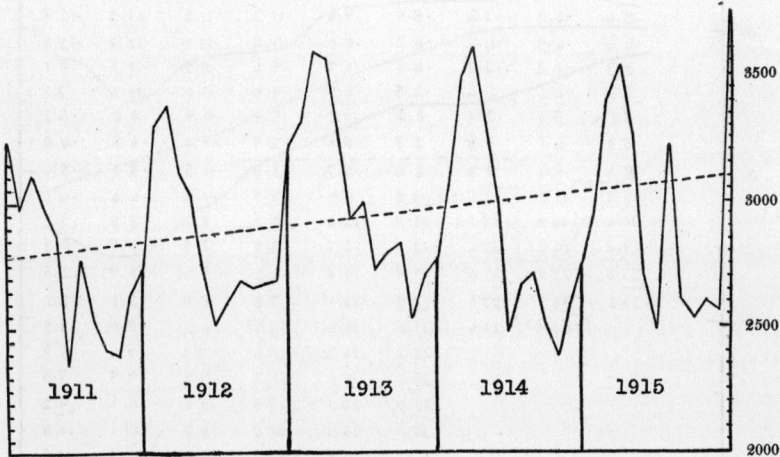

FIGURE 29.   Monthly Deaths in Chicago, 1911 to 1915

When the mean mortality rates had thus been computed for all the combinations of temperature and humidity that occur in a given region, the departures of these rates from the normal mortality were plotted in diagrams like Figure 30.   In order to avoid irregularities, however, the departures in Figure 30 and in all the similar diagrams have been smoothed by averaging the departure for any given position on the

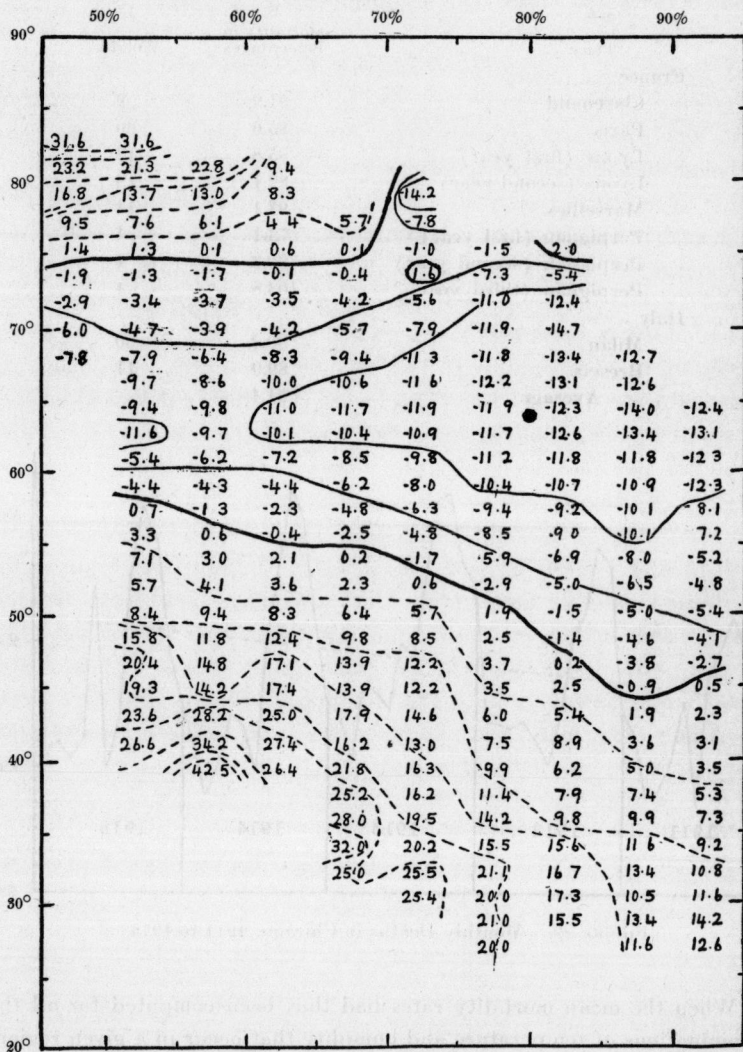

FIGURE 30.   Unsmoothed Climograph of France and Italy, 1899-1913, 3,700,000 Deaths

diagram with the eight adjacent departures. In every case the departures receive a weight in proportion to the number of people they represent. Figure 30 represents the final tabulation of about 3,700,000 deaths in France and Italy. For convenience in comparing with the American diagrams the Fahrenheit scale has been used, although the original computations were on the Centigrade scale.

Let us interpret Figure 30. We may begin by inquiring what degree of mortality prevailed during months when the mean temperature for day and night together was 75°F and the mean humidity 75 to 80 per cent. To find this we note at the top of the diagram the point where the humidity is between 75 and 80 per cent. Then we go downward vertically to a temperature of 75°, as indicated on the left. There we come upon the figure —1.5. This means that during the small number of months having this particular temperature and humidity the deaths were 1.5 per cent less than the normal. During the much larger number of months having the same humidity, but somewhat lower temperatures the mortality rate falls to —7.3, —11.0, and finally to —12.2 at a mean temperature of 66°. At lower temperatures the mortality increases once more, for the minus departures become smaller and smaller until at a temperature of about 51° the deathrate at this particular humidity is the same as the normal. Then at still lower temperatures we have plus departures showing that the number of deaths was more than normal when the weather became cool. Finally, when the mean temperature fell below freezing the deaths were more than 20 per cent above the normal. In similar fashion look at the deaths at a temperature of 48°. Beginning on the right of Figure 30 we see that when the mean humidity averaged over 90 per cent, the deaths were 4.1 per cent less than the normal. At slightly lower humidities conditions were still more favorable, for the mortality was —4.6 per cent. Farther to the left, however, conditions become less and less favorable. At a humidity of 80 per cent the mortality is normal, and then increases until in very dry months with a humidity of 50 to 55 per cent it is +15.8 per cent.

In order to bring out the salient features of Figure 30 lines have been drawn at intervals of 5 per cent. The heaviest or zero lines indicate the conditions at which the normal number of deaths occur.

One such line begins on the left at a temperature of about 74° and extends nearly straight to the right with a bend upward at the end. Just above it comes a dotted line. This means that although at 74° the mortality rate was normal, at 76° it had increased to 5 per cent more than the normal. The next dotted line shows a mortality rate of 10 per cent and so on. The dotted lines in this and in other diagrams indicate more than the normal number of deaths, while the solid lines indicate less. Such a diagram is called a "climograph." The lines may be called "iso-practs" or "lines of equal effect," from the Greek word "isos" meaning "equal" and "practicos" meaning "effective." They are analogous to the "iso-bars" or lines of "equal pressure" on a weather map. The isopracts divide the climograph into zones. Each zone indicates the degree of health to be expected among people living under its particular climatic conditions.

In the central portion of Figure 30 the isopractic lines are quite regular, for that part represents the temperatures and humidities that generally prevail. On the borders of the diagram especially at the top and bottom the isopracts become irregular because the number of months having such extreme conditions is small. In order to do away with the irregularity and the resulting confusion, the diagrams in the body of the text have been simplified. That is, the isopracts have been smoothed, the figures for departures have been omitted, and the zones between the isopracts have been shaded. The darkest shading indicates that the mortality is more than 10 per cent *below* the normal; the next shading indicates a mortality ranging from normal to —10 per cent, and so on. The degree to which the diagrams in the text have been smoothed may be judged by comparing Figures 8 A, 12 A, and 14 A with the corresponding diagrams numbered 8 B, 12 B, and 14 B.*

* The term "climograph" was introduced by Dr. Griffith Taylor in his interesting paper on "The Control of Settlement by Humidity and Temperature." (Commonwealth Bureau of Meteorology, Bulletin No. 14, Melbourne, 1916.) His climograph differs somewhat from the form here shown. (1) He uses wet bulb temperature instead of the ordinary dry bulb temperature. This gives double weight to humidity, and is of doubtful expediency. (2) He does not use isopracts. Instead of this he plots the points indicating the mean wet bulb temperature and the mean relative humidity for each month.

The twelve points thus fixed are connected by lines, thus forming a closed figure. In order to provide some standard of reference by which to judge whether the graph of a given place is favorable, Taylor adds to each of his climographs a standard graph based on twelve large cities in regions where the white man prospers. This is an admirable method of bringing out the salient characteristics of a climate.

The form of climograph used in the present paper was suggested by Mr. W. D. Pierce in a valuable paper on "A New Interpretation of the Relationships of Temperature and Humidity to Insect Development" (*Journal of Agricultural Research,* vol. 65, 1916, pp. 1183-1191), but it is modified by some features taken from Taylor's method. Pierce's climograph pertains to the cotton-boll weevil. It is based on the number of days required for development of that insect under different conditions of temperature and humidity. Although Pierce does not use the term "isopract," his terminology suggests it.

The climographs of both Taylor and Pierce are reproduced and described in *The Geographical Review,* vol. IV, November, 1917, pp. 402 and 403.

SUPPLEMENTARY NOTE

After the final proofs of this book had gone back to the printer the author learned that in *The Cairo Scientific Journal,* No. 50, vol. IV, November, 1910, Dr. John Ball published an article entitled "Climatological Diagrams." In this he used the same form of climograph that Taylor later developed more fully in Australia, except that Ball used dry bulb temperatures where Taylor used wet bulb temperatures. Hence, while Taylor apparently introduced the term "climograph" in this connection and was the first to apply the method on a large scale, the method itself should be ascribed to Ball.

APPENDIX C

EXTINCTION OF MAMMALS DURING THE GLACIAL PERIOD

THE accompanying table shows the basis of Figure 22. The first column shows the names of the geological periods from the beginning of Tertiary times down to the present. The next three show the length of the periods according to three diverse estimates. Sollas' estimate represents the wholly inadmissible idea that the various periods were of approximately equal duration. Matthews' estimate is based on fossil evidence supplemented by the thickness and character of the strata. Barrell has utilized these same data and also certain newly discovered facts as to the rate at which uranium and thorium lose their radioactivity and degenerate into a series of other metals ending in lead. The views of all three authors, together with references, are given in the paper by Barrell listed in Appendix D. Barrell's time-scale seems to the present writer the best yet available, but for our present purpose it makes no difference whether we use the figures of Matthew or Barrell.

In the columns headed "North American Genera" and "European Genera," the first column in each case shows the total number of genera of mammals listed by Osborn in his "Age of Mammals." The next shows the number which became extinct, and the third gives the percentage of extinction. Then come three columns showing the average percentage extinguished during one hundred thousand years according to each time-scale. According to both Matthew and Barrell the rate of extinction increased enormously during the Pleistocene or Glacial Period. This is illustrated graphically in Figure 22, where the solid line shows the rate of extinction according to Barrell, and the dotted line according to Matthew. In interpreting Matthew's figures the percentages at the right must be multipled by ten, while the names of the periods as given at the bottom must be crowded into the small horizontal distance occupied by the dotted curve. Incidentally the effect of a knowledge of radioactivity upon our conceptions of geological time is evident from the fact that according to Sollas and most of the earlier geologists our entire diagram would have to be crowded into the space occupied by the Upper Pliocene (U) and the Pleistocene (Pl) according to Barrell.

In studying Figure 7 the thoughtful reader may at once inquire whether the sudden apparent increase in the rate of extinction during the Glacial Period may not be due merely to the scantiness of our knowledge of earlier times. The reverse is actually the case. The less we know of the fauna of an early period the more probably its component animals will appear to have become extinct. In general the older faunas are less fully known than the later ones. This is evident from the following table which shows the approximate number of mammalian genera known in all parts of the world during each period since the beginning of the Tertiary:

Basal Eocene	.	.	47	Lower Miocene	.	.	67
Lower Eocene	.	.	47	Middle Miocene	.	.	84
Middle Eocene	.	.	67	Upper Miocene	.	.	148
Upper Eocene	.	.	85	Lower Pliocene	.	.	117
Lower Oligocene	.	.	84	Middle Pliocene	.	.	105
Middle Oligocene	.	.	64	Upper Pliocene	.	.	98
Upper Oligocene	.	.	83	Pleistocene	.	.	181

At the beginning of the Eocene the number of genera may not have been as great as in the Pleistocene, but surely the difference was nothing like so great as is indicated by the figures 47 and 181 in Table II. Hence the chances of finding new forms from the basal Eocene, for example, are much greater than from the Pleistocene. The chances are, however, that among these new forms the percentage that are not found in the succeeding period and hence are considered to have been extinguished in the earlier period will be the same as among the forms already known. On the other hand, there is a very large chance that among the many unknown forms of the Lower Eocene, for example, there will some day come to light a considerable number that have as yet been found only in the basal Eocene and are now wrongly

EXTINCTION OF MAMMALIAN GENERA DURING TERTIARY AND PLEISTOCENE TIMES

Period	Length of Period in Thousands of Years per			North American Genera			Rate of Extinction per Hundred Thousand Years in Percentages per			European Genera			Rate of Extinction per Hundred Thousand Years in Percentages per			Average Rate of Extinction in Americas and Europe per	
	Sollas 1909	Matthew 1914	Barrell 1918	Total	Extinguished	Per Cent Extinguished	Sollas	Matthew	Barrell	Total	Extinguished	Per Cent Extinguished	Sollas	Matthew	Barrell	Matthew	Barrell
Basal Eocene	500	900	5000	31	30	97%	19.4%	10.8%	1.94%	3	3	100%	20.0%	11.1%	2.00%	11.0%	1.97%
Lower Eocene	500	900	5000	39	25	64	12.8	7.1	1.28	11	11	100	20.0	11.1	2.00	9.1	1.64
Middle Eocene	500	900	5000	55	43	78	15.6	8.7	1.56	13	9	69	13.8	7.7	1.38	8.2	1.47
Upper Eocene	500	800	5000	33	32	97	19.4	12.1	1.94	42	21	50	10.0	6.3	1.00	9.2	1.47
Lower Oligocene	400	700	6000	37	14	38	9.5	5.4	0.63	44	30	68	16.5	9.7	1.13	7.6	0.88
Middle Oligocene	400	700	5000	35	18	51	12.8	7.3	1.02	33	10	30	7.5	4.3	0.60	5.8	0.81
Upper Oligocene	400	600	5000	49	37	76	19.0	12.7	1.52	37	15	41	10.3	6.8	0.82	9.8	1.17
Lower Miocene	500	1000	4000	24	16	67	13.4	6.7	1.62	37	14	38	7.6	3.8	0.95	5.3	1.30
Middle Miocene	500	1000	4000	37	10	27	5.4	2.7	0.68	52	22	42	8.4	4.2	1.05	3.5	0.87
Upper Miocene	400	1000	4000	46	12	26	6.5	2.6	0.65	56	23	41	10.3	4.1	1.03	3.4	0.84
Lower Pliocene	500	400	2000	39	23	59	11.8	14.8	2.95	47	16	34	6.8	8.5	1.70	11.7	2.33
Middle Pliocene	400	300	2000	19	4	21	5.3	7.0	1.05	41	6	14	3.5	4.7	0.70	5.9	0.88
Upper Pliocene	400	300	2000	20	4	20	5.0	6.7	1.00	41	5	12	3.0	4.0	0.60	5.4	0.80
Pleistocene	400	100	1000	67	23	34	8.5	34.0	3.40	58	18	33	8.3	33.0	3.30	33.5	3.35

reckoned as extinguished during that period.   Since practically all
living forms are known, however, there is almost no chance that any
of the Pleistocene forms now reckoned as extinct will be transferred
to the opposite category.   Hence while the percentage of apparently
extinct forms will steadily decrease in earlier periods, it will change
but slightly in the Pleistocene.   Accordingly, as knowledge increases,
the earlier, or left-hand portions of Figure 22 will fall steadily lower,
the greatest fall being in the earlier periods.   Thus it seems safe to
say that the rate of extinction of mammals during the last Glacial
Period was fully four times as rapid as the average during the preceding Tertiary Era.

APPENDIX D

REFERENCES

Abbott, C. F.: Various publications of the Smithsonian Institution.

Affleck, G. B.: The Ventilation of Gymnasia: A Preliminary Report: American Physical Educational Review, vol. XVII, 1912, pp. 455-463.

Ammon, Otto: Zur Anthropologie der Badener. Jena, 1899.

Antevs, Ernst: Die Jahresringe der Holzgewächse und die Bedeutung derselben als klimatischer Indicator, Progressus Rei Botanicae. Jena, 1917.

Aschaffenberg, Gustav: Crime and its Repression. Boston, 1913.

Babson, Roger W.: Barometer Letter and Babson's Composite Plots. Business Barometers used in the Accumulation of Money, Wellesley Hills, 1913.

Barrell, Joseph: Rhythms and the Measurements of Geologic Time. Bull'n Geol. Soc. Am., vol. 28, 1917.

Beveridge, W. H.: Unemployment, a Problem of Industry, Lon., 1909.

Boas, Franz: Changes in Bodily Form of Descendants of Immigrants. Report of the U. S. Immigration Commission, vol. 38, Wash., 1911.

Boas, Franz, and Helene M.: Head-forms of the Italians as influenced by Heredity and Environment. Am. Anthropol., vol. 15, 1913, pp. 163-188.

Bonger, Wm. A.: Criminality and Economic Conditions, Boston, 1916.

Cattell, J. McK.: Articles on men of Science in Popular Science Monthly, and in Science.

Chamberlin, T. C., and Salisbury, R. D.: Textbook of Geology. New York.

Chicago: Annual Reports of the Department of Health.

Chicago: Report of Chicago Commission on Ventilation, 1914.

Clark, A. H.: A Study of Asymmetry, as developed in the Genera and Families of Recent Crinoids, American Naturalist, vol. XLIX, 1915, pp. 521-546.

Cocks, Erhard H.: Experimental Studies of the Effect of Various Atmospheric Conditions upon the Upper Respiratory Tract. American Laryngological, Rhinological and Otological Society, 1916.

Colton, H. S.: The Geography of certain Ruins near the San Francisco Mountains, Arizona. Bulletin of the Geographical Society of Philadelphia, vol. 16, 1918, pp. 37-60.

Commons, John R.: Races and Immigrants in America. New York, 1908.

Connecticut: Annual Reports of the Department of Health.

Darwin, Chas.: Origin of Species.

Eliot, Sir Charles: Turkey in Europe. Lon., New Edition, 1908.

Ewing: Biol. Bulletin, vol. XXXI, 1916, pp. 63-112.

Fairchild, H. P.: Immigration and Crises. Am. Econ. Rev., vol. 1, 1911, pp. 753-765.

Ferrero, G.: History of the Rise and Greatness of the Roman Empire.

Fishberg, Maurice: Material for the Physical Anthropology of the Eastern European Jews. Memoir Am. Anthr. and Ethnol. Soc., vol. 1, 1905, pp. 1-146.

Fisher, Irving, and Fisk, E. L.: How to Live. New York, 1917.

Gale, H. S.: Notes on the Quaternary Lakes of the Great Basin. Bulletin No. 540, U. S. Geological Survey, 1914.

Gibbon, Edward: Decline and Fall of the Roman Empire. Ed. by J. B. Bury. New York, 1906-1907.

Greenberg, D.: On the Relation of Pneumonia to Meteorological Conditions MS.

Helland-Hansen, B., and Nansen, Fritzjof: Temperaturschwankungen des Nord-Atlantischen Ozeans und in der Atmosphäre. Christiania, 1917.

Hoge, Mildred A.: The Influence of Temperature on the Development of a Mendelian Character. Jour. Exp. Zoöl., vol. 18, 1915, pp. 41-298.

Huntington, Ellsworth: The Pulse of Asia. Boston, 1907.

Physical Environment as a Factor in the Present Condition of Turkey. Jour. Race Development, vol. 1, 1910, pp. 460-481.

Palestine and its Transformation. Boston, 1911.

The Climatic Factor: as illustrated in Arid America. Wash., 1914.

The Solar Hypothesis of Climatic Changes. Bull'n Geol. Soc. Am., vol. 25, 1914, pp. 477-590.

Civilization and Climate. New Haven, 1915.

A Neglected Factor in Race Development. Jour. Race Development, vol. 6, 1915, pp. 167-185.

Solar Disturbances and Terrestrial Weather. Monthly Weather Rev., vol. 46, 1918, March, April, and July.

Climatic Changes and Agricultural Decline as Factors in the Fall of Rome. Quarterly Journal of Economics, vol. 31, 1917, pp. 173-208.

Immigration Commissioner: Annual Reports of the Commissioner of Immigration, Wash.

Johnson, G. A.: The Typhoid Toll. Jour. Am. Water Works Ass'n, vol. 3, No. 2, June, 1916, pp. 249-326 and 791-868.

Jones, W. H. S.: Malaria: a Neglected Factor in the History of Greece and Rome, 1907.

Kammerer: Abstracts by Lull, Thompson, etc.

Knapp, M. C.: International Y. M. C. A. College, Springfield, Mass., Thesis.

Köppen, A.: Luftemperaturen, Sonnenflecke und Vulcanausbrüche; Meteorologische Zeitschrift.

Lehmann and Pedersen: Das Wetter und Unsere Arbeit. Archiv. ges, Psychol., Leipzig, vol. 10, 1907.

Liebig, Justus von: Die Chemie in ihrer Anwendung auf Agricultur und Physiologie. 9 te auflage, 1876.

Livi, R.: Antropometria Militare. Rome, 1896.

Loeb, Jacques: Studies in General Physiologie. Chicago, 1905.

Lull, R. S.: The Evolution of Life and of Worlds. New Haven, 1918.

Organic Evolution. New York, 1915.

MacDougal, D. T.: Annual reports and other publications of the Carnegie Institution of Washington.

Mason, Wm. P.: Water Supply (Considered principally from a Sanitary Standpoint). New York, 1916.

Massachusetts: Annual Reports of the Department of Health.

Moore, H. L.: Economic Cycles: Their Law and Cause. New York, 1914.

Morgan, T. H.: A Critique of the Theory of Evolution. Princeton, 1916.

Muir, Ramsay: Expansion of Europe: The Culmination of Modern Europe. Boston, 1917.

New York City: Annual Reports of the Department of Health.

New York Ventilation Commission: Preliminary Report. (Also several articles referred to under other names.)

Norlind, Arnold: Einige Bemerkungen über das Klima der historischen Zeit nebst einem Verzeichnis mittelalterlicher Witterungs erscheinungen. 53 pp. Lunds Univ. Arsskrift, N. F., vol. 10, 1914.

Osborn, H. F.: The Age of Mammals in Europe, Asia, and North America. New York, 1910.

The Men of the Old Stone Age. New York, 1915.

Palmer, Geo. T.: Are School Rooms Drier than Deserts? Proc. Am. Soc. of Heating and Ventilating Engineers, 1917.

Penck, A.: Die Alpen in Eiszeitalter. Leipzig, 1909.

Pettersson, O.: Climatic Variations of Historic and Pre-historic Times. Stockholm.

Plough, H. H.: The Effect of Temperature on Crossing-over in Drosophila. Jour. Exp. Zoöl., vol. 24, 1917, pp. 148-209.

Provost Marshal General: Report to the Secretary of War on the First Draft under the Selective Service Act, 1917. Wash., 1918.

Radosavljevich, Paul R.: Professor Boas' New Theory of the Form of the Head: A Critical Contribution to School Anthropology. Am. Anthropologist. N. S., vol. 13, 1911, pp. 394-436.

Study of the American and European Child. Proc. 2d Pan-American Scientific Congress. Section I. Anthropology, Wash., 1917, pp. 124-125.

Richards, Ellen: The Cost of Living. New York, 1905.

Ripley, Wm. Z.: The Races of Europe: A Sociological Study. New York, 1899.

Robertson, Dennis H.: A Study of Industrial Fluctuations. Lon., 1916.

Robinson, H. H.: Unpublished Charts of Prices on the New York Stock Market.

Rogers, J. E. Thorwald: History of Agriculture and Prices. Oxford, 1866 ff. 7 vols.

The Economic Interpretation of History. New York, 1889.

Ross, A. L.: The Old World in the New.

Schuchert, Chas., and Pirrson, L. V.: Textbook of Geology, New York.

Schuchert, Chas.: Geological Climates (In The Climatic Factor, Wash., 1914).

Sergi, G.: The Pretended Change in the Physical Forms of Descendants of Immigrants in America. (Reprint from Revista Italiana de Sociologia. Jan. and Feb., 1912.)

Simkhovitch, V. G.: Rome's Fall Reconsidered. Pol. Sci. Quart., June, 1916.

Standfuss, Maximilian: Beobachtungen an den schles. arten des genus *Psyche*. Namslau, 1879.

Stecher, Lorle Ida: The Effect of Humidity on Nervousness and General Efficiency. Columbia University Contributions to Philosophy and Psychology, vol. 25, 1916.

Sumner, Francis B.: Some Studies of Environmental Influence, Heredity, Correlation and Growth in the White Mouse. Jour. Exp. Zoöl., vol. 18, 1915, pp. 325-432.

Terman, Lewis M.: The Hygiene of the School Child. Boston, 1914.

Thompson, J. Arthur: The Wonder of Life. New York, 1914.

Tower, Wm. L.: Reports in Year Books of the Carnegie Institution of Washington.

Recent Advances and the Present State of Knowledge concerning the Modification of the Germinal Constitution of Organisms by Experimental Processes. (In Heredity and Eugenics, by Castle, Coulter, Davenport, East, and Tower. Chicago, 1912.)

Tyler, W. F.: The Psycho-Physical Aspect of Climate with a Theory Concerning Intensities of Sensation. Jour. Trop. Medicine. Apr. 1907.

Wall Street Journal.

Whipple, Geo. C.: Value of Pure Water. New York, 1907.

Typhoid Fever: Its Causation, Transmission, and Prevention. New York, 1908.

Winslow, Chas. E. A.: The Katathermometer as a Measure of the Effect of Atmospheric Conditions upon Bodily Comfort. Science, N. S., vol. 43, 1916, pp. 716-719.

Woodruff, L. L.: The Temperature Coefficient of the Rate of Reproduction of Paramœcia Aurelia. Am. Jour. Physiol., vol. 29, 1911, pp. 147-155.

Rhythms and Endomixis in various Races of Paramœcium. Biol. Bulletin, vol. 33, 1917, pp. 51-56.

APPENDIX E

PROPER AIR IN HOUSES

THE facts presented in this book make it clear that the quality of the air in our houses is even more important than is generally realized. Little has been said, however, about how different kinds of air *feel,* nor about methods of obtaining the right kind of air. Hence this appendix discusses the effect of different kinds of air upon our feelings, while Appendix F gives certain simple directions which will enable the householder to have the right temperature and humidity in his house with almost no outlay for equipment and with much greater comfort.

In order to realize the effect of moisture upon our feelings, step into a greenhouse. Even in the cooler rooms where pansies, pinks, and roses are growing, the air seems almost too warm, and has a fresh, springlike quality. You could sit there comfortably all day in summer clothing. Yet the thermometer stands at only 60° or at most 65°. In a dwelling-house in winter such a temperature would make everyone shiver. In the fall, however, dwelling-houses frequently have this temperature and people feel quite comfortable. It is moisture that makes the difference. The so-called "sensible" temperature, that is, the effect of the air upon our senses is very different from the actual temperature as measured by the ordinary thermometer. We see this illustrated again and again in summer. On a damp day a temperature of 90° often causes sunstroke. Yet in our dry western deserts the same temperature does not feel particularly uncomfortable. The evaporation there keeps people so cool that they can work actively in the sun.

One way of testing the relation between humidity and sensible temperature is to watch the thermometer during the spring and fall.

In September and October, or again in April and May, the thermometer at breakfast time frequently stands at about 60° not only out of doors, but in the house. Yet we feel comfortable without a fire.

Another test would be possible on a rainy day when the thermometer outside stands at about 55°. Let the inside temperature fall to 64°. Without telling the family what you have done ask them whether the house is too warm or too cool. Ten to one they will say it is all right. Yet if the outside temperature were 10° and the inside temperature 64°, they would all be shivering and urging you to open the draft of the furnace. Even if the outside temperature were only 30° they would still feel cool with the thermometer at 64° inside. It is all a matter of moisture, and thus of sensible temperature as opposed to actual temperature.

On a rainy day such as you have chosen for your experiment, the outside air has a relative humidity of nearly 100 per cent. When such air is brought into the house and heated to 64°, its capacity for moisture increases so much that its relative humidity would fall to 60 per cent if no new moisture were added. As a matter of fact, a little is added by people's breath and by evaporation from their bodies, as well as from plants or other sources. Hence when you try your experiment the house may have a relative humidity of nearly 75 per cent and a temperature of 64°. In other words, you have reproduced the optimum conditions, which are much like those in the cooler kinds of greenhouses. Suppose now that the outside air has a temperature of 30° and is bright and clear, so that the relative humidity is 70 per cent. If the air is heated to 70° in the house, its humidity will be 12 per cent, or perhaps 25 per cent if allowance is made for additions of moisture from other sources. Such air makes people feel cooler than does the air at 64° and 75 per cent, for it causes rapid evaporation from the skin and still more rapid evaporation from the delicate mucous membranes of the nose and throat.

These considerations lead us to ask whether it is possible to construct a table showing what combinations of temperature and humidity give approximately the same feelings of warmth. A brief account of two sets of experiments will illustrate the way in which this has been attempted. First, in Shanghai and Canton, China, in the summers of 1902 and 1904 W. F. Tyler, an English official interested in climatology, secured the coöperation of a dozen persons "of normal condition, regular habits, and equable temperament" whose occupations were such as to preclude rush and worry and to render the environment of all days essentially the same. Each noon they were asked to record their feelings according to a comfort scale in which zero means perfect comfort, while 10 means that the heat is almost unbearable. His results appear in the following table. I have added column E to show what temperature would correspond to each "hyther," or degree on the scale of comfort, if the relative humidity remained constant at 75 per cent.

Scale of Comfort or "Hyther"	Number of Days	Average Temperature	Average Relative Humidity	Estimated Temp. if Rel. Hum. were 75%	Definition of Hythers i. e. of feelings at each Point in the Scale
0 (0.4)	3	74°	73%	70°	No discomfort from heat when lightly clad and making no exertion.
1	17	80°	58%	76°	Slight discomfort. With European clothing and exertion the heat would be oppressive.
2	24	81°	73%	80°	
3	27	84°	75%	83°	Increasing discomfort.
4	23	85°	77%	86°	
5	17	89°	71%	88°	The slightest exertion causes perspiration with most people.
6	7	90°	75%	90°	Increasing discomfort.
7 (6.7)	3	92°	83%	92°	
8	0	?	?	?	Very great oppression.
9	0	?	?	?	
10	0	?	?	?	Almost unbearable.

Tyler's experiments were conducted in weather so warm that no days were perfectly comfortable for all his subjects. The humidity made a great difference, however, as appears from the following table, where the temperature is shown on the left and the relative humidity at the top, while the hyther, or comfort vote, together with the number of cases on which it is based, appears in the body of the table.

Temperature Relative Humidity	65% or Less		60-80%		81%	
	Cases	Hyther	Cases	Hyther	Cases	Hyther
91°-95°	5	4.9	10	5.5	2	6.7
86°-90°	10	3.2	21	3.9	5	5.2
81°-85°	10	1.5	16	2.3	13	3.7
76°-80°	7	0.8	7	1.9	10	3.5
71°-75°	2	0.5	0	?	1	2.7

Notice that no matter what the temperature, the degree of discomfort increases with higher humidity, that is, the hythers in each line become higher as one passes from left to right.

The second set of experiments was carried on by Affleck and Knapp at the Y. M. C. A. Training School at Springfield, Mass. They took a comfort vote after a class of young men had been exercising for about an hour and a half. Their scale of hythers consisted of only three points: (1) too cool, (2) just right, and (3) too warm. In the table, 30 means just right, while anything lower is too cool, and anything higher too warm. During the experiments the temperature ranged from 53° to 70° and the humidity from 20 per cent to 80 per cent. As a rule the temperatures and humidities were both much lower than those of Tyler. The results are as follows:

Temperature Relative Humidity	40% or Less		41-60%		61% or More	
	Cases	Hyther	Cases	Hyther	Cases	Hyther
66°-70°	16	37.6	11	41.1	5	42.5
61°-65°	29	34.1	39	34.3	4	28.7
56°-60°	1	27.2	4	26.7	3	20.6

For temperatures between 66° and 70° this table agrees with that of Tyler. Thus for all temperatures above the optimum there is agreement. For lower temperatures the data are not conclusive. Between 61° and 65° the air felt cooler at humidities below 40 per cent than at humidities of 41 per cent to 60 per cent. The difference between 34.1 and 34.3, however, is too slight to be important. At slightly higher humidities with a temperature of 61° to 65°, and at temperatures below 60° the table suggests that dry air feels warmer than that which is even moderately moist. The number of cases, however, is altogether too small to be conclusive. In passing, it is interesting to note that the young men at the Y. M. C. A. gymnasium felt most comfortable at a temperature of about 58° when the humidity was above 65 per cent and at a temperature of about 61° when the humidity fell below 20 per cent. The fact that they had just been actively exercising accounts for the apparently low optimum.

On the basis of these experiments and others I have prepared the following table. It shows the approximate dry bulb temperature that would be necessary in a house under different conditions of weather in order to make people feel as warm as they would feel with a temperature of 64° and a relative humidity of 75 per cent.

TABLE OF EQUIVALENT TEMPERATURES

A Temperature of Outside Air	B Relative Humidity of Outside Air	C Approximate Temperature to which Air must be Heated in the House in order to feel as warm as Greenhouse Air (64°, 75% Humidity), provided no moisture is added except from the human body	D Approximate Relative Humidity of Air thus Heated
64°	75%	64° (Optimum)	75% (Optimum)
50°	70%	67°	55%
40°	80%	70°	45%
30°	80%	72°	35%
20°	90%	74°	30%
10°	90%	76°	20%

Column C shows that on very cold winter days with the thermometer at 10°, the air in the house will have to be heated to 76° in order to feel as warm as greenhouse air. It would then be as dry as the air of the driest deserts. Such conditions prevail frequently in our houses. That is why we shiver in cold weather even when the thermometer is comparatively high in the house. That appears also to be one chief reason why we catch so many colds, suffer so much from winter sickness, and have so much poorer complexions than our English cousins. The English, be it noted, live most of the time in fairly moist air; we, on the contrary, parch our poor mucous membranes to such an extent that they cannot resist the attacks of germs. The matter can scarcely be put too strongly. Recall how disagreeable the dryness of the air feels when the heat is first turned on. The heat itself may be grateful, but it gives the nose and throat a disagreeable feeling. Consider, too, how many people suffer from rough skins and from cracks around the finger nails. The outside temperature may have something to do with this, but apparently the indoor dryness is a much more potent cause.

These considerations lead to the conclusion that humidification of the air in houses should be universal during the winter. If the air has a humidity of 60 per cent and a temperature of 64°, that is ample for both health and comfort. Such air can cool down to 55° at night without danger of depositing moisture except on the windows. Even if the humidity is no more than 50 per cent, our health and comfort will be greatly increased.

If we would have the very best health, however, we must remember that it is not wise to preserve a uniform temperature and humidity. The right average must be secured by varying the temperature first one way and then the other. The air in the ideal house should fluctuate back and forth from about 60° to 68° at irregular intervals. Such fluctuations may not seem pleasant at first if begun in the middle of the winter after people have become softened by dry air and uniform temperature. So long as the windows are kept open, however, they prevail naturally in the fall at the very time when people's health is best. If the conditions of those fall days, with their optimum temperature, their comparatively high humidity, and their variability could prevail all winter, it seems probable that the appalling increase in our winter deathrate would be much diminished.

Another important consideration is the degree of movement of the air. In many houses the air moves so little that the upper part of a room may have a temperature of 75° while on the floor the thermometer records only 65°. Such a condition is of course undesirable. It can be avoided only by a proper system of ventilation.

Having seen the nature of the atmospheric conditions most favorable to health, the next step is to secure them. The first and greatest requisite, as we have seen, is proper temperature. Today 70° is the standard indoor temperature, although wise people see that 68° would be better. Our study of health shows that an average of 64° is apparently high enough. If this were the only element in the problem we could simply reduce our coal consumption until our rooms averaged 64° instead of 70° during the hours when we are not sleeping. That in itself, if we may judge from the experience of the New York schools, would decrease the number of colds by nearly half. Such a result would be due not merely to the more favorable temperature, but also to the more favorable humidity. The average outside temperature in New York City from October to April, the months when houses are usually heated, is almost exactly 40°, while the relative humidity is about 75 per cent. When such air is taken into the house and heated to 70°, its relative humidity is reduced to about 16 per cent, provided no new moisture is added. Even with the addition of a little moisture from people's breath, from pans in the furnace, or from other sources, such air is as dry as that of the driest deserts and is very harmful to the mucous membranes. When the same air is heated to 64°, its relative humidity without the addition of other moisture becomes about 30 per cent. This is altogether too dry, but it is much better than 16 per cent.

In a crisis like the war which is coming to an end as these lines are written, it is necessary to conserve coal in every possible way. It would seem as if the practice of having cooler air in our houses would be one of the best ways to accomplish this. Normally the people of the United States burn about 120,000,000 tons of coal each year in their houses. If the inside temperature were kept at 64° instead of 70°, the air taken in from outside would have to be warmed 24° instead of 30°, or only four fifths as much as now. That would mean a corresponding decrease in the consumption of coal, or a saving of 24,000,000 tons per year. In order to be comfortable under such conditions we should have to dress more warmly than at present. We should also need to take more exercise in the morning and again toward night in order to set the blood in motion.

At times when conservation of coal is not one of the most pressing demands, which means in all ordinary times, the humidity as well as the temperature should be right. That means that when the winter air at an average temperature of 40° and a humidity of 75 per cent is taken into our houses it should not only be heated to 64°, but should be caused to evaporate enough water to raise its humidity to about 50 per cent. Strange as it may seem, the latent heat required for the evaporation of water is so great that more heat is required to bring the air to a temperature of 64° and a humidity of 50 per cent than to bring it to 70° without humidification. The writer himself, in an article prepared hastily at the request of the United States Fuel

Administration, failed to appreciate the importance of this factor. There is a distinct difference, however, between the conservation of coal arising from the healthful practice of keeping the temperature down to about 64°, and the somewhat increased consumption of coal arising from the much more healthful practice of keeping the temperature down to 64° and at the same time giving it the most favorable conditions of humidity. Yet this matter of humidity is so vital to human health that it seems wise to insert Appendix F. Directions are there given whereby the householder who cannot afford a patented humidifier can, at very slight expense, improvise a system that will give him a close approach to the right conditions. As time goes on, far better methods will be developed. The author would be most grateful if his readers would send him suggestions along these lines.

Finally, there is need of constant variety of temperature. This, as we have seen, can perhaps be brought about by direct window ventilation. In addition to that, however, the air in the ordinary house should be kept moving so that the temperature on the floor and at the ceiling is the same. This is now done in theaters and other public buildings, but it ought also to be the rule in dwellings. Some day our heating arrangements will be so far perfected that the air will always be right in both temperature and humidity; it will automatically be warmed and cooled so that we may enjoy due variety; and it will be kept constantly but gently in motion. When that day comes we may expect that our health and ability in winter will be almost as great as is now the case in the best days of the autumn.

APPENDIX F

DIRECTIONS FOR VENTILATION AND HUMIDIFICATION

I. Ventilation

THE studies outlined in this book indicate that the best and simplest method of ventilation is by means of ordinary windows. At frequent intervals the top should be lowered a little and the bottom raised about the same amount. It is important, however, to avoid drafts. Therefore every window should be fitted with a board at the bottom. If such a board is placed an inch or two from the window and has a height of five or six inches, it will prevent the air from blowing directly into the room, and yet will allow a complete change of air within a moderately short time.

II. Humidity

A. *Houses Heated by Steam or Hot Water*

1. Take a piece of absorbent cotton cloth. Cut it as if you were going to make a curtain to place between your radiator and the wall. Make it long enough to lie five or six inches on the floor. Make a hem so that a curtain rod, string or wire can be run through it.

2. Fasten a sash curtain rod horizontally behind each radiator, and hang the curtain from it. If you have no curtain rods, simply run a string or wire through your little curtain, and tie the string around the radiator. Put a little block of wood under the string at either end to hold it out from the radiator. This will let the curtain hang freely between the radiator and the wall.

3. It may be necessary to place an additional rod or string near the bottom of the radiator in order to prevent the moist cloth from striking against the wall and damaging the paper. A tuck can be made at this level and the rod or cord run through it.

4. Under the radiator, place a pan as deep as the radiator will allow and large enough so that it comes to the front. Ordinary dripping pans will do excellently. Fill them with water morning and evening.

5. Gather the cloth together at the bottom so that it will lie in the pan, and spread it out at the top.

6. From time to time it is well to wash the curtains, for otherwise they lose the power of absorbing water. If your walls are cold, it may be a wise precaution to place oilcloth behind each radiator to prevent possible injury from the condensation of moisture.

When the pans are filled with water, the absorbent cloths will draw the water up, thus giving a large evaporation surface. The air that is heated by the radiator naturally moves upward, and the movement is greatest back of the radiator. Thus there will be a constant current of warm air moving along the surface of the cloth and causing abundant evaporation.

This simple contrivance gives all the humidity required at a very small cost. In using it, remember that if you succeed in getting much moisture into the air, you must avoid letting the room get too hot; not over 65°. If the room gets up to 70° or over, the humidity makes the air uncomfortable and when the room cools down, a little of the moisture in the air may condense and harm the wall paper.

B. *Houses Heated by Hot-Air Furnaces*

Method I. For registers near the wall or in protected parts of the room:

1. Lift up the iron grating of the register.

2. On the floor beside the register, lay a piece of stiff oilcloth a little smaller than the grating. Put it on the side next the wall and let the edge project an inch over the opening of the register. The oilcloth is designed to protect the floor and also to keep the wet cloth off the metal parts of the register.

3. Put a brass bowl, or other dish of water, close to the register on the oilcloth.

4. Put the end of a piece of absorbent cloth into the bowl and weight it down so that it will not pull out. Spread the other end over the edge of the oilcloth and let it hang down a foot or more into

the register, taking pains that it is spread out as much as possible. Weight the lower corners of the cloth to prevent it from being blown up by the draft from the furnace.

5. Put back the grating, arranging it in such a way that the side toward the cloth is propped up a little with bits of wood or wads of paper.

Method II. For registers in exposed situations where a bowl of water would be likely to be kicked over:

1. Inside the register, and a foot or two below the grating, place some kind of receptacle for water. The receptacle should not be large enough to prevent the flow of air. It may be hung from the grating if necessary.

2. From the grating, suspend one or two little curtains like those already described. If two curtains are placed parallel the water can be poured into the pans between them, and will not be likely to slop over.

3. In using this device, it is important to fill the pans carefully in order to avoid pouring water down the hot air flue.

C. *Houses Heated by Stoves*

Keep an open kettle on each stove. A pan and curtain such as are described under A, above, may be placed back of the stove provided care is taken to avoid the danger of fire, should the cloth get dry.

INDEX

Abbott, C. F., cited, 129
Abnormality, 154 (see Mutation)
Adana, massacres at, 210 f.
Affleck, G. B., cited, 269
Agriculture, in ancient Rome, 192 ff., 197, 203 ff.
Air, effect of dry, 85 f.;
  effect on head-form, 181;
  proper in houses, 266 ff.;
  relative importance of, 58 ff., 105
Alcohol, and health, 33
Alexander, advantages of environment to, 228
Alpine Race, entrance to Europe, 122, 141
Alytes, mutations of, 157
Ammon, O., cited, 180
Amorites, intermarriage with Jews, 170
Amphibians, evolution of, 109
Amphioxus, asymmetry among, 163
Anableps, asymmetry among, 163
Anæmia, effect of food on, 135
Ancestral types, reversion to, 151, 158
Andrea Pisano, 147
Anglo-Saxons, variability among, 168
Animals, origin of new, 148 ff.
Annapolis, mental optimum of students, 75
Antevs, E., cited, 187
Antonines, 204
Apes, asymmetry among, 163
Aphids, relation to temperature, 156
Arabs, relation to Turkish Government, 215 f.
Aridity, effect on beetles, 152;
  effect on evolution, 109 ff.;

in Devonian Period, 109;
  in Glacial Period, 140
Ariosto, 147
Armenians, character of, 214;
  massacres of, 208, 210 f.
Art, and climate, 146 f.;
  in prehistoric Europe, 122
Ashkenazim, described, 169 ff.
Asia, Glacial climate of, 144 f.;
  Great Plague in, 136 ff.;
  home of primitive races, 141 f.;
  origin of human races in, 122
Asiatic Cholera, 136
Assyria, conquests of, 227
Asymmetry, origin of, 163
Athenian Plague, 136
Augustan Age, 202 f.
Australia, effect of drought in, 138 f.
Austria, strength in Great War, 229
Axylon, plain of, 218 f.

Babylonia, conquests of, 227
Baker, Miss, cited, 102
Baltic Sea, in 14th century, 132 f.
Bank clearings and health, 37;
  deposits and health, 38 f.;
  secular trend of, 245 f.
Barbarian invasions, 205
Barrell, J., cited, 115, 256 ff.
Baths, compared with changes of temperature, 93
Beersheba, drought in, 220
Beetles, mutations of, 152 f.
Belgium, seasonal variations in death-rate, 71;
  strength in Great War, 231
Bey Shehir, irrigation at, 209

Gale, H. S., cited, 131
Gallic War, 193
Geological evolution, 107 ff.;
  Time-scale, 256 ff.
Germany, and her neighbors, 227 ff.;
  compared with Rome, 238;
  comparison with United States, 47;
  economic cycles in, 47 ff.;
  expansion of, 23 f.;
  government relations to business, 49;
  health in, 22, 48;
  malnutrition in, 135;
  physical character of Jews in, 172;
  seasonal variations in deathrate, 62 f.;
  strength in Great War, 229 ff.
Germplasm, response to environment, 161
Gibbon, Edw., cited, 205
Giotto, 147
Giovanni, 147
Glacial mammals, 257 f.
Glacial Period, causes of evolution in, 162;
  effect on evolution, 115 ff.;
  effect on man, 140;
  extinction of mammals during, 256 ff.
Glaciation, causes of, 144;
  effect on mutation, 152
Goats, in ancient Rome, 201
Government, as a panacea, 17
Gracchi, 198 f., 202
Grain, in Rome, 194, 199, 201
Great Plague, 136
Great War, comparison of nations in, 229 ff.;
  health of drafted men in, 21;
  nature of opponents, 208 ff.;
  relation to climate, 227 ff.
Greece, causes of expansion, 228
Greeks, character of, 214, 218 f.;
  complexion of, 170 f.

Greenhouse, air in, 266
Greenland, during 14th century, 132
Gregory, H. E., cited, 139

Hadrian, 204
Hampton Institute, experiments at, 79
Harput, 221
Hawaiian Islands, climate of, 75
Head-form (see Cephalic Index);
  effect of New York upon, 177 ff.;
  geographic variations of, 170, 172 ff.
Health, and bank clearings, 37;
  and bank deposits, 38 f.;
  and business, 26 ff.;
  and civilization, 19;
  and Civil Service examinations, 32 f.;
  and climate, 58 ff.;
  and immigration, 39;
  and mental power, 34 f.;
  and prices, 38;
  and prosperity, 39 f.;
  and school attendance, 37;
  and temperance, 33;
  and victory, 227;
  care of, in Turkey, 225 f.;
  compared with crops, 53;
  curve of, 1870-1910, 32;
  economic effect, 51;
  effect of climate in Turkey on, 221 ff.;
  effect of malnutrition on, 135;
  effect of variable climate on, 89 ff.;
  fluctuations in England, 46;
  in ancient Rome, 192 ff.;
  in Germany, 22, 48;
  of drafted men, 21;
  of school children, 20;
  relation to Great War, 227 ff.;
  variations in, 1870-1910, 29
Heat, effect on butterflies, 150 ff.
Hebrews (see Jews)
Heidelberg man, 117 f.